101 674 719 5

£50.50

ONE WEEK LOAN

18 NOV 2005

1 2 APR 2002

1 9 MAR 2002

13 MAY 2002

2 8 OCT 2002

10 JAN 2003
2 6 FEB 2003

1 5 AUG 2003

9/1/04

ITY

D0303085

Tennessee Williams

A Casebook

CASEBOOKS ON MODERN DRAMATISTS
Kimball King, General Editor

CHRISTOPHER HAMPTON
A Casebook
edited by Robert Gross

HOWARD BRENTON
A Casebook
edited by Ann Wilson

DAVID STOREY
A Casebook
edited by William Hutchings

PAUL SHAFFER
A Casebook
edited by C. J. Gianakaras

SIMON GRAY
A Casebook
edited by Katherine H. Burkman

JOHN ARDEN AND
MARGARETA D'ARCY
A Casebook
edited by Jonathan Wilke

AUGUST WILSON
A Casebook
edited by Marilyn Elkins

JOHN OSBORNE
A Casebook
edited by Patricia D. Denison

ARNOLD WESKER
A Casebook
edited by Reade W. Dornan

DAVID HARE
A Casebook
edited by Hersh Zeifman

MARSHA NORMAN
A Casebook
edited by Linda Ginter Brown

BRIAN FRIEL
A Casebook
edited by William Kerwin

NEIL SIMON
A Casebook
edited by Gary Konas

TERRENCE MCNALLY
A Casebook
edited by Toby Silverman Zinman

STEPHEN SONDHEIM
A Casebook
edited by Joanne Gordon

HORTON FOOTE
A Casebook
edited by Gerald C. Wood

SAMUEL BECKETT
A Casebook
edited by Jennifer M. Jeffers

WENDY WASSERSTEIN
A Casebook
edited by Claudia Barnett

WOODY ALLEN
A Casebook
edited by Kimball King

MODERN DRAMATISTS
A Casebook of Major British,
Irish, and American Playwrights
edited by Kimball King

PINTER AT 70
A Casebook
edited by Lois Gordon

TENNESSEE WILLIAMS
A Casebook
edited by Robert F. Gross

Tennessee Williams

A Casebook

Edited by Robert F. Gross

Routledge
New York • London

Published in 2002 by
Routledge
29 West 35th Street
New York, NY 10001

Published in Great Britain by
Routledge
11 New Fetter Lane
London EC4P 4EE

10   9   8   7   6   5   4   3   2   1

Library of Congress Cataloging-in-Publication Data

Tennessee Williams : a casebook / edited by Robert F. Gross.
        p. cm. – (Casebooks on modern dramatists; v. 31)
        Includes bibliographical references (p.) and index.
    ISBN 0-8153-3174-6 (acid-free paper)
Williams, Tennessee, 1911–1983—Criticism and interpretation. I. Gross, Robert
F. II. Series.

    PS3545.I5365 Z84514 2001
    812'.54—dc21

                                                            2001018068

To the memory of
James Gulledge
(1932–2001)

"I still say that I'm not a bird, Mr. Shannon. I'm a human being and when a member of that fantastic species builds a nest in the heart of another, the question of permanence isn't the first or even the last thing that's considered . . . necessarily? . . . always?"

—Tennessee Williams, *The Night of the Iguana*

Contents

General Editor's Note

Tennessee Williams: A Casebook offers a series of perceptive essays about one of the great dramatists of the twentieth century. A plethora of books and articles on Williams focus on biographical parallels of events in the playwright's life with scenes and images underscored in his plays, or they explore canonical works, such as *The Glass Menagerie* or *A Streetcar Named Desire* at the expense of less well-known masterpieces, like *Out Cry*, *Vieux Carré*, or *Spring Storm*. Furthermore, critics have been identified as Tennessee Williams scholars, when, in fact, Williams's oeuvre and influence are an inescapable legacy in all contemporary theatrical history. The editor of *Tennessee Williams: A Casebook*, Robert F. Gross, has been a frequent contributor to the Casebook Series. He edited the fourth volume in the series, *Christopher Hampton: A Casebook*, in 1990, when that playwright's latest triumph was *Les Liasons Dangereuses*; and he has contributed individual essays to a dozen other volumes, both in the Casebook series and in the Studies in Modern Drama series. In 1996, Gross published a research and production source book on S. N. Behrman, an appropriate book topic for a professor of drama and theatre director at Hobart and William Smith Colleges in Geneva, NY. Many of the essays in *Tennessee Williams: A Casebook* assert that the chaos and disorder some critics have objected to in Williams's work as excessive or even melodramatic are essential ingredients of his world view. The "messiness" of life is highlighted in painful but moving analyses of modern existence. Throughout this casebook a "new" Williams is uncovered in unlikely pairings of famous with nearly forgotten plays, in gender studies, and in the exploration of death as a force that molds his dramaturgy.

Kimball King

Acknowledgments

First, thanks are due to Kimball King, the editor of this series, who first suggested the volume, and has supported it every step along the way. Second, to the students and colleagues who have contributed immensely to my understanding of Williams by collaborating on productions at Hobart and William Smith Colleges. Third, to the Faculty Research Council at Hobart and William Smith Colleges, which supported this project with a research grant. Finally, to Jim Gulledge, whose enthusiasm for the works of Tennessee Williams, support of me, and unfailing patience with the maddening minutiae of editing, brought this book from initial conception to reality.

Chronology

1911   Thomas Lanier Williams is born 26 March in Columbus, Mississippi, son of Cornelius Coffin and Edwina Dakin Williams.

1919   Family moves to St. Louis, Missouri.

1928   "The Vengeance of Nitocris" published in *Weird Tales.*

1929   Enters the University of Missouri. Receives honorable mention in contest for his play *Beauty is the Word.*

1935   *Cairo! Shanghai! Bombay!* performed by Memphis Garden Players.

1936   Enrolls at Washington University, St. Louis.

1937   *Candles to the Sun* and *The Fugitive Kind* performed by Mummers, an amateur theatre in St. Louis. Writes *Spring Storm.*

1938   Graduates from University of Iowa with B.A. degree, major in English. Writes *Not About Nightingales.*

1939   Four one-act plays under the title *American Blues* wins $100 in a contest organized by the Group Theatre. Plays submitted to competition under name, "Tennessee Williams." Wins a Rockefeller Foundation grant of $1,000.

1940   Enters advanced playwriting seminar under John Gassner at the New School, where students produce *The Long Good-Bye. Battle of Angels* plays briefly in Boston.

1943   *The Glass Menagerie* written, submitted to, and rejected by Metro-Goldwyn-Mayer. *You Touched Me!* plays in Cleveland.

1944   *The Purification* directed by Margo Jones in Pasadena. Poems appear in *Five American Poets*, third series. 26 December, *The Glass Menagerie* premieres in Chicago 26 December.

1945   25 March, *Stairs to the Roof* premieres at Pasadena Playbox. 31 March, *The Glass Menagerie* opens in New York (561 performances) and wins New York Drama Critics Circle Award. 25 September, *You Touched Me!*, written with Donald Windham, opens in New York (100 performances).

1947   8 July, *Summer and Smoke* opens in Dallas. 3 December, *A Streetcar Named Desire* opens in New York (855 performances), winning New York Drama Critics Circle Award and Pulitzer Prize.

1948   *One Arm and Other Stories* published. 6 October, *Summer and Smoke* opens in New York (100 performances).

1950   Williams's first novel, *The Roman Spring of Mrs. Stone* published.

1951   3 February, *The Rose Tattoo* opens in New York (306 performances).

1953   19 March, *Camino Real* opens in New York (60 performances).

1954   *Hard Candy and Other Stories* published.

1955   24 March, *Cat on a Hot Tin Roof* opens in New York, (79 performances), winning New York Drama Critics Circle Award and Pulitzer Prize.

1956   Williams's first collection of poetry, *In the Winter of Cities* published. *Sweet Bird of Youth* plays at Studio M. Playhouse in Coral Gables, Florida. *Baby Doll*, with a screenplay by Williams and direction by Elia Kazan, premieres in December.

1957   21 March, *Orpheus Descending* opens in New York, (68 performances).

1958   7 January, *Garden District*, a double bill composed of *Suddenly Last Summer* and *Something Unspoken*, opens Off-Broadway. 29 December, *Period of Adjustment* begins pre-Broadway tryouts in Miami.

1959   10 March, substantially rewritten version of *Sweet Bird of Youth* opens in New York (95 performances). 2 July, one-act version of *The Night of the Iguana* premieres at Spoleto Festival in Italy.

1960   August, full-length version of *The Night of the Iguana* prepares for New York run at a series of venues, accompanied by substantial revisons, beginning at Coconut Grove Playhouse, Miami. 10 November, *Period of Adjustment* opens in New York (132 performances).

1961   28 December, *The Night of the Iguana* premieres in New York (316 performances), winning New York Drama Critics Circle Award.

1962   11 July, *The Milk Train Doesn't Stop Here Anymore* plays at the Spoleto Festival..

1963   16 January, *The Milk Train Doesn't Stop Here Anymore* premieres in New York, (69 performances).

1964   25 June, *The Eccentricities of a Nightingale* premieres at Tappan Zee Playhouse, Nyack, New Jersey.

1966   *The Knightly Quest,* a collection of short fiction, is published. 22 February, *Slapstick Tragedy*, a double bill of *The Mutilated* and *The Gnädiges Fräulein*, premieres in New York (7 performances).

1967   12 December, *The Two-Character Play* premieres at Hampstead Theatre Club, London.

1968   27 March, *The Seven Descents of Myrtle* premieres in New York (29 performances).

1969   11 May, *In the Bar of a Tokyo Hotel* premieres in New York (23 performances).

1971   2 July, *Out Cry* premieres at Ivanhoe Theatre, Chicago.

1972   2 April, *Small Craft Warnings* premieres in Off-Broadway production in New York (200 performances).

1973   1 March, revised version of *Out Cry* premieres in New York (13 performances).

1974   May, *The Latter Days of a Celebrated Soubrette*, a revision of *The Gnädiges Fräulein,* premieres Off-Broadway (1 performance). July, revised version of *Cat on a Hot Tin Roof* premieres in Connecticut, and moves to New York in September. 3 November, a revised version of *Battle of Angels* opens at Circle Repertory Theatre in New York. *Eight Mortal Ladies Possessed*, a book of short fiction, is published.

1975   Williams's *Memoirs* and a second novel, *Moise and the World of Reason* are published. 6 March, *Kingdom of Earth*, a revised version of *The Seven Descents of Myrtle*, premieres at McCarter Theatre, Princeton, New Jersey. 18 June, *The Red Devil Battery Sign* opens in Boston—New York opening postponed.

1976   A second volume of poetry, *Androgyne, Mon Amour* is published. 16 January, *This Is (An Entertainment)* premieres at American Conservatory Theatre, San Francisco. Revised version of *The Red Devil Battery Sign* plays in Vienna. *Eccentricities of a Nightingale* opens in New York (24 performances).

1977   11 May, *Vieux Carré* premieres in New York, 11 May (5 performances). June, after further revisions, *The Red Devil Battery Sign* plays in London.

1978   16 May, *Tiger Tail* premieres at Alliance Theatre, Atlanta, Georgia. 5 June, *Creve Coeur* opens at the Spoleto Festival in Charleston, South Carolina.

1979   10 January, *A Lovely Sunday for Creve Coeur*, a revision of *Creve Coeur*, plays in New York at Hudson Guild Theatre (36 performances). 27 September, *Kirche, Kutchen und Kinder* premieres at Jean Cocteau Repertory , New York.

1980   24 January, *Will Mr. Merriweather Return from Memphis?* premieres at the Tennessee Williams Performing Arts Center, Key West. 26 March, *Clothes for a Summer Hotel* opens in New York (15 performances).

1981   Spring, *A House Not Meant to Stand* premieres at Goodman Theatre, Chicago. 24 August, *Something Cloudy, Something Clear* premieres in New York, at Jean Cocteau Repertory. 12 September, early draft of *The Notebook of Trigorin* premieres at Vancouver Playhouse.

1983   Dies night of February 24, at Hotel Elysée, New York, choking on a bottle cap.

1996   5 September, *The Notebook of Trigorin* premieres at the Cincinnati Playhouse in the Park. 26 October *Spring Storm* receives staged reading at Ensemble Studio Theatre, New York.

1998   5 March, *Not About Nightingales* premieres at Royal National Theatre, London, followed by runs in Houston and New York.

Introduction

Tennessee Williams is both too well-known and not nearly well-known enough, too often performed and too often passed over, written about incessantly and repeatedly ignored. As the author of *The Glass Menagerie*, *A Streetcar Named Desire* and *Cat on a Hot Tin Roof*, he is a much loved and respected Master of the Canon. As the author of *The Milk Train Doesn't Stop Here Anymore*, *Clothes for a Summer Hotel* and *Vieux Carré*, he is often dismissed with a mixture of embarrassment, condescension and pity. Embraced as a genius and dismissed as a neurotic, substance-abusing failure, it is hard for readers to fuse the two figures into one. Studying his works and their reception, one often seems to be seeing with two eyes—something cloudy, something clear.

The canonical works tend to suffer from overfamiliarity these days. They sometimes need some help to allow us to encounter them afresh as the fascinating works they are. So, some of the essays in this volume provide new perspectives by pairing well-known plays with less famous ones—Frank Bradley on *Streetcar* and *Camino Real*, Thomas Gregory Carpenter on *Cat* and *Not About Nightingales*. Stephanie B. Hammer takes *The Glass Menagerie*, the play most often rendered mute by innumerable rote productions and excruciating scene study projects in acting classes, and treats it to a thorough defamiliarization through the lenses of bourgeois tragedy, female impersonation and New Age creativity.

For the neglected Williams, the challenge is different. Here, it is not only a matter of making cases for works that have been attacked and marginalized, but also showing that the attention paid to these works have made significant contributions to our understanding of Williams's entire oeuvre. Rhonda Blair's essay on *The Notebook of Trigorin* not only illuminates a lesser-known play, but uses it as an occasion to submit the well-worn critical comparison of Williams and Anton Chekhov to painstaking (and rewarding) scrutiny. Similarly, Kalliopi Nikolopoulou's reflections on the widely undervalued *Out Cry* leads to a deepened appreciation of the dramatist's place in the symbolist tradition.

But, whether they deal with the canonical or non-canonical Williams, the essayists in this volume repeatedly place Williams in new contexts. For both Bradley and Hammer, Williams is the inheritor of the problematics of Enlightenment drama, whether articulated by Denis Diderot (Bradley) or Friedrich Schiller (Hammer). Blair watches Williams engaging with Chekhovian realism, Nikolopoulou senses "Mallarmean echoes" in *Out Cry*, Bruce J. Mann finds reinscriptions of Rilke and Hart Crane in the late autobiographical plays, and Linda Dorff reads the imagery of *Clothes for a Summer Hotel* against similar images in the works of August Strindberg and D. H. Lawrence.

For other contributors, the context is less literary than social and ideological. Lauren Friesen sees the recently rediscovered *Spring Storm* as an early instance of Williams's life-long project of dramatizing sexual desire. Carpenter interprets American masculinities as seen in the plays. Ann Wilson questions the appellation of Williams as a "gay playwright," charting the anxious and ambivalent play of desires and representations in *Sweet Bird of Youth*. Michael R. Schiavi, turning to a number of rarely discussed short stories, begins by examining the social prejudice against large women, and then turns to see how Williams deals with this stereotype, leading us through a gallery of fascinating, appetitive women, and showing another aspect of Williams's depictions of desire. John Gronbeck-Tedesco works up a rich context for the appreciation of *The Rose Tattoo*, not just in relationship to the "Politics of Normality" (his phrase) that dominated the post-World War II era, but against a far wider vista that includes the Declaration of Independence, *The Scarlet Letter* and a contemporary tattoo parlor in San Francisco—and opens out onto the future.

Certain concerns occur repeatedly in the volume. Williams emerges, not as an isolated, original voice, but a figure wrestling with his age, and his literary and theatrical forbearers. Concerns of gender and sexuality are central to the insights of Wilson, Hammer, Schiavi, Carpenter, and my own contribution to the volume. For Dorff, Nikolopoulou, Mann, Wilson and myself, death becomes a major presence in the work, shaping character, imagery and dramaturgy. Mann, Carpenter, Hammer, Wilson, Gronbeck-Tedesco and Bradley all turn to Williams's life to help chart the dynamics of his plays.

With an author as productive as Williams, some works will inevitably be passed over in a volume of this length. I would have liked to have included some essays on the one-acts: on *The Night of the Iguana* (an important and eloquent play that largely vanishes here), the wistful and charming *Will Mr. Merriwether Return to Memphis?*, and the lusty *Tiger Tail*, to name only a few. But I console myself that the perspectives offered by the contributors suggest approaches to the works that received short shrift. I have also included references in the bibliography to the works that we have neglected.

As with Williams's work, so it is with Williams scholarship. There is a rich expanse of work there, far too much for me to cover in the space allotted here. I have used the space to point to some particularly valuable reference volumes, essays that suggest new critical approaches, and give attention to lesser-known works. The Bibliography, taken together with the Notes and Works Cited at the end of each essay, should give the newcomer to Williams criticism some interesting points of entry, as well as uncover a new source or two for the long-time enthusiast.

We continue to discover Williams. Three early plays have recently been published for the first time, and New Directions has announced its plans to expand their edition of the Collected Plays to include more of the late work, including previously unpublished plays. Critical debates will continue, and, most importantly, good productions will give us opportunities to experience the vitality and richness of these plays, and provide new insights.

—Robert F. Gross
Hobart and William Smith Colleges

We All Have to Paint Our Nudes

The Iconography of Sexual Longing in *Spring Storm*

Lauren Friesen

When Thomas Lanier Williams read the entire manuscript of *Spring Storm* in a playwriting workshop at the University of Iowa, Professor Mabie reportedly responded with that memorable and curt dismissal, "We all have to paint our nudes" (Williams and Mead, 70). The playwright, vulnerable in that moment of exposure, had anticipated a more positive response. Even though the Professor's intention may have been to merely cut through the silence that followed the reading, it had a lasting effect on the young playwright. The comment may have intensified Williams's self-perception as a misfit in that academic environment and possibly served as the crystallizing factor in his decision to end formal studies.

Now that nearly three quarters of a century have passed since that statement was uttered, it has become evident that Mabie identified with considerable precision the central dimension of Williams's dramatic investigations: undressing male and female sexual desire. What began as a classroom dismissal would become a central motif and the primary mark of distinction in one of America's premiere playwrights. For all of its weaknesses, *Spring Storm* boldly charts the terrain over which subsequent Williams characters would struggle: misguided actions and continual psychological battle between alienation and sexual longing.

Mabie's comment also serves to remind us that Williams was a young student at the time when he wrote *Spring Storm*. The play has a number of features that reveal the author's youthful perspective: lack of structural unity, time sequence problems, a mixture of styles, sudden plot shifts and the use of symbols that seem forced upon the play rather than motivated by action or character intentions. Even with these apparent problems, the play serves to introduce the reader to those elements in Williams's writing that would later become the identifying features of his work. In this early play, Williams is already exploring the imagery of sexual desire, the volatile mixture of longing and rejection, and the chasm between the personal and social needs of men and women.

Another major theme in this play is rooted in Williams's love of poetry. In this play as in well as a number of later ones, a main character, Arthur Shannon, expresses a strong devotion to poetry—but with a self-critical eye. Even though Shannon's insecurity emerges when he comments on his work, "My poetry, it isn't a terrific volcanic eruption—No—it's just a little bonfire of dry leaves and dead branches," (25) it introduces a major motif—the struggle for art to fully express the dimensions of human passion.

Although the play explores the themes that would later dominate Williams's literary corpus, it is inappropriate to expect this early play to have the refined features of his highly successful work. He was, after all, a struggling student. Therefore, thorough comparisons between this play and his highly successful ones may only disappoint the reader. If comparisons are to be made, a fair one might be Eugene O'Neill's student-written play, A Wife for a Life, (O'Neill, 1–16) because it also shares many of the character and structural problems of Spring Storm. Even though O'Neill's work is much shorter, it also has sudden shifts in plot, an experimentation with various styles and a reliance on devices that appear to be out of proportion with the plot. Both plays explore loneliness and isolation, and the human need for belonging. While there are many small differences between these two plays, the one great difference is Williams's proclivity for undressing psychological dimensions of sexual nuance and desire. Spring Storm began Williams's long journey to present characters that are primarily motivated by their sexual urges and desires. This was new territory for the American stage.

The irony of Professor Mabie's observation is that he identified the central theme not only in Spring Storm but also in those plays yet to be written. Esther Merle Jackson notes that Williams's uniqueness is the development of his "iconology in the explication of contemporary problems [. . .] a vivid and comprehensive sexual symbology" (131). Williams continued to paint semi-clad characters with more carefully chosen colors and to explore a dramatic iconography of sexual desire. In Spring Storm, the sexual themes become central to the identities of the characters. They don't just seek marriage and social respectability, they are searching for sexual expression and fulfillment. In writing about the later plays, C. W. Bigsby notes that "He [Williams] deployed the iconography of the romantic: fading beauty, the death of the young, a dark violence, a redeeming love" (33). Those themes are already present in this early work and within a decade after writing Spring Storm, Williams would emerge as a new voice, and the emotional nudity of his characters would become a primary motif. What is often overlooked is that if an artist wants to excel in painting the human figure, they must initially develop the ability to paint the nude. Williams appears to have understood that, while the class under Professor Mabie apparently did not.

The plot in Spring Storm relies on a variety of stylistic conventions including melodrama, naturalism and the well-made play. While Williams employs the devices of the well-made play and melodrama, he appears to be influenced the most by late-nineteenth- and early-twentieth-century naturalism. Even though this is no evidence that Williams read Hermann Sudermann's *Honor* and *Magda,* there are many parallels between the early plays by both authors.[1] Sudermann also employs elements of melodrama, naturalism and the well made play with the intention of unmasking the power of sexual attraction across the boundaries of class and social status. While Sudermann delights in subjecting his characters to strokes, illnesses and untimely deaths, *Spring Storm* uses the melodramatic devices—storms, disappearances, and a suicide—as dramatic reversals. Both authors show signs of wanting to leave melodramatic devices behind in order to address more profound human struggles but at the same time appear to rely heavily on these devices for their dramatic effect.

Spring Storm is a story that explores the sexual passions, insecurity, and alienation of four young people in the South during the Great Depression. Their lives are marked by a series of contrasts: poverty versus privilege, aimlessness and responsibility, the forces of nature and those of the intellect, unfulfilled desires and the suppression of passion. The four main characters: Heavenly Critchfield, Arthur Shannon, Dick Miles and Hertha Neilson are studies in contrast. Heavenly is beautiful and sensual, Arthur is insecure and nonathletic, Dick is a muscular dreamer and Hertha Neilson is intelligent, nervous and excitable. The bond that links all of these characters is their sexual desire: Arthur for Heavenly, Heavenly for Dick, Hertha for Arthur, and Dick Miles, who once gave his undivided attention to Heavenly, is now obsessed with unknown conquests that beckon when he sees barges flowing by on the Mississippi River. In this small southern town the summer heat has stimulated two sets of lovers to fantasize and act on their sexual inclinations. A church picnic at the top of the show soon ensnares all four into a love triangle that will eventually seal their fates.

The contrasts between Shannon and Dick, Hertha and Heavenly are not merely personality differences; they are rooted in the social fabric of a small town where everyone knows each other's personal business. Dick and Heavenly have already explored the pleasures of sexual intimacy, and their night at Moon Lake Lodge soon becomes common knowledge for all who wish to know. Due to Arthur's social status, he has pursued a long courtship with Hertha that retains respectability. Because Shannon, the banker's son, will inherit the mantle of wealth and power and he understands the necessity of living up to the community expectations, his reticence with Hertha isn't solely due to his social status but grounded in his own ambivalence toward her. Her love of books and his love of poetry is not enough to ignite the fires of passion in Arthur. Marriage with Hertha would be a step downward, but that might not deter the socially inept Arthur. His ardor is stifled, not by social class, but by his infatuation with the unattainable: Heavenly. In contrast to Hertha, Heavenly avoids all things studious and values those experiences that provide physical pleasure. In contrast to Arthur Shannon, the restless Dick Miles is weighing a very different decision. Shall he continue his affair with Heavenly, even marry her, or shall he escape small town life in exchange for the mysteries of the Mississippi River? He would prefer both, of course, and assumes that Heavenly will join him if he hops onto a barge. The contrasts between Heavenly and Hertha, Arthur and Dick reflect various social, economic, vocational and educational, and family backgrounds.

The only family that we encounter is Heavenly's. Her father is ill and they are on a downward economic spiral. Her mother is desperately trying to create a match between Arthur and Heavenly before their financial condition becomes too well known. The bonds between these two families have a long history. A Critchfield ancestor saved the town from destruction during the Civil War and thereby established the Shannons as the leading banking family in the area. Heavenly's aunt, Lilly, had an affair with Arthur's father before he married (40). Heavenly, at twenty-five, is still beautiful and with her respectable family background her mother, Esmeralda, cannot understand why a romance between Arthur and Heavenly has not blossomed. Esmeralda's persistence only forces Heavenly to admit that she is in love with Dick and that if he intends to jump a river barge, she may join him. She dislikes the idea of living on a barge but has to weigh to the alternatives: to be with a man you love (Dick) in a place you scorn, or with a man you scorn (Arthur) in a place you might be too loveable (his mansion).

In her desperation for a quick solution to their financial situation and Heavenly's prospects for marriage, Esmeralda insists that Heavenly give her one reason why she can't marry Arthur. Heavenly elects to be honest: her sexual liaison with Dick is the reason for her hesitancy. Heavenly's family is scandalized by her sexual freedom and her attachment to a man without any prospects. They want her to climb the local social ladder and link up with Arthur Shannon even though she doesn't feel any passion for him. Arthur Shannon, on the other hand, has a deep and abiding crush on Heavenly and, even in the middle of the Depression, pays eighty dollars for her cake at a church picnic. This purchase is viewed by everyone as an expression of love but in extremely bad taste, since Hertha is there by his side. This extravagant demonstration of love illustrates Shannon's social awkwardness and his divided loyalties that eventually result in disastrous decisions. He is unable to communicate in person his attraction to Heavenly and so the extravagant purchase of the cake becomes a highly public, although passive, declaration of love. He mustered the courage to take one step toward claiming Heavenly but it is a false step. The only one who is genuinely thrilled with this purchase is the priest, because the proceeds from the sale will go to the parish.

Two powerful forces motivate Heavenly's actions, define her character and guide her decisions: the pursuit and enjoyment of sexuality, and the fear that she might have to spend her adult life on the porch as a single woman, watching the pleasures of the world pass her by. While she is aware of Arthur's infatuation with her, she does not have the patience to wait for him, and even if she had the patience, she does not view him as an attractive candidate for romance. Her interests in romantic feelings outweigh her need for financial security. Heavenly's attitude toward sexuality do not conform to the conventions of the day. "'Faithful unto death' isn't the sort of thing I want on my tombstone," (17) she announces to Dick while he dreams of traveling around the world in a cattle boat. Even if she marries him, she will continue to explore where sensual pleasures may lead her.

Dick Miles fears that he will be forever chained to poverty in this town and therefore desires to seek his fortunes wherever the river might flow. Even though

Heavenly's father has arranged an offer of a job at a local pharmacy, he responds with disdain. Stacking shelves and pouring cokes is not his idea of living. Work, for Dick, consists of living in the outdoors where the powers of nature require resilience, strength and uncertainty. Heavenly reminds him that hopping a barge will bring him face to face with other destitute and marginal people, but he persists in his fantasy. In every scene where Dick appears, his desire to go places, cruise around the world, or watch "things goin' places" is always on his lips. The restlessness of his spirit was not fulfilled by the promise of steady employment nor by Heavenly's willingness to share the same bed.

In contrast with Heavenly and Dick, Hertha Nielson suppresses her passions by devoting her energies to the local library. Her great pleasure comes from reading children's stories, which, in turn, may prepare her for a future role of a community respectable socialite. Her role in the small town is severely circumscribed because of her family's recent immigrant status, her father's early death from alcoholism and their continual poverty. She is deeply in love with Shannon, who shares her love of poetry and literary imagination. Only at the end of the play does she realize that while she has viewed their long talks as prelude to romance, he has viewed her merely as a companion and a conversationalist.

The undeveloped form of *Spring Storm* is demonstrated in the way Williams experimented with devices from several styles. The melodramatic elements are easily recognizable: the tension between Dick and Shannon suddenly erupts into a fight and it is over as quickly as it started. Even though Dick wins this fistfight, it does not convince Heavenly to run away with him for a life on the barge. Had Williams truly wanted a melodrama, this action would have ended with Heavenly and Dick running off together, but the consequences of this fight are never fully realized.

The use of trees on a hill facing the Mississippi and Hertha's outstretched arms against the background of a lightning storm appears as a forced religious symbol that appears once and is never referenced again. Williams may have intended this crucifixion tableau as a device to foreshadow Hertha's suicide at the end of the play. Even though Hertha suffers from Arthur's rejection, her death does not have religious significance. Williams introduces this melodramatic image, complete with a thunderstorm, as a means of bringing Act I to a close. The use of this religious spectacle seems rooted in the devices of melodrama rather than realism or naturalism.

Williams's naturalism emerges in the characters of Heavenly and Dick. They are both following the urges of their bodies in search for sexual fulfillment and freedom from society's constraints. They act on their sexual inclinations and, while Dick is mute about his sexual desires, he openly yearns for freedom on the barge. Heavenly freely states her desire to find sexual fulfillment and her view that life on the barge would be a form of enslavement. The only kind of slave she wants to be is described when she states, "I've been reading *The Sheik*—I wanted to be pursued an' captured an' made a slave to passion!" (12). Heavenly expresses a willingness to live on the edges of acceptable social behavior but she cannot take that further step and live on the boundaries of society. Dick, on the other hand, repeatedly voices his willingness to leave civilization behind and live on the edges of society. Heavenly sees the paradox of a fleeing not as freedom but as servitude and refers to life on a barge as a "nigger's life." While the racism of that term is offensive to all modern sensibilities, she appears to deliberately use the term as a means to shake Dick from his obsession. The shocking effect of the word appears to be Williams's intent (Isaacs, xxii). But Dick cannot be diverted; the pull of the river is greater than his desire for Heavenly or his interest in establishing a future in a small town.

Like a good Chekhov, the choices the characters make have a deep impact on the plot, but each decision heightens the degree of alienation. Arthur Shannon decides to express his love to Heavenly and buys the cake that insults her and causes eyebrows to be raised. Later when he finds Hertha alone in the library he kisses her passionately but because he is drunk, he runs away. When Heavenly asks him to kiss her with passion, he does so with mechanical precision. As with Chekhov's characters, Arthur Shannon appears incapable of acting effectively on his intentions. Hertha, on the other hand, acts on her skills and desires. She works, she reads to the children in the library and at church picnics, while her passion for Arthur becomes an obsession. Dick Miles was at one time obsessed with trains but now his mind is fixed on the river and the freedom that life on a barge promises. His two actions include striking Arthur Shannon and knocking him to the ground, and eventually fleeing to the river with the hope that Heavenly will join him for a life of adventure. While Heavenly's family wants her to climb the social ladder and marry Arthur, she has decided not to wait for him and his indecisive advances. Once when she pleads with him to "kiss her boldly," he does so but only because she has demanded it and not because he was driven by inner passions. She, on the other hand, is drawn to the spirit of adventure and the raw masculinity of Dick Miles. As Mrs. Lamphrey says, "He has that—that sort of—primitive masculinity that's enough to make a girl lose her head!" (21). (Hints of what would eventually become Stanley Kowalski.) Heavenly has made the great sacrifice in a puritanical society: she has traded her virginity for the hope of marriage. But her sexual liaison with Dick is not merely a social contract; she has explored sexual pleasures for the sake of pleasure. In her frame of thought, marrying down, if that someone stokes life's passions, is far more attractive than the alternative. Arthur Shannon buys the cake and thereby seals his fate. After such a bold and expensive act, he pursues Heavenly with a lame approach. She seems nearly willing to accept the social respectability and financial stability that Shannon has to offer, knowing full well that she may not be able to control or limit her desires to one man.

Dick Miles's decisions are reflected in his comments on lights. He views candles at weddings in the following manner: "June weddin's you see written up in sassiety columns with everything white an' sweet smellin' an' candles an' lilies an' yards an' yards of white lace for you to walk down like a queen . . ." (20). The sarcasm of this speech is immediately followed by a sense of excitement and anticipation when Dick looks out on the Mississippi River and says, "See those lights goin' on down there? One of them'll be ours!" (20) With this juxtaposition in comparing the oppressiveness of candles at a wedding with the lights of boats on the Mississippi, the direction Dick's life will take becomes obvious. He will only marry if he can follow the "lights . . . goin' on down there!"

The problems with the characters reflect Williams's stylistic indecision. Heavenly is the only fully developed character in the script. She is guided in her thoughts and actions by the forces of nature in that she explores sexuality and passion with a natural ease. Dick Miles appears as a combination of romanticism and primitivism. He is motivated by his desire to flee and take up life as a hunter and gatherer. In the meantime he conveniently enjoys the sensual moments that Heavenly offers. Miles serves the plot as a foil for Arthur Shannon and a preoccupation for Heavenly's affections. Arthur Shannon is more developed than Dick but there are imbalances in how his character is developed. By imbalances I refer to the affair Arthur had at Oxford University that seemingly does not inform him on how to initiate a romance with Heavenly. His interest in poetry implies that he is an introspective character who had benefited little from his introspection. His social awkwardness may be rooted in his poetics—he prefers the formalism of the Victorians to the passion of the Romantics. The slightest character is Hertha Neilson even though she ends Act I with the Golgotha tableaux, and her suicide at the end creates the paralysis that engulfs Arthur and Heavenly. The magnitudes of her melodramatic actions are not fully in proportion to the slight attention that the remainder of the plot affords her character.

The problems with the plot also reflect a struggle to refine a style. While the play certainly has the features of Williams's later poetic realism, there are many elements that suggest that he was attracted to other stylistic devices. The sudden fight between Arthur Shannon and Dick Miles occurs during the one and only time these two characters meet. The buildup to the fight and the effect it has on both men is never fully developed. Arthur Shannon's interest in poetry establishes a character who is searching for meaning and beauty but he becomes an ignored character element in his pursuit of Heavenly. The attempt at religious iconography (Golgotha) with the use of real trees also hints at this pivotal image rooted in naturalism. By ending an act with this image, Williams implies that it may have greater significance in the subsequent action. Because this image is ignored in the subsequent acts, it raises questions about the meaning of intent the of the image. Even though Hertha does end her life at the end when Arthur rejects her, it would be a significant leap to refer to it as a Christological event. Williams appears to be struggling with various plot elements, naturalism, poetic realism, and symbolism without coming to a decision on focusing on one as the definite style.

The directions the characters take lead them all on to paths of alienation. Toward the end, when Arthur thinks he has lost Heavenly to Dick he becomes drunk. In that condition he goes to the library to visit Hertha and he kisses her wildly but then thrusts her aside when guilt overtakes him. He flees to Heavenly's house to discover that she did not leave for a life on the barge and instead wants to reconsider prospects with Dick. In the midst of their meeting, a phone call interrupts them. The caller reports that a drunk accosted Hertha Neilson in the library and that she left the library and ran to the railroad tracks and there she died. Upon hearing this Arthur is overcome with guilt and cannot continue his conversation with Heavenly, who then has the last line, "I'm going to sit on the front porch till one of them comes back" (148).

The ending, like the ending of Act I, is highly melodramatic and seems to break the realistic conventions that dominate this work. It seems apparent that Williams was experimenting with various dramatic styles. The characters and their conflicts are compelling and the hints of later genius are certainly evident. The play provides an excellent window into the early education of a major playwright. With this play and those that followed, Williams established the presence of sexual desire as a major theme in the American theatre. And so Professor Mabie, it now seems very clear: everyone has to paint their nudes.

NOTE

1. For examples of Sudermann's work, see *Die Ehre* and *Magda* in works cited.

WORKS CITED

Bigsby, C. W. E. *Modern American Drama*. Cambridge: Cambridge University Press, 1998.

Isaac, Dan. Introduction to *Spring Storm*. New York: New Directions, 1999.

Jackson, Esther Merle. *The Broken World of Tennessee Williams*. Madison: University of Wisconsin Press, 1965.

O'Neill, Eugene. *Ten "Lost" Plays*. New York: Dover, 1955.

Sudermann, Hermann. *Die Ehre*. Berlin: J. O. Cotta'sche, 1929.

———. *Magda*. New York: Samuel French, 1895.

Williams, Dakin, and Shepeard Mead. *Tennessee Williams: An Intimate Biography*. New York: Arbor House, 1983.

Williams, Tennessee. *Spring Storm,* ed. Dan Isaac. New York: New Directions, 1999.

"Stop! I'm a Family Man! I've Got a Daughter! A Little—Girrrrl!"

Prefiguring the Patriarch in *Not About Nightingales*

Thomas Gregory Carpenter

In 1938 the inmates of a Philadelphia County prison in Pennsylvania launched a hunger strike to protest the prison's bad food. Twenty five of the leaders of the strike were corralled into a block of cells known as the "Klondike" where the prison officials raised the temperature on the steam radiators. When this version of appetite stimulation was completed, four men were dead. In St. Louis, an outraged Tom Williams[1] began writing almost immediately, spurred on by a combination of newspaper headlines and an admitted overindulgence in coffee (Leverich, 274). His feverish reaction to the prison scandal resulted in one of his earliest full-length plays, *Not About Nightingales*. With no attempt to disguise his inspiration, Williams focuses the play on a prison where a number of inmates decide to protest the prison's bad food with a hunger strike. The warden, Boss Whalen, orders five of the ringleaders to the "Klondike," killing all but one. Williams conceived the play as a vehicle for the Mummers, a theater group in St. Louis, but it was never performed. Shortly thereafter, he revised it as part of a young playwright's competition sponsored by the influential Group Theatre.[2] The play then languished for more than five decades until in 1998 it was finally published and performed in England to much acclaim.[3] Williams uses the basic facts of the prison scandal in order to write a play that is both political and personal. He uses the incident to "make a statement" about both the need for prison reform and the horrors of what Blanche DuBois might call "deliberate cruelty." Williams even dedicates the play to Clarence Darrow,[4] as if to underscore further his own connection with humanitarian and social protest causes.

Such overt political content is certainly unusual for Williams, who, when asked about his own reluctance to write explicitly about the civil rights movement, chose to term his aesthetic as "oblique" (*Conversations,* 129) when confronting any political or social issues. Williams's own comments as well as several decades of criticism have conditioned most readers to view his writing as outside of the political and social issues of his time, focusing instead on internal themes, autobiographical allusions, and psychoanalytic interpretations of his characters, perhaps best represented by Nancy Tischler's early critical biography, *Tennessee Williams: Rebellious Puritan.* Even Lyle Leverich's biography of Williams begins with a quotation from Williams, printed as an epigraph, about how "the major theme" in his work is "the affliction of loneliness (xxvii)."

Thus, for many readers, *Not About Nightingales* comes as a bit of a surprise. Its dramatic pedigree appears to owe more to Clifford Odets than to Williams's usual inspiration, Anton Chekhov. Given its politically charged subject matter, it is tempting to try to explain away this early play as an anomaly or as a cynical attempt to pander to the political tastes of the Group Theatre in order to win a prize.[5] In the final draft, Williams certainly seems to have a canny understanding of his immediate audience, and as Allean Hale points out, Williams's reference to Group Theatre alumnus "Jules Garfield"[6] in a stage direction seems less than a coincidence (xix). Some contemporary theater reviewers have chosen to dismiss the play for these suspicions:

> Nightingales is mainly notable as a lesson in the ways even a self-generating, poetically fecund talent like Williams can learn by mimicking the currently popular models, and shaping his sensibility to his idea of the market taste. Though streaked with hints of the real Williams to come, the play is chiefly an imitation of something else—a standard-issue '30s prison movie—carpeted up to please somebody else. (Feingold, 135)

Even reviewers who do not stress the connection to the Group Theatre contest, such as Robert Brustein, still reject the play for being derivative: "Writing partly under the influence of O'Neill's sea plays, Williams had also been watching a lot of *Big House* [prison] movies when he conceived *Not About Nightingales*" (30). For the reader who sees Williams solely as the "personal" playwright dedicated to originality and poetic expression, it may indeed be tempting to reclassify this play as an aberration which predates Williams's discovery of his own "voice" as a dramatist. As such, it would seem to offer little to a contemporary audience, and its place in the Williams's canon would involve only its historical significance.

However, more recent scholarship has succeeded in expanding the relevance of Williams's body of work beyond personal expression and into the political arena. As Philip Kolin notes in his review of recent Williams scholarship, "[g]one is the image of Tennessee Williams, the rebellious Puritan. . . . In the 1990s, Williams is often lauded for being egregiously rebellious" ("Tenn" 3). Kolin goes on to state that "[t]he refrain in much earlier Williams criticism—that Tenn was not a political author, never had been, never will be—has been happily muted in the 1990s" (3–4). Recent critical works such as John M. Clum's review of male homosexuality in modern drama and David Savran's analysis of the politics of masculinity in the works of Williams and Arthur Miller have helped to solidify a number of different ideological readings of Williams's plays.[7] In place of the popular perception of Williams as the personal poet of the stage, we now often see Williams considered as a persistently subversive social critic.[8] Savran even goes so far as to suggest that Williams possesses a more active political consciousness than Miller: "[U]nlike Miller, who (at least in testimony before the House [Un-American Activities] Committee) renounced his former leftist associations, Williams, in his *Memoirs* and in interviews dating from 1940 until the end of his life, insisted on his continued commitment to radical political change" (79). Savran actually takes his cue from Williams himself, who, despite his desire to be "oblique," nevertheless wished to present himself in more self-consciously political terms. In early interviews, he repeatedly casts himself in the tradition of the socially conscious dramatist: "I try to write all my plays so that they carry some social message along with the story" *(Conversations,* 5). When asked in 1945 how to improve the human situation, he clearly responds as an artist with very pragmatic political ideas: "It's a social and economic problem, of course . . . not something mystical. I don't think there will be any equity in American life until at least ninety percent of our population are living under different circumstances" *(Conversations,* 15). Even during the 1970s, when his plays were becoming more and more introspective, he persists with many of his earlier attitudes. While being interviewed for the highly political *The Red Devil Battery Sign,* Williams explains his disenchantment with recent United States history:

> It's the moral decay of America, which really began with the Korean War, way before the Kennedy assassination. The main reason we were involved in Vietnam was so two hundred billion dollars worth of equipment could be destroyed and would have to be bought again. We're the death merchants of the world, this once great and beautiful democracy. People think I'm a communist [for saying this], but I hate all bureaucracy, all isms. I'm a revolutionary only in the sense that I want to see us escape from this sort of trap. (Conversations 292)

As a result of these recent critical trends, as well as many of his own comments, the highly charged political content in *Not About Nightingales* should make the play seem less of an anomaly in the Williams canon and more like an introduction to the social conscience that reappears throughout his later work.

Yet, in some ways his "oblique" style is still present. Certainly, if one reads the play solely as a treatise on penal reform, Williams "puts his cards on the table" plainly enough to please even Stanley Kowalski. However, if one looks beyond Williams's surface-level presentation of a "social issue," the play begins to demonstrate much of Williams's more subtle political approach. Savran provides the most compelling argument available for reading Williams as a political writer, even in the playwright's

more "oblique" work. Savran's basic thesis suggests that Williams's political sensibilities come into his work as a result of Cold War gender prescriptions. Taking his cue
from the social historian Elaine Tyler May, Savran points to a "domestic form of
containment" (7) dominating American culture after World War II which enforced
a "strict prescription of masculine and feminine roles defined by the interrelation-
ship of men and women in both home and marketplace" (7). Savran sees Williams
struggling within this social framework and attempting to challenge "these same
constructions by offering subtly subversive models of gender and sexuality that, I
believe, suggest a way beyond those 'sex roles' that continue to exercise a powerful
hold over the American domestic *imaginaire*" (9). Savran's reliance on the particu-
larities of Cold War domestic policy has little to do with *Not About Nightingales*, but
by drawing attention to Williams's treatment of masculinity, he does prompt a
Williams's reader to look at the playwright's handling of men in this early, male-
dominated play. As an early work, *Not About Nightingales* provides an ideal opportunity to find the heart of Williams's notions of masculinity in the broad strokes
often typical in a writer's early stages. The play presents one of the earliest examples
of Williams's explorations of the link between power and practiced masculinity. His
artistic mission is to exploit the dramatic and theatrical potential of characters with
great power, to link their power with practiced masculinity, and then to deconstruct
those characters, exposing flaws, contradictions, and inconsistencies in order to
explore the problems facing men's identity in twentieth-century America.

In *Not About Nightingales,* Williams focuses on two levels of narrative: he presents a politically charged story which details the struggle between an all-powerful
prison warden, Boss Whalen, and a group of inmates who rebel and are punished;
and he writes a more personal story about Canary Jim, a young inmate and inform-
ant for the warden who, only a month away from parole, falls in love with Eva, the
newly hired receptionist. The latter story is most familiar to Williams's readers. Jim
is a budding writer, much like Valentine Xavier in *Battle of Angels*, and he is educat-
ing himself, much like Jim O'Connor in *The Glass Menagerie*. Jim and Eva's conversations provide the play's philosophical moments, as well as the inspiration for
the title of the play. Unlike John Keats, Jim believes that literature should be real and
gritty, and thus, not about nightingales (98). Due to its familiar trope many reviewers, anxious to link the play to Williams's later work, have focused on Jim's plight.
Kolin points out the similarities by labeling Jim as a "true Williams revolutionary"
(Review 833) and connecting his final action to other Williams revolutionaries: "At
the end of the play, Jim jumps from the warden's office into the harbor around the
prison. He is the survivor, the fugitive hero, the would-be poet—all roles Williams
would flesh out in Kilroy, Val Xavier, and even Chance Wayne" (833). Likewise,
Matt Wolf links Jim to Tom Wingfield and connects Butch O'Fallon, the "tough
guy" inmate, with both Stanley Kowalski and Blanche DuBois (E2). However, the
political story of Boss Whalen and his exercise of institutional power provides an
equally compelling means of connecting the play to the rest of Williams's work
through his treatment of masculinity and power.[9]

The political story is less familiar to Williams readers, and it also carries with it a healthy share of the awkwardness of a young writer. The inmates consist of stock characters with predictable, and perhaps even inevitable names: the tough guy leader, Butch; the homosexual, Queen; the athlete, Swifty; a blonde female apparition from Butch's past, Goldie; the former Navy recruit, Sailor Jack; and so on. Allean Hale correctly identifies Williams's inspiration as the conventions of 1930's prison films, such as *The Big House* (xviii),[10] hardly the richest source of inspiration for a young playwright. And yet, it is this archaic, clumsy, and rickety social storytelling that jumps off the page because in it we see the heart of the melodrama that Williams would later perfect in his theatrical collaborations with Elia Kazan, the violence that permeates much of his early work, the passion of his convictions, and most significantly for this study, the exploration of the different ways in which masculinity manifests itself. Williams, at the time of the writing, was coming into his own. He had escaped from his father's shoe factory in St. Louis, he had finally completed his formal education, he had begun writing plays, and he was on the verge of establishing his sexual identity. At this time of impending maturity, he turns to this archetypal gathering of men and begins his exploration of power and practiced masculinity.

To the extent that power and patriarchy walk hand in hand, the prison's patriarch is Boss Whalen, the warden.[11] With Boss Whalen, Williams introduces a chain of social patriarchs that will include Big Daddy in *Cat on a Hot Tin Roof* and Boss Finley in *Sweet Bird of Youth*,[12] and he consistently defines these men's power in terms, not only of societal position, but also as an expression of gender. These are all men who wield tremendous influence over others due, in part, to their hierarchical positions in society and/or their wealth, and they exercise that power as an expression of their masculinity. Boss Whalen, whose title suggests his relationship with the others in the play, establishes his power through his position in the prison hierarchy. However, he views his role in a much broader social context than life in a prison. When Eva first applies for a job by explaining her difficulties in finding work during the Depression, Whalen interrupts her and clearly establishes his own view of his position: "Next time you apply for a job don't pull a sob story. What your *business executive* is interested in is your potential value, not your—your personal misfortunes!" (15, italics mine). Interestingly, Whalen chooses to classify his position of prison warden as a "business executive," which creates an analogy between a capitalist corporation and a penal institution (an analogy with which Williams might very likely agree, considering his hatred for working in his father's shoe factory), as well as linking Whalen's position as an institutional patriarch with the broader social world. In this moment of conflict between Whalen and Eva, Williams emphasizes their gender roles in a stage direction. While Eva *"in breathless haste"* (14) attempts to make her case, her words spill forth equally with the contents of her purse. Williams uses this opportunity to underscore the gender roles played by Eva, through her purse, and consequently by Whalen, the "business executive," who *"takes a cigar"* (15) while administering his corrective lecture. When Whalen speaks of proper interviewing techniques, he speaks as both a "business executive" and as a man.

This pattern becomes clearer in a later scene after Whalen has already hired Eva. He begins by emphasizing his power over previous women who have worked for him by insisting that he normally gets rid of female employees within two weeks if they don't "measure up to the job" (78). When Eva boasts of her own efficiency, he corrects her by stating the proper requirement for a woman in her job: "Personality! You're in a position where you got to meet the public. Big men politically come in this office—you give 'em a smile, they feel good—what do they care about the tax-payers' money?" (78–79). Just as he has connected his own societal position with male business executives across the country, he now connects that source of eco-nomic power with the political, linking his office to a chain of "big men politically" throughout the country. He simultaneously elevates his own power while reducing the role of the woman in his office. Her job is to make men feel good and, thus, add a sense of virility to similarly powerful men.

By establishing Whalen's power as being connected to the power of men throughout the country, Williams can then turn to the microcosm of Whalen's deal-ings with the other characters in the prison to comment on the nature of power and patriarchy in society at large. Williams introduces Whalen as "*a powerful man, rather stout, but with coarse good looks*" (13), who demonstrates his relation to others in his first appearance in the play by entering his office and tossing his coat to Jim. It is understood that Jim will take his coat and put it in a clean, safe place for him. He does not verbalize his desires. Clearly, Jim is used to anticipating and taking care of Whalen's daily needs. Shortly thereafter, he also refers to Jim as "Jimmy boy" (13), assuming a paternal position while simultaneously casting Jim in the role of a child by using the diminutive version of his name and adding the tag, "boy." As a "boss," Whalen has assumed the power of the chief in a tribe of men, a god who holds the ability to grant manhood to others. He has become the father to the son who can never see himself as a man until his father calls him a man. This paternal position-ing reemerges whenever Jim attempts to express himself equally. For example, when Whalen asks Jim to describe the food in the prison and Jim responds a bit too col-orfully, Whalen takes it as an affront to his own dominant position. Feeling that Jim is getting too comfortable with himself, Whalen seeks to embarrass him in front of Eva: "Look here, Jim. You're talking too uppity. Showing off for Miss Crane, I guess—'s at it?" (61). Whalen not only becomes the disciplining father figure, but he also exploits the sexual tension in the room. Like an animal, he marks his terri-tory and attempts to eliminate Jim as a sexual rival. Thus, his power again manifests itself along gender lines.

As we have already seen in two of his interchanges with Eva, Whalen's expres-sion of power exploits gender difference when dealing with women. Williams simi-larly takes careful note to develop the gender distinctions when Mrs. Bristol, the mother of Sailor Jack, comes to plead her son's case before Whalen, unaware that her son has been transferred to a mental institution after suffering the rigors of the Klondike. Unsure of Sailor Jack's identity, Whalen orders Jim to read the informa-tion off the son's file card. When Jim begins to improvise an explanation for Sailor Jack's breakdown, Whalen interrupts him: "Read what's on the card, that's all!" (32). Here, we see one of the principal exhibitions of power in the Williams canon—the ability to control all information.[13] When Mrs. Bristol reacts emotionally to the

news of her son's breakdown, Whalen complains that he has no time for such outbursts: "I got all the sympathy in the world for *you women* that come in here, but
this is a penal institution and we simply can't be taking time out from our routine
business for things like this" (32, italics mine). As Jim helps her out of the office,
Whalen christens his victory by lighting another cigar. Again, Whalen demonstrates
the extent of his power, and then defines that power in terms of gender by contrasting his "penal institution" with "you women," and then signing his work with
the ever-manly cigar.

However, it is in Whalen's confrontations with Eva that Williams fully exploits
the ways in which the warden's societal power is linked with his practiced masculinity. In his first scene, after tossing his coat to Jim, Whalen notices Eva, whom he has
not yet met. He takes steps not only to consolidate his own position of power, but
also to demonstrate male dominance in the office. He begins speaking to Jim about
the difficulties he has encountered while inspecting the grounds of the prison,
unaware that Jim has already told Eva that the warden has been drinking beer at
Tony's, a popular gathering place. As Whalen speaks this lie, seemingly to Jim but
intended for Eva, Williams includes the following stage direction: "*He winks at Jim,
then belches*" (13). These two actions both reinforce the sense of Whalen's power in
the play and position of his power within the realm of gender. Despite Jim's subservient position to Whalen, he nevertheless rates higher than a visiting female.
Whalen shows he can trust Jim by lying to someone else and acknowledging that lie
to his male friend. The wink suggests a shared knowledge and thus an intimacy. It
is a source of bonding that they have which necessarily excludes the woman. The
belch, on the other hand, draws more clearly the line between men and women. By
committing such a social *faux pas*, Williams links Whalen to one of the oldest tropes
in American culture, including Huckleberry Finn, Stanley Kowalski, and Oscar
Madison, by contrasting the rough, naturalistic man against the feminizing practice
and manners of the domestic woman.[14] His belch also ties him to a tradition of practiced masculinity that prizes non-verbal communication over actual conversation. In
his analysis of masculinity and twentieth-century literature, Peter Schwenger argues
that the rise of self-consciousness in modern life has had a direct impact on modern
notions of masculinity: "The role has become that of the 'natural' man. Its particular gestures are increasingly less civilized, reveling in rough edges; fists replace
rapiers, blue jeans replace silk breeches, obscenity replaces wit" (9). Whalen
embraces the behavior of this more crude, "natural man" in order to make the visiting female less comfortable and to demonstrate the full extent of his power.

Whalen's subtle attack against Eva is not yet complete. After having removed
his coat, he then begins to unbutton his shirt and loosen his tie. At this point, he
finally addresses Eva directly: "Excuse me, *lady*, I'm going to do a striptease" (13 italics mine). Williams will repeat a variation of this moment in *A Streetcar Named
Desire* when Stanley first confronts Blanche. Stanley's undressing is partly intended
to arouse Blanche, but also it is an attempt to test the boundaries of acceptable
behavior around the visiting sister-in-law and reinforce his own ability to do as he
pleases in his own home. In a sense, he is daring her to object. While Williams gives

no indication that Whalen hopes to arouse Eva in this first scene, the warden does acknowledge that she is a different sex, and that certain actions of a man, such as the removal of his clothes, are inappropriate around a "lady," a term which moves beyond the identification of her sex and carries connotations of traditional gender expectations. Yet, he implies that he might do so anyway. He does not apologize for a past action, but instead for his future behavior: "I'm *going* to do a striptease." At this point, the seemingly innocuous "joke" becomes a threat of future actions and a demonstration of his power, and most significantly, because of the sexual nature of the threat, Williams links Whalen's power with his gender.

Whalen also denies Eva a voice in the office. When he incorrectly assumes that she is a reporter, Eva attempts to correct him, but he cuts her off in mid-sentence:

> EVA: To begin with I'm not—
> WARDEN: You've probably come here to question me . . . (14)

Thus, it falls to Jim, the other man in the office to clarify the situation: "She's not a reporter" (14). Whereas Eva begins with a clarifying clause, Jim must directly state the facts in order for Whalen to take notice. The communication rules are quite clear. The woman has no voice in Whalen's office unless she is granted special permission to speak. Only after Jim corrects Whalen's assumption does the warden grant her such an opportunity: "Aw.—What *is* your business, young lady?" (14). However, just as with his reduction of Jim to "Jimmy Boy," he also manages to emphasize her youth and her sex role, underscoring everything she is about to say with the understanding that her words are the words of a non-adult, non-man.

Having retgained control of the conversation, he lectures her about approaching "business executives" before "*biting and spitting out the end of the cigar*" (15), reinforcing his command over the room. Eva, demoralized by Whalen's lecture, seemingly recognizes the significance of the phallic shaped emblem of masculine power and begins to leave. Whalen, with all the assurance of absolute power, now decides to reverse himself as an act of whimsy and considers offering her a job. He prompts Jim to explain the one requirement of working for him: "The ability to keep your mouth shut except when you're given specific instructions to speak!" (15). Whalen uses this rule to reinforce the notion that he controls all information, communication, knowledge, and reality. Comfortable in his socially sanctioned position of power, safe within the confines of his office, and armed with a cigar, Whalen defines truth as he sees fit, creating reality in prison by *fiat*.

Once Eva leaves, Williams provides us with a further demonstration of Whalen's unequal but valued bond with Jim. Whalen asks Jim what he thinks of Eva, but he prompts the nature of Jim's answer by including the tag, "okay, huh?" (16) at the end of his question. When Jim agrees, Whalen interrupts with the final line of the scene: "Yes, Siree! Dizzy as hell—But she's got a shape on her that would knock the bricks out of a Federal Pen!" (16). With this statement, Whalen reduces her value to her sexual attractiveness, while Williams subtly casts that attractiveness as a threat to the warden's own kingdom. While Whalen encourages Jim to appreciate her as a sexual object, Williams positions the warden's power as the patriarch of a "Federal Pen" in opposition to the power of her "shape." Throughout this scene, Williams works hard to establish Whalen's position within the institution, the extent of his power, and the link that power has to gender. He closes the scene with Whalen's "*booming laughter*" (16), leaving the reader with the final conclusion that just as Whalen can control the nature of truth within the prison, he also defines what is funny, so long as he amuses himself.

As the play progresses, the subtle linking of Whalen's institutional power with his expression of masculinity becomes more blatant and sexual. In one of Jim's private conversations with Eva, he points to an inner room in the office and tells her about Whalen's relationship with his previous receptionist: "He *had her* in there the first week" (44, italics mine). Jim, who is a budding writer and presumably is careful with words, sees Whalen's sexual practices as another expression of power. Jim's use of the phrase "had her" to describe sexual intercourse expresses the view of women in the all-male environment, and Jim's recognition of the speed with which Whalen "had" the women adds to this sense of possession. Williams follows up this description of Whalen's sexual practices by allowing the cock to crow himself. When Whalen is alone with Eva, he begins to brag about his own sexual prowess, citing past experiences: "Well, it might surprise you to know how well I go over with some of the girls! . . . I had a date not so long ago—girl works over at the Cattle and Grain Market—'bout your age, build, ev'rything— [*He licks his lips.*]—When I got through loving her up she says to me— 'Do it again, Papa do it again!'" (79–80). Not only does he emphasize the degree of sexual pleasure he is capable of supplying, but he also clearly takes on a paternal relationship with this last conquest, denoted by her reference to him as "Papa." He plays the role of patriarch not only with the "boys" in the prison, but also with the "girls" of the inner room.

As the tensions in the prison escalate, Whalen consolidates his social and sexual power in order to thwart the threatened riot. He begins enforcing his power by ordering the leaders of the hunger strike to be sent to the Klondike and closing access to the prison. When Eva prepares to leave for home, he exerts his control over the situation. He begins by belching, the masculine expulsion again. He then informs her of his plans for the prison while the hunger strikers are in the Klondike: "Quarantine! A bad epidemic's broken out! Twenty-five cases are going to be running a pretty high fever tonight so I've put this place under quarantine restrictions— nobody's gonna leave the grounds till the epidemic is over" (130). When she protests, he elaborates: "I've ordered the boats to take no passengers on or off the island without my special permission" (131). He then boasts that he has no limits to his power: "Times of emergency I can do what I damn please" (131). He has even disconnected the phones in order to solidify his position as the king of the island. His connection to business executives and "big men politically" is apparent in his actions. He has the power of the business executive and the politician, and as Williams has demonstrated, that power is the power of manhood.

At this moment, Williams moves from the social to the personal. In one of the play's most audacious moments, Whalen culminates his control over the elements by seducing Eva, calming her fears with a powerful physical massage (133). Feingold, in reviewing the Broadway production of the play, describes Whalen's charismatic abilities as "a gaze of hypnotic power, in the Gothic-monster tradition" (135). At the moment when he demonstrates his greatest institutional power over people's lives, in the role of the all-powerful warden, Williams reminds us that Whalen's power also permeates even to the individual level and is based, in part, on his sexual prowess and charisma.

However, Williams implies that Whalen's playing of the patriarch has extended too far. Not only does he amass all of his power in the prison as an extension of his masculinity, but he also attempts to extend this power to the domestic world. We learn that Whalen has a young daughter which, if left at that, might simply reinforce his sexual virility as an effective propagator of the species. However, in a scene where Whalen talks to what he terms his "baby doll" (60) on the telephone, Williams demonstrates the ways in which Whalen interacts with her. Suddenly, the belching, abusive man who seemed incapable of gentility when talking to the new receptionist, devolves into "baby talk," doting on his daughter with seemingly unashamed abandon: "Puddikins? Popsy dust wanted to know if oo was bein' a dood little durl! Oo are? Dat's dood. Popsy'd dot somefin fo dood little durls! No. Not a stick-candies. Oo see when Popsy dets home, 'es oo will! Bye-bye now! Bye-bye!" (60). While Williams's overwritten baby talk reduces Whalen to a figure of ridicule, it also emphasizes his attempt to control aspects of his home. By playing the doting father to his "little durl," Whalen reinforces traditional gender roles. He urges her to play her role and be a "dood little durl." His boast that he has "somefin fo dood little durls" emphasizes that, just as in the prison, in his domestic life he is the one with the power to bestow gifts, whether they are rubber ducks, as is the case here, or "copper" (merits) in the prison, which he gives to Jim for playing the role of informer.

Whalen's desire to play the role of the patriarch at home was not unusual at the time of *Not About Nightingales*. As Michael Kimmel points out, during the Great Depression American men demonstrated an increased desire to play domestic roles. With the fear of losing one's job and, thus, becoming a "failure" eminent, a number of men looked to the security of their positions at home: "The workplace was too unreliable to enable men to prove their manhood; in fact, it eroded their authority at home" (201). Williams's glimpse of Whalen the family man busily perpetuating gender stereotypes foreshadows the specter of loss circulating around his institutional position. If common men were losing their jobs and attempting to solidify their positions at home, perhaps a warden could too. This idea of failure in the social world was not alien to Williams. Nor was it something he read about in social theater or saw in prison movies as many of the reviewers would have it. Rather, at the time he was writing this play, Williams watched his own patriarch, his father Cornelius Williams, who attempted to rule young Williams's life both at home and in the institution of the shoe factory, fail. By all accounts Cornelius was an abusive, uncommunicative father to whom Williams could never relate until after his death. However, in 1938, rather than the all-powerful and abusive patriarch, Williams began to witness the capitalist failure of his father, whose shoe business was collapsing:

> What Tom presently saw was a man defeated, retreating and impris-
> oned by his own hand. . . . Tennessee was to say that his failure to stand
> up to his father and his overt fear of him were interpreted by the old
> man as weakness and cowardice and that he loathed his son for it. But
> now, in December of 1938, the tables were turning. During all the
> years of his youth, Tom had looked upon C. C. as an overpowering fig-
> ure of strength. But once the son had become a young man, he began
> to perceive in his father the same weakness and cowardice that the old
> man had attributed to him. This knowledge was enough to give Tom
> the courage he needed to leave and to say, once again, good-bye to St.
> Louis. (Leverich, 273)

Significantly, as Williams finds his own maturity, and thus his manhood, he recognizes the fragility and fluidity of such concepts. He finds a way to use elements
from his own life to address the more broad social concerns of the time. If the fear-
some "C.C." could return home, decimated by the collapsing economy, then most
any traditional concept of masculinity must be in jeopardy.

At this point, Williams is fully ready to break this, the first of his many great
patriarchs. As the prison riot escalates, Whalen is finally confronted by his
Doppelgänger in the prison, Butch O'Fallon. Butch is the ringleader of the riot and
the lone survivor of the Klondike. He is presented repeatedly as a "tough," whose
masculinity becomes most fully defined when he accepts the challenge of the
Klondike, becomes an animal himself, and attacks the radiator: "[*He springs on the
radiators and grapples with them as though with a human adversary—he tries to throt-
tle steam with his hands—he's scalded—screams with agony—backs away, his face contorted, wringing his hands.*] SSSSS! SSSSS! SSSSS! [*He is crazily imitating their noise*"]
(145). As Butch enters Whalen's office, Williams underscores the mythical nature of
their face off: "*The two rulers face each other for the first time*" (157). However, like
many American men in the Great Depression, Whalen faces insurmountable opposition and, like Cornelius, fails. He turns to Jim, attempting to reestablish their
bond, insisting that he was Jim's friend, but Jim responds defiantly: "I wasn't yours!"
(157). As Butch begins to whip him with the warden's own whipping hose, Whalen's
demeanor changes drastically. First, he boasts that he has the backing of the United
States army, calling on all of his authority as an institutional patriarch. When Butch
shows little concern, Whalen's position crumbles and he retreats to his other realm:
"[*cowering to the floor*]: Stop! I'm a family man! I've got a wife! A daughter! A little—
girrrrl! [*The final word turns into a scream of anguish as Butch crouches over him with
the whip beating him with a demoniacal fury till he is senseless*"] (158). In this key
reversal, the sadist has become the receiver, and the proud patriarch hides behind his
family—his wife to whom he has been repeatedly unfaithful and his daughter,
whom he attempts to mold into the epitome of girlhood with an inflatable rubber
duck. He also voluntarily allows himself to be defined by his relation to his family.
Williams breaks his patriarchal figure of power by demonstrating the instability of
the masculine role exerted by many institutional patriarchs.

Clearly, in Williams's view the concept of masculinity becomes very slippery. In many of his interviews, he concedes his belief in striving for the androgynous: "You can seek it but never find it. However, the androgynous is the truest human being" ("Conversations," 212). He seems to indicate, in an era when gender was being rigidly prescribed, that gender is fluid. By deconstructing the most powerful of men, men who link their masculinity to their expression of power, Williams creates his most dramatic opportunity for exposing the social construction behind our most visible embodiments of gender. Even at an early age, Williams demonstrates a keen understanding of the technique that he continues to employ in many of his later, more celebrated plays. One can best observe this continued exploration of power and masculinity by looking briefly at his depiction of Big Daddy in *Cat on a Hot Tin Roof*, and Boss Finley in *Sweet Bird of Youth*.

In *Cat on a Hot Tin Roof*, Williams uses all of his skills to build up Big Daddy into one, loud, bombastic titan of masculine achievement.[15] Big Daddy possesses a tremendous amount of power, and like Boss Whalen, he attempts to exert that power on two fronts. As a successful plantation owner "of twenty-eight thousand acres of the richest land this side of the valley Nile!" (86), he has amassed great wealth and possesses social power similar to an institutional patriarch. Moreover, since his plantation is also his home, he appears in the role of a domestic patriarch as well. As a success in the social world, Big Daddy's wealth touches so many others that even though his extended family (as well as Reverend Tooker) have gathered to welcome him home and celebrate his birthday, in reality, most have gathered for positioning in Big Daddy's will. As a domestic patriarch whose wealth also lends social power, Big Daddy controls everyone in the play. As Colby Kullman explains: "Big Daddy Pollitt appears to have tyrannical control over his Delta plantation empire, seeming to rule without pity his wife, Big Mama; sons, Brick and Gooper; daughters-in-law, Maggie and Mae; his grandchildren; his doctor; and his minister" (668). Unlike Boss Whalen, who desperately attempts to hold on to his crumbling institution, Big Daddy's empire continues to flourish, and his only fear is, like that of Augustus, Claudius, and Marcus Aurelius, that he will not have anyone as capable as he with whom to leave his empire.

Moreover, demonstrating a tendency for Butch's machismo, Big Daddy boasts of his longevity and connects his ability to rule as an expression of his own physical prowess: "I got fifteen years or twenty years left in me! I'll outlive *you* [Brick]! I'll bury you an' have to pay for your coffin!" (126). He further links his monetary success to his virility as a heterosexual male: "I'm going to pick me a choice one [woman], I don't care how much she costs, I'll smother her in—minks! Ha ha! I'll strip her naked and smother her in minks and choke her with diamonds! Ha ha! I'll strip her naked and choke her with diamonds and smother her with minks and hump her from hell to breakfast. *Ha aha ha ha ha!*" (96). He can "buy" a woman, and then smother, strip, and choke her (all feats of physical power), by exercising his power through the purchase of the most expensive items. In this statement, Big Daddy expresses the power of his wealth in terms of his ability to combine heterosexual activity and violence.

Williams demonstrates the extent of Big Daddy's power as a domestic patriarch most clearly through his control of communication. Just as Boss Whalen can control the nature of information and truth in his prison, Big Daddy comes to dominate the language used in his home. When Big Mama finally tries to assert herself after learning that Big Daddy is dying, she calls on Brick to help coach her diction:

> BIG MAMA. I say—what is it Big Daddy always says when he's disgusted?
> BRICK (from the bar) Big Daddy says "crap" when he's disgusted.
> BIG MAMA (rising). That's right—CRAP! I say CRAP too, like Big Daddy! (156)

Likewise, when she confronts Gooper with his box of "official" papers for rearranging the estate, she similarly adopts the language of Big Daddy: "And Gooper you put that away before I grab it out of our [sic] hand and tear it right up! I don't know what the hell's in it, and I don't want to know what the hell's in it. I'm talkin' in Big Daddy's language now; I'm his *wife*, not his *widow*, I'm still his *wife*! And I'm talkin' to you in his language" (155). Big Daddy's sphere of influence overwhelms the members of the house to the extent that whether he is present or not, and whether he performs or not, his ideology will be performed by others in the home—particularly by his "*wife*" as Big Mama puts it, emphasizing their sex roles.

Yet, by reversing audience expectations Williams places distance between popular notions of patriarchy and his use of it in the play. At first glance, Big Daddy appears to follow the tradition of what Michael Kimmel terms "the Self-Made Man, a model of manhood that derives identity entirely from a man's activities in the public sphere, measured by accumulated wealth and status" (16–17). According to Kimmel, this model of obtaining manhood through effort and material success becomes increasingly difficult after the turn of the century. As a result, American men seeking manhood through this model turn to discriminatory practices in order to maintain their increasingly precarious position of privilege: "to many men, that tide that threatened to wash over American manhood and dash their hopes for self-making included other groups (besides immigrants) as well, among them women and homosexuals" (90). Presumably, any successful Self-Made Man would have built his empire on a number of exclusionary principles, including racism, sexism, and homophobia. However, Williams's opening stage directions remind his readers that Big Daddy's "richest land this side of the Valley Nile" was built, not by the current patriarch, but rather by his former employers, whose bedroom provides the set for the entire play: "It hasn't changed much since it was occupied by the original owners of the place, Jack Straw and Peter Ochello, a pair of old bachelors who shared this room all their lives together. In other words, the room must evoke some ghosts; it is gently and poetically haunted by a relationship that must have involved a tenderness which was uncommon" (15). Even though the plantation may be flourishing under the rule of an all-powerful patriarch, Williams broadens the concept of such patriarchy by reminding his readers that the empire was established, not by white, bigoted, Self-Made Men, but rather by two loving homosexuals.

Williams adds to the complexity of manhood in the key confrontation between Big Daddy and Brick. Brick, the former athlete with possible homosexual desires becomes the mouthpiece for the intolerant, homophobic culture, while Big Daddy, the successful patriarch of the culture, suggests an ambiguous personal history and a becomes a bastion of tolerance. As Clum points out, "[t]he exchange is a brilliant reversal of expectation: the object of suspicion will not listen to expressions of understanding and tolerance, countering them with heterosexist ranting" (158). When Brick vehemently attacks the idea that he and Skipper were lovers, Big Daddy interrupts him: "Now, hold on, hold on a minute, son.—I knocked around in my time" (115). As Brick expresses his dismay, Big Daddy pushes even further, defying all expectations of a 1950s Self-Made Man: "[I've] [a]lways, anyhow, lived without much space around me to be infected by ideas of other people. One thing you can grow on a big place more important than cotton!—is *tolerance*!—I grown it" (120). Significantly, his statement implicitly rejects the tendency of many Self-Made Men to incorporate discrimination into their power base. Instead, he insists that his success, which has given him the "space" of a "big place," has fostered the concept of tolerance. In other words, Big Daddy sees masculine success as a natural source for gaining understanding.

In effect, Big Daddy is rejecting his model of masculinity in favor of an older tradition. According to Kimmel, the first archetype of American manhood is the Genteel Patriarch: "To the Genteel Patriarch, manhood meant property ownership and a benevolent patrarchal authority at home, including the moral instruction of his sons. A Christian gentleman, the Genteel Patrarch embodied love, kindness, duty, and compassion, exhibited through philanthropic work, church activities, and deep involvement with his family" (16). This model provides an awkward fit at times for the "Mississippi redneck" (53), as Maggie identifies him, but it demonstrates an inner dissatisfaction with contemporary concepts of masculinity. As he watches his son struggle with the dominant homophobic ideology of the time, Big Daddy finds his own masculine model as a Self-Made Man utterly inadequate.

Likewise, his insistence that Brick communicate with him more fully without the reliance on alcohol also appears somewhat out of character. In his study of communication in all-male cast plays, Robert Vorlicky notes that men generally limit their conversation to "social dialogue" including such topics as "employment, consumerism, families, women, and their own active identification with the cultural ideal of male virility" (16). This type of dialogue offers protection from what he terms "self-disclosing dialogue," which results "in the characters' articulation of personal truths" (7). Vorlicky notes that most men only turn to self-disclosing dialogue when affected by "alcohol, drugs, and violence" (7). In the play, Big Daddy encourages Brick to challenge gender prescriptions and speak more openly. However, Brick notes that their past attempts at communicating have been less than successful: "We talk, you talk, in—circles! We get no where, no where! It's always the same, you say you want to talk to me and don't have a ruttin' thing to say to me!" (102). Just as Big Daddy's attempts to take on the somewhat ill-fitting mantle of the Genteel Patriarch provide mixed results, his attempts to expand the traditional forms of communication between men also fall somewhat short. When Big Daddy finally learns of his cancer and retreats from the play (in Williams's original version), Williams leaves the audience with a sense of failure. Just as Boss Whalen cannot maintain his masculine power on two fronts, Big Daddy cannot fully overcome mid-twentieth-century trends in masculinity.

With *Sweet Bird of Youth*, Williams's vision of power and masculinity seems to have lost the sense of hope partially raised in *Cat on a Hot Tin Roof*, and he returns to the dilemma presented first in *Not About Nightingales*. Like Boss Whalen and Big Daddy, Boss Finley has power and attempts to exert it in both the public and private world. As an institutional patriarch, he has amassed a combination of wealth and political power which has manifested itself in particularly masculine terms as seen in Williams's description of his magisterial house: "*There is only essential porch furniture, Victorian wicker but painted bone white. The men should also be wearing white or off-white suits: the tableau is all blue and white, as strict as a canvas of Georgia O'Keefe's*" (56). He also notes that the terrace to the house is represented by a doorframe and "*a single white column*" (56). The Spartan decorations of "only essential" furniture follows in the tradition of Self-Made Man who has more power than taste, and the single column evokes a phallic image, helping to define Boss Finley's power along terms of gender. Moreover, the constant repetition of "whiteness" provides the first suggestion that Boss Finley, unlike Big Daddy, will fully embrace the exclusionary ideology of the twentieth-century model of the Self-Made Man.

Finley's nickname comes from his position as a Mississippi political boss, replete with mythical and religious connotations which help to solidify his position as an institutional patriarch: "when I was fifteen, I come down barefoot out of the red clay hills as if the Voice of God called me. Which it did, I believe. I firmly believe He called me. And nothing, nobody, nowhere is gonna stop me, never" (73). As a political boss, he has the invulnerability of an agent of God, and his primary agenda involves fighting against miscegenation. His solution, castration of African-American males, serves as an expression of his masculinity. Like Boss Whalen, who holds the power of manhood over the inmates, and Big Daddy, who tries to usher Brick through his guilt over his relationship with Skipper, Boss Finley is the keeper of manhood in the state of Mississippi. Specifically, he places himself as the protector of white manhood, as evident in his television speech: "And what is this [my] mission? I have told you before but I will tell you again. To shield from pollution a blood that I think is not only sacred to me, but sacred to Him [God]" (106). Whereas Big Daddy attempts to spread tolerance, Boss Finley fully embraces discrimination.

And yet, he too feels the strain of attempting to negotiate the expression of his masculine power in both public and private spheres. Just as Boss Whalen's inability to maintain his institutional power threatens his role as a domestic patriarch, Boss Finley's failure to control his domestic world threatens his position as an institutional patriarch: "It's a curious thing, a mighty peculiar thing, how often a man that rises to high public office is drug back down by every soul he harbors under his roof. He harbors them under his roof, and they pull the roof down on him. Every last living one of them" (63). Both of his children, Tom Junior and Heavenly, threaten to expose the hypocrisy behind his public image—Tom Junior, through his repeatedly injudicious behavior (overseeing castrations, drunk driving, flunking college classes), and Heavenly, through her affair with Chance Wayne and the resulting "secret" operation, the scandal of which threatens to dismantle Finley's political reputation. Both of his children's actions reflect directly on Finley's masculine role. He is unable to train Tom Junior in the practicalities of becoming a Self-Made Man, and as a patriarch, he is unable to protect the purity of his daughter. Heavenly refuses to follow his mandates and is, in a sense, Boss Whalen's young daughter from *Not About Nightingales* all grown up and refusing to be a "dood little durl," despite her father's admonitions.

Williams also undercuts Boss Finley's manhood through Miss Lucy, Finley's mistress. According to Tom Junior, Miss Lucy has written on the wall of the hotel restroom that his father "is too old to cut the mustard" (65). However, Williams in not content merely to question Finley's sexual virility. He also casts doubt on the political boss' domineering presence by contrasting his boast that "nobody, nowhere is gonna stop me, never" with a contradictory description of Finley's exit as he goes to settle things with Miss Lucy: "*A sad, uncertain note has come into his voice on this final line. He turns and plods wearily, doggedly off at left*" (73). Boss Finley's position as the most powerful political figure in the land backed up by God, going to wreak justice, hardly matches Williams's description of his "wearily dogged plodding," suggesting to the reader that such seemingly invulnerable institutional patriarchs may be resting uncomfortably behind a façade.

Moreover, even his final, most memorable action in the play, his order to castrate Chance Wayne, is not carried out without complications. As the keeper of the phallus in this small coast town, castration seems to Finley to be the ultimate threat, punishment, and solution to problems. If other men will not follow his will, he will deny them their manhood. Yet, when he finally places the order to emasculate Chance Wayne, Williams de-emphasizes the importance of the threat. Shortly before Finley's men arrive, Chance informs Alexandra Del Lago that he no longer fears Finley's threats: "That [castration] can't be done to me twice. You did it to me this morning, here on this bed" (120). The ultimate symbol of Finley's power, tied directly to a sense of masculinity, is trumped, if only metaphorically, by a woman. With his political future crumbling, his relationships with Heavenly and Miss Lucy in disarray, and his ability to grant and eliminate manhood now being circumvented, by the play's conclusion it is Boss Finley who is emasculated.

Consequently, what we see in *Not About Nightingales* is the beginning of Williams's lifelong essay on American power and masculinity. Repeatedly he focuses on the struggle of men with tremendous power who are unable to maintain it. He links their power with their masculinity, and then exploits the weaknesses in that concept of masculinity. For Boss Whalen that means using the power of the institution to express his manhood, and thus, attempting to live the life of an institutional patriarch while, in a moment of crisis, trying to rely on his role as a domestic patriarch for protection. Big Daddy looks into the abyss and tries to reject the shackles of the Self-Made Man in favor of a more benevolent, older tradition, but his efforts appear to be too little, too late. And Boss Finley fully embraces all of the negatives of maintaining the image of the Self-Made Man, only to see it crumble because of its inner corruption and his inability to maintain any authority in his private sphere. The message seems clear. Tennessee Williams uses his drama in part to expose the facade of masculine power while demonstrating the difficulties and shifting tensions of discovering and performing masculinity in the twentieth century.

NOTES

1. Williams first began using the nickname "Tennessee" after completing the play.

2. The Group Theatre was, along with Orson Welles's Mercury Theatre, the most influential theater company in the 1930s. Its members included Harold Clurman, Lee Strasberg, Stella Adler, Clifford Odets, John Garfield, and the young Elia Kazan, years before he would begin directing Williams's plays. The group was best known politically for its leftist goals and aesthetically for its dedication to realism. While *Not About Nightingales* did not win the competition, another part of Williams's submission, a collection of one-act plays, *American Blues,* did receive a special mention and merited a small cash award.

3. Much of the credit for the play's recovery belongs to the actress Vanessa Redgrave. See her foreword in the edition of the play.

4. The dedication to Darrow also carries further implications. The famed defense attorney in the Scopes Monkey Trial was equally well known for arguing passionately against the death penalty on behalf of Leopold and Loeb. It is conceivable that, for Williams, Darrow represented not only a voice for the humane treatment of criminals, but also a voice against homophobia.

5. Williams did lie about his age in order to apply for the contest, subtracting three years in order to qualify. According to Leverich, Williams felt "that he had every right to deduct the three lost years of enforced labor at the shoe company" (274).

6. John Garfield, who first gained attention as a member of the Group Theatre, was a pioneer for "method" actors in American films, paving the way for more "naturalistic" actors including Montgomery Clift, Marlon Brando, Rod Steiger, Julie Harris, and James Dean. He was also the first choice to play Stanley Kowalski. His most memorable films include *Four Daughters, The Postman Always Rings Twice, Gentlemen's Agreement, Body and Soul,* and *Force of Evil.* See Vineberg in works cited.

7. As proof of current trends, see Colby Kullman's essay as cited. In the essay, Kullman neatly links many of Williams's powerful characters to the power regimes present in George Orwell's *1984* and Joseph Heller's *Catch-22.* Given the past history of Williams's scholarship, it seems unlikely that anyone in an earlier era would have linked Williams with such an overtly political writer as Orwell without needing an extraordinary amount of justification.

8. Nor are these readings purely "new" or reflective of contemporary concerns. See Arthur Miller's contemporaneous reading of *Cat on a Hot Tin Roof* in Bigsby, 88–92.

9. Though he devotes much more space to linking Jim with other "fugitives," Kolin does include one sentence to identify Whalen with Jabe Torrence and Boss Finley, *et al.* However, he does not pursue the idea, probably because of the physical restraints of such a brief review.

10. Hale also identifies this genre of prison films as *film noir*. While the sort of Warner Brothers social issues films and prison films of the 1930s may share some similarities in theme with the tradition of *film noir*, they should not be confused with the latter. The French critics who first started identifying *film noir* were looking at films during and after World War II, often filmed on small budgets (hence the low level of lighting), and were generally pessimistic or cynical in tone (think *Double Indemnity, Out of the Past*, or Orson Welles' much later *Touch of Evil*). For more on the genre, see Katz in works cited.

11. For a broader analysis of the dynamics of masculine power in the play, one could also consider Canary Jim, who, despite his subservient position with Whalen, nevertheless exerts a subtle degree of influence while still maintaining an air of sensitivity often lacking in both Whalen and Butch.

12. See Kullman as cited for an overview of others, such as Jabe Torrence in *Orpheus Descending*, as Williams's own memories of his father.

13. Many examples abound: Amanda's "romantic" memories of her past, and Tom's desire to present "truth" as an "illusion" in *The Glass Menagerie*; Blanche's careful filtering of information and Stanley's discovery of the "truth" about her; Brick's need to put a "spin" on the nature of his friendship with Skipper in *Cat on a Hot Tin Roof*; and Mrs. Venable's control over her son's memory in *Suddenly Last Summer*. . . .

14. In *The Odd Couple*, Neil Simon reverses the gender of Oscar's foil, but the nature of the conflict remains the same. For an example of this trope in American Drama, see Carpenter, 13–17.

15. The character overwhelms the play to such an extent that the Broadway director, Elia Kazan, pushed Williams to rewrite the third act in objection to Williams's having excluded the character.

WORKS CITED

Brustein, Robert. "The Artifact Museum." *New Republic*, 5 April (1998): 29–31.

Carpenter, Greg. "A Streetcar Named Wildfire: Tennessee Williams' Fulfillment of Paulding's *The Lion of the West*," *Publications of the Mississippi Philological Association* (1996): 13–17.

Clum, John M. *Acting Gay: Male Homosexuality in Modern Drama*. New York: Columbia University Press, 1992.

Feingold, Michael. "Private Prisons." *Village Voice*, 9. (1999): 135.

Hale, Allean. Introduction to *Not About Nightingales*, by Tennessee Williams, ed. Allean Hale. New York: New Directions, 1998 xiii–xxii.

Katz, Ephraim. *The Film Encyclopedia*. New York: Harper, 1994.

Kimmel, Michael. *Manhood in America: A Cultural History*. New York: Free Press, 1996.

Kolin, Philip C. Review of *Not About Nightingales*, by Tennessee Williams. *World Literature Today* 72 (1998): 833–834.

———. "Tenn in the '90s: Recent Scholarship on Tennessee Williams." *Publications of the Mississippi Philological Association* (1997): 1–6.

Kullman, Colby. "Rule by Power: 'Big Daddyism' in the World of Tennessee Williams's Plays." *Mississippi Quarterly* 48 (1995): 667–76.

Leverich, Lyle. *Tom: The Unknown Tennessee Williams.* New York: Crown, 1995.

Savran, David. *Communists, Cowboys, and Queers: The Politics of Masculinity in the Work of Arthur Miller and Tennessee Williams.* Minneapolis: U of Minnesota P, 1992.

Schwenger, Peter. *Phallic Critiques: Masculinity and Twentieth-Century Literature.* London: Routledge and Kegan Paul, 1984.

Tischler, Nancy M. *Tennessee Williams: Rebellious Puritan.* New York: Citadel, 1961.

Vineberg, Steve. *Method Actors: Three Generations of American Acting Style.* New York: Schirmer Books, 1991.

Vorlicky, Robert. *Act Like a Man: Challenging Masculinities in American Drama.* Ann Arbor: University of Michigan Press, 1995.

Williams, Tennessee. *Cat on a Hot Tin Roof.* Volume 3 of *Theatre.* New York: New Directions, 1971. 1–215.

———. *Conversations with Tennessee Williams,* ed. Albert J. Devlin. Jackson: University Press of Mississippi, 1986.

———. *Not About Nightingales,* ed. Allean Hale. New York: New Directions, 1998.

———. *Sweet Bird of Youth.* Volume 4 of *Theatre.* New York: New Directions, 1972. 1–124.

Wolf, Matt. "Finding out How Tennessee Williams Got That Way." *New York Times* 21 Apr. 1998, late ed.: E2.

"That Quiet Little Play"

Bourgeois Tragedy, Female Impersonation, and a Portrait of the Artist
in *The Glass Menagerie*

Stephanie B. Hammer

If I might open my lips, Walter, I could tell you things . . . I could . . .
but harsh destiny has bound my tongue as well as my love . . .

(Schiller, *Intrigue and Love*, 7)

Laura is very different from other girls.

(Williams, *Glass Menagerie*, 187)

Far from being a brain-numbed soldier, our artist is actually our child
within, our inner playmate [. . .] In order to work well, may artists find
that their workspaces are best dealt with as play spaces? Dinosaur
murals, toys from the five-and-dime, sea . . . tiny miniature Christmas
lights [. . .]

(Cameron, *The Artist's Way*, 153–4)

Probably no Tennessee Williams play is better known to American audiences and
more often produced on American stages—both amateur and professional—than
The Glass Menagerie, first staged in Chicago and then in New York in late 1944.
Nonetheless the playwright seems to have disliked the drama intensely. Exhibiting
at once frustration and obsession, the dramatist's correspondence with friend
Donald Windham testifies to the ongoing drama of creating the play that was to
represent Williams's breakthrough into success and which also presented a terrible
burden to its creator.

A letter from April 1943 describes a typical day at work on *Menagerie*:

> I have been writing with a tigerish intensity on "The Gentleman
> Caller" every day, and today I felt like I was going to just blow up, so
> I quit. What I am going to do to that quiet little play I don't know.
> (Windham 60)

Williams paints a portrait of himself as both a wild animal, and a bundle of
emotional dynamite ready at any moment to explode. But this violent emotionality
is apparently nowhere to be found in the actual artistic creation. Rather, the emotions of the artist contrast enormously with the work he is constructing, the "quiet
little play" that:

> remains my chief work but it goes slowly . . . It lacks the violence that
> excites me, so I piddle around with it. (Windham, 91)

Work on the play dragged on through the summer of 1944, with Williams talking increasingly about the play as a dreary exercise rather than a piece of artistry:

> It is not a very exciting business but it keeps me occupied while I wait
> for the energy to do something more important. (Windham, 140)

In this same July letter Williams makes an odd comment about himself, admitting he does not want to travel and yet poignantly, feels unstable and rootless:

> I do not feel in such a Gulliver mood—more like an Alice-Sit-By-The-
> Fire—only I can't find the right fire, none of the chimneys seems to
> draw very well. (Windham, 143)

In this fleeting moment, Williams reads himself as both a man and a girl; he
tellingly juxtaposes two images: on one hand, Jonathan Swift's epitome of masculine
motion and outwardness encased in the picaresque adventure of one of Anglo-
America's greatest prose narratives; on the other hand, a distinctly feminine figure of
motionless and domesticity—vaguely reminiscent of Lewis Carroll's famous little
girl hero. In this particular epistle, Williams clearly aligns himself with the latter,
with a quiet girl sitting by a fireplace or rather with a little girl who would sit by the
fire, if she could just find the correct heart—a girl not unlike Cinderella, the orphan,
beleaguered by false siblings and a cruel stepmother, waiting for a prince and a glass
slipper. He is also citing *Alice Sit-by-the-Fire*, the play that Laurette Taylor—eventually the star of *The Glass Menagerie*—closed in New York because of her opening
night appearance on stage, completely drunk (Leverich, 582).

The invocation of this highly successful 1920s play is interesting on a number
of levels. First, the reference suggests that Williams was already thinking seriously of
Laurette Taylor for the production of *Menagerie*. Secondly, *Alice Sit-By-The-Fire* was

composed by James M. Barrie, the author of *Peter Pan* and *The Admirable Crichton*; this figure presents an interesting point of comparison with Williams and a historical trajectory of theater created by gay dramatists. Deeply closeted and yet brilliantly insightful into the workings of bourgeois English society,[1] Barrie delighted in odd kinds of gender and genre bending creations, which combined aspects of narrative and traditional drama in unorthodox ways. *Alice Sit-By-The-Fire* is part novel, part drama, and part comedy, and features the complex dynamic between a belle-of-the-ball young mother and her thoughtful, artistically gifted adolescent daughter. This dynamic clearly looks forward to the relations between Laura and Amanda in *Menagerie*. At the end of the play, the mother, Alice (played in the New York production by Laurette Taylor) makes the following poignant speech:

> It's summer done, autumn begun. Farewell summer, we don't know you any more. My girl and I are like the little figures in the weather-house; when my Amy comes out, Alice goes in. Alice Sit-by-the-Fire henceforth. The moon is full tonight, Robert, but it isn't looking for me any more. Taxis farewell—advance, four-wheelers. (316)

Is Barrie's Alice really so sad to stay home? The overt theatricality of the speech and its melodramatic emphasis suggest that it is at least partially ironic, and the action of the play thus far has shown us clearly that party-girl Alice is in large part overjoyed to remain at home with her daughter and two younger children, now that she at last has the chance to do so.

If we know anything at all about Williams's career and demise, we cannot help a frisson of foreknowledge reading these lines against the playwright's description of himself in the letter to Windham. Throughout his stormy career, Williams was very much like Barrie's Alice; an avid pursuer of beautiful young men. A spectacular and notorious figure, he would indeed appear to wander like Gulliver, but at heart he seems to have been continually searching for the right person and the right place to retire to, never finding either. He would die alone in a New York hotel room, an alcoholic, plagued by writers' block and depression, alienated from and disenfranchised by the many people he knew. He never came back from behind the looking glass.

The double image of Gulliver and Alice—with Williams leaning strongly toward the latter—hints that in that quiet little play that is the *Glass Menagerie* the playwright speaks to us in a feminine rather than masculine voice. At the same time, this vocal affiliation, although appealing, proves unsatisfying and unable to root the nomadic identity of the gay male artist.

Another valuable hint as to how to read *Menagerie* lies in Williams's disparaging comment about the play once he finished it:

> No doubt it goes in my reservoir of noble efforts. —It is the last play I shall write for the now existing theatre. (Windham, 148)

Williams's self-irony accompanies his awareness that the play represents the end, rather than the beginning of a theatrical tradition; Williams is clearly thinking of the American trajectory of realist drama, which has its origins in the bourgeois tragedy. And this tradition is precisely the one he critiques and disclaims, as his production notes to the play make clear:

> When a play employs unconventional techniques, it is [. . .] attempting to find a closer approach, a more penetrating and vivid expression of things as they are. The straight realistic play with its genuine Frigidaire and authentic ice-cubes, its characters who speak exactly as its audience speaks, corresponds to the academic landscape and has the same virtue of a photographic likeness. Everyone should know nowadays the unimportance of the photographic in art [. . .] (131)

Seen through the dual lenses of genre and gender *Menagerie*, proves to be a complex dramatic exercise which on one hand both invokes and dismantles the bourgeois drama, and on the other hand paints a displaced, poignant, portrait of the gay artist in terms of a disabled, partially silenced feminine psyche.

Lens 1 – Genre: Menagerie *and the Bourgeois Tragedy*

> Now that we come to the grapple we wish we could give you what you want, for you do want it, you have been used to it, and you will feel that you are looking at a strange middle act without it. (*Alice Sit-By-The-Fire*, 277)

Certainly, part of the ongoing power of *Menagerie* derives from William's shrewd utilization of the tradition of the bourgeois tragedy. This type of drama emerged during the eighteenth century in Anglo-Europe and proliferated in the nineteenth century in the subspecies of melodrama and bourgeois realism. Simply put, bourgeois tragedy proclaimed itself as serious drama containing a tragic catastrophe brought about by family conflicts (often between father and daughter), and which consistently demonstrated "middle class virtue." Bourgeois tragedy also often manifested some aspects of a seduction plot as well as elements of class conflict (Hart, xi). George Lillo's *The London Merchant* was an early exponent of this kind of theater, and the tradition moved on through the work of Ibsen, Chekhov, and Shaw.[2]

Some of these ideas should already immediately resonate with any casual reader of *Menagerie*, but the degree to which Williams invokes and then dismantles the bourgeois tragedy may be seen more clearly by comparing it to a work that stands at the center of this tradition. Friedrich Schiller's 1783 classic *Intrigue and Love* (*Kabale und Liebe*) has been regarded by such theorists as Erich Auerbach as a quintessential example of the bourgeois tragedy:

> The world here revealed to the spectator is desperately narrow, both spatially and ethically. A petty-bourgeois parlor; a duchy so small (as

we are repeatedly told) it is only an hour's drive to the border; and class dictation of propriety and ethics in its most unnatural and pernicious form . . . The prevailing order of society is viewed by the duke's subjects— including Luise herself [the play's heroine]—as a "general and eternal order." Servile submission is everywhere a matter of Christian duty . . . (439)

In addition to the radically small and small minded world it depicts, Schiller's play boasts characters and situations which are also "small"—imperfect persons who would become the recognizable stereotypes of nineteenth century melodrama, and who would figure in film dramas and television soap operas in the twentieth century. The play is peopled by the following familiar characters: a virtuous young middle class girl encased firmly in the domestic sphere (beautiful, but modest, soft spoken and somewhat shy); a male love interest from a higher, superior, and decadent class (a good man, but tending to be arrogant and impulsive); overbearing and controlling parents (a grasping, ambitious, talkative but somewhat dumb mother and either an hysterical, powerless, possessive father or a bitter, unloving, power-mad one [or both, as in the case of Schiller's play]); a hostile public world bent on keeping the lovers apart; and a smart, sexy "bad girl" who wants the love interest for herself. In this play, as in others like it, the lovers are successfully blocked by outside forces, and both die at the end of the play—through the somewhat bathetic device of poisoned lemonade.

Against the constricted worldview of the play, the romantic lead, Ferdinand von Walter asserts a seductive combination of *fin de siécle* republicanism, rugged individualism, and heterosexual love. Contemplating possible exile, Ferdinand envisions himself as a self-made man, a deistic citizen of the world freely ranging with his beloved at his side:

Will this eye not sparkle just as ravishingly, whether it is mirrored in the Rhine or in the Elbe, or in the Baltic Sea? My fatherland is where Luise loves me; your footprints in wild, sandy deserts are more interesting to me than the cathedral in my native land . . . Will we miss the splendor of cities? Wherever we may be, Luise, a sun rises and a sun sets . . . spectacles beside which the most exuberant flight of art grows pale. If we no longer serve God in any temple, night will arise with inspiring awesomeness, the changing moon will preach us penance, and a reverent churchful of stars will pray with us. Shall we exhaust ourselves in conversations of love? . . . A smile of my Luise's is matter for centuries, and the dream of life is over before I have fathomed this tear. (3. 4)

No obstacle, according to the hero, can stand in love's way. He is, at least at the beginning of the play, a wide-eyed optimist, but of course his privilege and rank enable an attitude which may be a luxury for others. Schiller makes this point clearly by juxtaposing Ferdinand with Luise, who betrays her class affiliations by being a much terser speaker (she actually speaks less than any other major character). The play contrasts Ferdinand's rhetorical extravagance with her own much more economically minded discourse of modesty and renunciation.[3] Correspondingly, if Ferdinand's great act is to leave his family for Luise, Luise's great heroic act, in her own mind, is to give up her aspirations of marrying Ferdinand, which as he himself notices—she is almost *too* willing to do. Compare her more modest, self-disparaging mode of speech:

> Let me be the heroine of this moment . . . giving back a runaway son to his father . . . renouncing an alliance that would rend asunder the seams of the bourgeois world and bring the universal and everlasting order down into ruins . . . My heart has been given to wanton, foolish desires . . . my unhappiness is my punishment; but leave me now the sweet, flattering illusion that it was my sacrifice . . . Will you begrudge me that pleasure? (3. 4)

Two extreme idealistic impulses are therefore represented by the main characters of Schiller's play: the male aristocrat who wants to escape society and affirm desire, the other—the female bourgeoise—who substitutes virtue for pleasure and who bases virtuous identity on her ability to renounce and sacrifice desire for the good of society. Significantly, the wills of both blocked by the shenanigans of two overbearing fathers, and the *Machtweib* or power-woman of the piece. Lady Milford, the dangerous femme fatale has designs on Ferdinand herself, although she is already the mistress of the all-powerful ruler of the province—the duke—whom we never once see on stage.

When we use Schiller's play as a generic template, it becomes evident that the plot and characters of *Menagerie* have a lot in common with *Intrigue*. Here too the principal action revolves around a lower class girl encased in the domestic sphere who longs for a boy from a higher sphere, and as in Schiller's play, the final call paid by the Gentleman Caller takes up the entirety of the last act. Here too the most petty of petty bourgeois values continually raise their banal heads: chewing one's food slowly is rated next to godliness, as are working a job and going to night school, learning how to type, doing without excitement, paying the bills on time and getting married.

On the rhetorical level, Williams invokes the position and function of the characters we saw in *Intrigue* and then radically compresses and thematizes them—telegraphing to the audience rather than histrionically elaborating upon their essential properties with key, clichéd phrases. Ferdinand's dream of unlimited possibility with Luise is stripped down to the following—still retaining something of the eighteenth century work's sense of adventure and rhapsodic nocturnal imagery:

> I go out all the time with a girl named Betty. She's a home-girl like you, and Catholic, and Irish, and in a great many ways we—get along fine. I met her last summer on a moonlight boat trip up the river to Alton,

on the Majestic. Well—right away from the start it was—love. [. . .]
Being in love has made a new man of me! (230)

In this manner, the smooth talking Ferdinand transformed by passion is meta-morphosed into the equally slick, if not so smart Gentleman Caller, also transformed by love. This romantic interest who waxes eloquent and enthusiastic about the business world and how he is going to make something of himself in terms not so different from the wild republicanism of Schiller's Storm and Stress hero. Both he and Ferdinand base their enthusiasm on the notion of the self-made man, the rugged individual, who only needs the will and the right gal to make his dreams come true.

A more radical reduction occurs in the case of the dramatic heroine. In *Menagerie*, the speech of the beleaguered young woman is further reduced to mere truncated words, as Laura's final words—uttered three script pages apart—signify: "A—souvenir" (231) and "Yes!" (234). Yet, Luise's position as bourgeois domestic angel, hampered by her social low status in a feudalistic society based on birthright, clearly looks forward to that of Laura, the poor "stay at home girl" who is physically and financially crippled in a society where looks and money are everything. For very real social reasons, neither can realistically hope to marry the dashing man of their dreams—a man shown from the outset to be "out of reach." Like Luise, Laura too lives to renounce; her act of sacrifice manifests itself in two steps: her gracious acceptance of the accidental breakage of her favorite glass figure, the unicorn, whose horn is broken off during a dance—and her subsequent decision to present the Gentleman Caller with the broken unicorn as a farewell gift.

The blocking figure of Williams's piece seems at first glance to be Amanda, the bourgeois heroine's mother, rather than the Schillerian fathers. Incorporating both the ambition of the parental figures of Schiller's play as well as the blocking, sexual threat of the duke's mistress, Amanda is at once maternal controller and aging femme fatale. In one early scene in Schiller's play, Lady Milford tells of her sexual power over the duke—a power which she used to mitigate his oppression of the people—announcing to Ferdinand that she outlasted even the duke's "giddy parisienne" mistresses because "I was more a coquette than all of them!" (2. 3. 32). Amanda proclaims a similar sexual power in her obsessive ruminating over her past life as a Southern belle of the ball:

One Sunday afternoon in Blue Mountain—your mother received—seventeen—gentlemen callers! Why, sometimes there weren't chairs enough to accommodate them all. (148)

And yet the ultimate power and blocking figure of *Menagerie* is —as in *Intrigue*—the person who is never seen on stage. Constantly referred to but never seen, it is the Duke who is ultimately to blame for the terrible state of affairs of the principality depicted in Schiller's play. The same may be said for Mr. Wingfield; is it not the father who serves as the ultimate evil authority— the one who has cast the family into its dire straits? This too is telegraphed to us at the beginning of the play : "This is our father who left us a long time ago" (145).

Finally, even Schiller's tragic lemonade also appears toward the end of *Menagerie*—a drink "poisoned" by an entire jar of maraschino cherries and juice. In the same way that the entire evening is tainted by the "overkill" saccharine efforts of the mother, in her girlish dress and false Southern accent.

At the same time however, Williams is clearly taking great liberties with the bourgeois tragedy—tweaking it in odd ways, and forcing it into strange and unexpected modalities. Once positioned within the bourgeois drama paradigm, the characters of *Menagerie* immediately begin to drift out of the category in which they have been situated—toward some far more disturbing and indistinct destination. The characters drift, because the stock types of *Intrigue and Love* find themselves transported into a social simulacrum where the socio-political values they want to incarnate and the resulting typological categories they want to inhabit have become slippery and problematic—making the characters into freakish anachronisms—glass unicorns in a very modern zoo.

This sense of anachronism—as well as the degree to which the past is being retroactively criticized—is announced at the beginning of the play by the narrator who self-consciously places the scene back in time before the world war in which the original audience was deeply enmeshed:

> To begin with, I turn back time. I reverse it to that quaint period, the thirties, when the huge middle class of America was matriculating in a school for the blind. (145)

Anachronism is emphasized visually throughout the play by the use of projections on a screen—a device not used in the actual first production, but an important indicator nonetheless of Williams's aesthetic intentions. In Brechtian fashion Williams calls for projected words to alienate the spectator from the emotionalism of the characters by anticipating and previewing key statements before they are actually uttered. This technique causes whatever the characters' affect to appear worn out and old fashioned, hackneyed and clichéd. Moreover, the use of the screen serves another important anachronising function; it indirectly reminds audiences of the primacy of a new kind of spectacle which has replaced live theater, namely film—the excitement of which is directly referred to by Tom himself.[4] Strangely, the stage itself emerges as an anachronism in Williams's play, as a medium that is now somehow beside the point, trite, overused, an impersonation of itself—like the characters.

Within such a self-problematizing structure, it is no surprise that traditional good and bad categories of bourgeois society are interrupted and bypassed by other considerations—all of them financial. While Luise's meekness and desire to remain within the bounds of the home are virtues in Schiller's play, in Williams's drama Laura's painful shyness is a negative rather than a positive, marking her as both unattractive to potential husbands and unhireable by potential employers. There is even a sense that this old-fashioned shyness is deviant in a way that Amanda regards, perhaps not wrongly, as defiance—as a neurasthenic refusal of the work-ethic, which as Mark Seltzer has argued, can be a significant means of individual resistance to capitalism.

In this way, Laura's determination to remain in the domestic sphere is shown from the outset as problematic, at least within the context of the family in the play. The opening conflict between mother and daughter revolves precisely around this question, and reverses the usual order of dramatic situation—where the daughter wants to go OUT and the parent wants the daughter to stay IN. Here mother wants her daughter to work and earn money—either as a wife or as a secretary—but this daughter actually wants to stay at home. Thus, Laura is shoring up traditional middle class views of womanhood as the lady of the house that we saw as operative in *Intrigue and Love*. But her mother won't have it. No one in this play can afford to be a "lady," and there are, unfortunately, good reasons for this economy, as Amanda explains:

> What is there left but dependency all our lives? I know so well what becomes of unmarried women who aren't prepared to occupy a position [. . .] little birdlike women without any nest—eating the crust of humility all their life! (156)

The mother by her own admission works like a "darkie," and her desperate vamping and flights of memory are the flip side to the drudgery of her life as a saleswoman at Famous Barr, and seller of subscription magazines inhabiting a run-down tenement. Her mean circumstances indicate that she is not wrong to be caught up in questions of money and class.

Once financial concerns become both overtly visible, and a value onto themselves—rather than upholding freedom, dignity, and the way of democracy—the bourgeois drama threatens to fall apart (as it will ultimately and absolutely in *Death of a Salesman*); deprived of their ideological moorings, the characters fall further and further out of their expected social orbit. The character most completely out of sync from the start is, of course, Tom, the narrator-actor, a one-man Greek chorus who functions much like the narrative voice-over of the much invoked film dramas; he has no part in the bourgeois tragedy paradigm and he operates as an awkward observer.

The gentleman caller is another example this "slippage" out of the crumbling theatrical paradigm. A failure at just about every role he is supposed to play, Jim is a suitor who is no suitor, a high school teen idol who is not at all handsome, a supposedly talented singer, who is just an ordinary salesman. Gabby but ineloquent when it counts (remarkably, whenever Laura *does* talk, he responds inadequately, if at all), Jim proves to have no romantic interest in Laura, and we aren't quite certain why he came to dinner in the first place. But he isn't a heartless seducer either. He is neither a seducer nor a cruelly indifferent high school idol. Rather, he is a businessman in the making, a curiously and rather flatly "normal" man drawn—sincerely, if momentarily—to a woman who is very different and special. The nature of this attraction is itself complicated—being neither the brotherly love Jim insists it is, nor the more recognizable heterosexual passion driving the bourgeois dramatic and melodramatic couple. Jim himself hints at its strangeness when he notes:

You make me feel sort of—I don't know how to put it! I'm actually pretty good at expressing things, but—this is something that I don't know how to say! (227)

What is this desire that is so different from Jim's feelings for Betty? What is this attraction that has no name, and that once expressed, is immediately denied and dispensed with? We will return to this question shortly.

Lens 2 – Gender: Menagerie *and the mask of femininity*

ALICE: I played the girl in the Wellington boots.
COSMO (blinking): Mother, I played the girl in the Wellington boots.
ALICE (happily): My son—this ought to bring us closer together. (Barrie, 269)

In contrast to the two male characters of Williams's play, the two female characters spend large portions of the play in disguise—pretending, and playacting at being something that they are not. This quality of disguise—or masquerade—most evident in Amanda, a mature woman with children, who recreates her Southern belle role with such exaggeration that the performance approaches the grotesquerie of camp rather than of serious drama:

I think light things are better fo' this time of year. The same as light clothes are. Light clothes an' light food are what warm weather calls fo.' You know our blood gets so thick during th' winter—it takes a while fo' us to adjust to ou'selves!—when the season changes . . . It's come so quick this year. I wasn't prepared . . . I ran to the trunk an' pulled out this light dress—terribly old! Historical almost! But it feels so good— so good an' co-ol, y'know . . . (203)

This is mimicry which, as Carole Anne Tyler has noted, deconstructs and distances as much as it invokes the lost or even impossible original. No longer a "real girl," Amanda impersonates girlishness in a manner that is embarrassing for the young people, and visibly, one might even say frighteningly inauthentic, for all its emotional intensity and strong sexual charge.

But Laura masquerades too. Dressed in a fancy new dress, with her hair styled, Laura consistently goes through her paces, albeit halfheartedly as a pretty, available girl—at the same time she is very aware that this is precisely what she is not. But Laura masquerades in other ways as well. Lying to her mother about typing class with surprising facility, Laura goes through the motions of pretending to be a would-be secretary, and, for that matter, a dutiful daughter, while in fact not doing any of these things. Amanda herself comments that her daughter is a mystery, seemingly content to "drift"—a state of affairs she herself finds unbearable.

What does the daughter want? This question haunts Schiller's play and is neither directly addressed nor completely resolved. It is this madding mysteriousness on this score that makes Luise's goodness seem suspect to Ferdinand, and it is this ambiguity of desire, which, ultimately, impels him to murder her. Laura's desire is even harder to get at. Everyone else in Williams's drama has a clear wish: to escape, to get somewhere, to have something. But Laura's desire is something and somewhere else. Seemingly happy with her collection of glass, Laura tends her miniature animals and listens to old records; during the day she walks and looks at the animals in the zoo. In short, when Laura is not pretending, she is playing, and, remarkably, her play is a kind of pretending also.

Laura's playfulness stands in stark contrast to all of the other characters, and lies at the heart of her odd, regressive self-sufficiency. The encounter with the Gentleman Caller partially reveals the content and character of her play and as such forms the epicenter of Tom's memory, making her—the quietest character—the most important one.

Laura's terse but surprisingly playful conversation with Jim reveals that she is doing a lot more than polishing her glass menagerie:

> LAURA: There now—you're holding him gently! Hold him over the
> light, he loves the light! You see how the light shines through him?
> JIM: It sure does shine!
> LAURA: I shouldn't be partial, but he is my favorite one.
> JIM: What kind of a thing is this one supposed to be?
> LAURA: Haven't you noticed the single horn on his forehead?
> JIM: A unicorn, huh?
> LAURA: Mmmmm-Hmmmm!
> JIM: Unicorns ... aren't they extinct in the modern world?
> LAURA: I know!
> JIM: Poor little fellow, he must feel sort of lonesome.
> LAURA: Well if he does, he doesn't complain about it. He stays on the
> shelf with some horses that don't have horns and all of them seem to
> be along nicely together.
> JIM: How do you know?
> LAURA: I haven't heard any arguments among them! (223)

Laura indicates that she is secretly spending her time creating dialogic make-believe; in short she is creating plays involving her glass characters. In this manner, her actions, more than those of any one else in the play, align themselves with those of Tennessee Williams himself. Of all the characters, it is Laura who possesses the sensibility of an artist. It is she who has the most refined aesthetic sense, and it is she who plays—very literally—at the art of play crafting.

Traditionally criticism of *The Glass Menagerie* has tended to see the Wingfield family as an exact replica of Williams's own, with the play's characters representing Williams's mother, Edwina, his sister Rose, and himself respectively. But after inspecting the play and comparing its "memory" to the actuality of Williams's own life—strange things happen—things which return us to the question of Laura and to Williams's own troubled view of himself as more Alice than Gulliver. As a child, it was Tennessee, and not Rose, who was frequently characterized as painfully shy, who clung to mother and sister; quiet, antisocial, he spent hours in his room dreaming and reading, according to Williams's sympathetic biographer, Lyle Leverich. When the siblings approached adolescence it was not Tennessee who struck out on his own—as the play suggests—but Rose, his sister, who was extraverted and sexual, to a fault, as biographers would have it. The youthful Tennessee hung back shy as ever, abandoned and deserted by the sister who was his one and only companion.

Other information is even more telling. Aggravated by his son's lack of masculine aggression, C. C. Williams (Tennessee's father) frequently called him, sarcastically, Miss Nancy, pointedly making Williams junior a girl rather than a boy through his mode of address. Most revealing is the fact that it was Tom and not Rose who suffered from a debilitating childhood illness, which left him unable to walk for almost a year:

> In the summer of 1916, Tom was stricken with diphtheria and almost died [. . .]When finally Tom was permitted to get up, it was discovered that he was unable to walk, the result of Bright's disease, an acute inflammation of the kidneys. Sitting on a little stool, he tried to push himself about [. . .] He had to learn gradually how to walk again [. . .] (Leverich, 43)

But Williams describes the period in very different terms:

> My sister and I were gloriously happy. We sailed paper boats in washtubs of water, cut lovely paper dolls out of huge mail-order catalogs, kept two white rabbits under the back porch . . . collected from neighboring alleys and trash-piles bits of colored glass that were diamonds and rubies and sapphires and emeralds. (Leverich 43)

The game of collecting glass shards obviously looks forward to Laura's glass collection in *Menagerie*, and Williams's juvenile delight in the game suggests strongly that Laura represents a lost part of Tennessee Williams, rather than that of his sister, Rose.

And the limp? Mark Lilly argues that Laura's limp manifests gay identity on a number of levels, but does not explain the profound resonance of that choice of metaphor—both for Williams himself and for the literary tradition he is both working in and working against (154). Throughout Western literature, physical deformity in male characters has suggested sexual deviance as well as the magical-sexual ability of the shaman. From blind, breasted Tiresias onward to Frankenstein, Quasimodo, and the Phantom of the Opera, male characters marked by deformity or handicap often incarnate essential otherness, as well as an uncanny brilliance, sensitivity or some other emotional, sexual, or uncanny non-quantifiable aptitude. The limp is what makes Laura unfit as a woman, the dragging foot making her noticeably different and monstrous, as well as possessing displaced phallic connotations. It is, from a number of symbolic points of view, an apt way to suggest without directly showing William's own queer desire—a desire he was in fact unable to directly represent on stage (Lilly, 154)—as well as his own equally problematic identity as an artist.

Elsewhere, in his less public writing, Williams directly links the crippled, the queer, and the artistic. A moving poem composed for Paul Bigelow in 1941 makes this chain of connections clear:

> I think the strange, the crazed, the queer
> Will have their holiday this year,
> I think for just a little while
> There will be pity for the wild.
>
> I think in places known as gay
> In secret clubs and private bars,
> The damned will serenade the damned
> With frantic drums and wild guitars.
>
> I think for some uncertain reason,
> Mercy will be shown this season
> To the lonely and misfit,
> To the brilliant and deformed—
>
> I think they will be housed and warmed
> And fed and comforted for a while
> Before, with such a tender smile,
> The earth destroys her crooked child. (Leverich, 419)

Williams could not safely speak in these terms on the American stage of the 1940s or even the 1950s, as James Fisher has argued in his persuasive reading of Williams and his impact on the depiction of homosexuality in American theater (16–17). Given the severity of what Gore Vidal characterized as both "fag-baiting" and Williams's own vicious press (Fisher, 16), what better way was there to begin to talk about queer desire than through a girl who isn't a girl? Laura is an Alice-by-the-fire who is indeed Tennessee wanting to be someone other than Gulliver but not having the means to say who and how.

Thus, Laura represents an autobiographical performance, but not of Williams's sister. Laura is the hidden aspect of Williams himself: the hysterical, withdrawn, secretly desirous, feminine crippled artist. As such she offers a fascinating if displaced portrait of a queer genius that cannot express itself directly. Small wonder that Williams hated writing the play. Years later he commented, "It is the saddest play I have ever written. It is full of pain. It's painful for me to see it" (Leverich. 591)

This use of a "mask of femininity" is not, however, without problems. Lilly sees the lameness metaphor and the depiction of Laura in general (as well as that of Blanche in *Streetcar*) as resoundingly negative:

> Gay desire, which can be seen as the sub-text informing the fortunes of both women, may survive fitfully in hugger-mugger, but must ever shun the light of day [. . .] It is in fact the closet that he portrays [. . .] As gay readers of today, we . . . must determinedly turn away from their negative conclusion. (163)

Certainly, Williams's play is disturbing from Lilly's contemporary "out" gay perspective and as much if not more so from a feminist point of view. In his depiction of women trying and failing to successfully impersonate feminine qualities, Williams shows us that the mask of femininity is just that—a mask. But there is also something profoundly unkind about the portrait. There is no mercy for these characters that are grotesque, pathetic, inadequate, and doomed to poverty and marginality. They are given no redeeming features. Failures as incarnations of classed femininity, and yet trapped within the social construction of being female, Williams's women are situated even more squarely and claustrophobically within the patriarchal domicile than Schiller's women, and the stripped down dramatic rhetoric offers them no way out. Lady Milford possesses greatness, and her decision at the end of the play, to abandon the duke and leave the court causes us to admire her even as we fear for her future. In a showstopping set of speeches that Schiller liked so much he used them again in *Maria Stuart*, Lady Milford says her good-byes:

> Put to shame Emilia Milford may be . . . but disgraced never
> . . . How good I feel, how relieved, how exalted all of a sudden . . .(4. 8)

We have already seen that Luise's words are also not without a certain admirable quality; she attempts at least to take control of a destiny severely out of her control.

In contrast, Williams's drama deprives the women and particularly the sister—his anima, his feminine queer side,—of any agency at the end of the play, by situating the two together and then effectively silencing them—having Tom talk over them, as they perform in dumbshow. In so doing Williams literally deprives us of their speech and makes an even more severe figurative intervention. We are effectively prevented from coming to any conclusions about the meaning of that last interaction, which we suspect to be quite important; who in fact is comforting whom is one of several questions which emerge from viewing the final scene of mother and daughter together, and the clear fact that the daughter deeply loves the mother (and vice versa) is also partially erased by our lack of access to their speech.

Seen from this point of view Williams's representation of women here and elsewhere in his oeuvre seems to be a strange and not altogether successful kind of masquerade.[5] Through a displaced mode of female impersonation—a poetic invasion of the body snatchers whereby the playwright's words inhabit the female bodies of actresses such as Laurette Taylor and Mia Farrow—Williams "drags" femininity in a manner which shows the lie of gender[6] but which also—almost sadistically—seems to delight in depicting the downfall, suffering, enclosure, and submission of the characters constructed as women.

My point is not to accuse Williams of misogyny, but to indicate both what is gained and what is lost by inflecting his female characters with a displaced gay male identity. As Carole Anne Tyler has already persuasively argued, the politics of gay drag (which Lilly himself seems to see as troubling) do not always correspond to the progressive politics of feminism, much as we wish they would. *Menagerie* is a wonderful example of that problem; it dramatizes the attempt of a gay male artist to depict himself, his desire, and his mode of creation in the interstices of the feminine, but this gambit tends to make the female characters at once scapegoat and sacrifice. The problems surrounding such a choice will become even clearer in Williams's subsequent play, *A Streetcar Named Desire*.

Lens 3: Laura's Candle

Despite these critical objections, Laura remains a haunting figure—haunting Tom the narrator, Tennessee the playwright and us. As the very personification of the quiet little play that her creator so wished to deny and destroy, Laura retains an ability to play, to imagine, and to dream. Her quiet little deviance, her small, consistent acts of generosity (surprising given how bereft she seems to be) suggest the presence of desire, pleasure, and emotional psychological reserves at odds with standard understandings of *jouissance*—heterosexual or homosexual. Laura performs a kind of pleasure not driven by lightning but by something fragile and yet persistent. Laura's art is a candle flame that illuminates a small space, but which casts a tiny flicker that casts shadows, that enables intimacy for the few who share its light.

Through Laura, Williams paints a compelling and nuanced portrait of the artist. The artist's ability to observe the world and then to delve into himself or herself and find that secret, solitary, and self-sufficient pleasure of creation marks him or her as a "freak:" as someone at once silly and subversive, as lazy, ridiculous, and non-productive (for what marketably useful thing does the artist make?), but also as "special," "unique" and even necessary. Williams seems to have honestly held this understanding of the artist's nature and function, as the report of a conversation with Oliver Evans suggests:

> "We ought to be exterminated" said Oliver, "for the good of society." I argued that if we were, society would lose some of its most sensitive, humanitarian members. "A healthy society does not need artists," said Oliver. [I replied,] "What is healthy about a society with no spiritual values?" (Leverich, 421)

At such moments, Williams's passionate defense of art and the artist as both necessary to and endangered by modern Western society looks both backward to Romantic notions of the artist as hero, and forward to the "creative living" credo of

New Age icon, Julia Cameron, who also emphasizes the difficult, potentially soul-deadening position of the artist in a social order based on money and power. Cameron pointedly sees the artistic impulse as a child, and the therapies offered in her best-selling work, *The Artist's Way* are not unlike the play-practices of Laura, the seemingly antisocial cripple. And interestingly, the two other playwrights pointedly invoked in this essay—Schiller and Barrie—also believed in both the essential playfulness of art, and in the primacy of childhood as the ever-fertile source of artistic creation.

Finally, it is important to note in closing that at the time Williams was composing *Menagerie*, the world really was literally being "Lit by lightning" (237)—the lightning of the Blitzkrieg and of Hitler's campaign for world domination. Surely Williams grasped that in a world lit by fascism, he didn't stand a chance—that gays were positioned with Jews and for that matter with the handicapped as first in line for extermination. This unwelcome connection was brought home to Williams on a trip to Mexico—usually a site of sexual adventure with beautiful Mexican drag queens. But on this journey, Mexico was overrun with German Nazis on vacation, and in a hotel where Nazis proliferated Williams was—to his horror—mistaken as a Jew by a female prostitute. He wrote about the experience to Joe Hazan:

> If the whole world falls into this state—and some people say we must be Fascist to fight Fascism—it will well nigh be impossible to live in during the remainder of our generation. Gentle ideals were impotent enough before—what will become of them now? What will become of us? What will become of our passion for truth in this great Battle of Lies? Who can we speak to, who can we write for—what can we say?" (Leverich, 377)

Seen from this point of view Laura, her glass, and her candle represent not only Williams but also those "gentle ideals" so in danger of being snuffed out by the political ideologies of the twentieth century. In this way, Willliams's marginalized portrait of the artist, not as young man, but as crippled young girl contains a quietly anarchistic and inclusive component—extending outward toward an "us" whose constituency may include many types of people regarded as different, special, marginalized, and who accept this difference, and who, as Laura does, in a gentle way affirm it. The subtle power of Laura's character may be in the end the most tantalizing and revolutionary feature of William's quiet little play. For this reason, and for many others not touched upon in this essay, Williams's memory-play remains a significant cultural artifact of the twentieth century American theater.

> You know, then, that the public Somebody you are when you "have a name" is a fiction created with mirrors and the only somebody worth being is the solitary and unseen you . . . (Williams, 140)

As grey, as controlled, as dreamless as we may strive to be, the fire of our dreams will not stay buried. The embers are always there, stirring in our frozen souls. (Cameron, 196)

NOTES

1. See my discussion of Barrie, homoeroticism, and Peter Pan in "As You Desire Me?" Forthcoming in *Nursery Realms*.

2. In his fine essay, Gunn discusses the similarities between *Menagerie* and *The Seagull*, noting that both seem to be invoking the same "narrative pattern" (319)— a pattern which, I contend, is that of the bourgeois tragedy

3. This is a common feature of bourgeois tragedy. See my discussion of rhetoric in *The London Merchant* in "Economy and Extravagance."

4. Frank Durham notes the importance of film for the play (Bloom 63).

5. The fact that Williams actually knew and had a crush on a man named Stanley Kowalski suggests again that one of his most famous female creations— Blanche Dubois—is a female stand-in for the author himself. Such connections oblige us to rethink how gender works in Williams's drams.

6. This ability to show the "mask" of gender may be why such unconventional and "unfeminine" actresses as Talullah Bankhead and Katharine Hepburn were particularly drawn to Williams's work.

WORKS CITED

Auerbach, Erich. *Mimesis: The Representation of Reality in Western Literature*. 4th edition. Princeton: Princeton University Press, 1974.

Barrie, J. M. *Alice Sit-By-The-Fire*, in *The Plays of James M. Barrie*. New York: Charles Scribner's Sons, 1928: 247–316.

Cameron, Julia. *The Artist's Way: A Spiritual Path to Higher Creativtiy*. New York: Tarcher/Putnam, 1992.

Durham, Frank. "Tennessee Williams, Theatre Poet in Prose," in *Tennessee Williams's The Glass Menagerie*, ed. Harold Bloom. (New York: Chelsea House, 1988), 59–73.

Fisher, James. "'The Angels of Fructification': Tennessee Williams, Tony Kushner, and Images of Homosexuality on the American Stage." *Mississippi Quarterly* 49.1 (Winter 1995–1996): 13–32.

Gunn, Drewey Wayne. "'More than just a little Chekovian': *The Sea Gull* as a Source for the Characters in *The Glass Menagerie*." *Modern Drama*, 33.3 (1990): 313–321.

Hammer, Stephanie. "Economy and Extravagance: The War of Words in *The London Merchant*." *Essays in Theatre* 8.2 (May 1990): 81–94.

———. "As you desire me? Nasty Boys and Mourning the Mother in *Peter Pan* and *The Witching Hour*." In *Nursery Realms*. University of Georgia Press. In production.

Hart, Gail. *Tragedy in Paradise: Family and Gender Politics in German Bourgeois*

Tragedy 1750–1850. Columbia: Camden House, 1996.

Leverich, Lyle. *Tom: The Unkown Tennessee Williams*. New York: Norton, 1995.

Lilly, Mark. "Tennessee Williams: *The Glass Menagerie* and *Streetcar Named Desire*," in *Lesbian and Gay Writing: An Anthology of Critical Essays*, ed. Mark Lilly. (Philadelphia: Temple University Press, 1990), 153–63.

Schiller, Friedrich. *Intrigue and Love and Don Carlos*. Ed. and trans. Walter Hinderer. New York: Continuum, 1983.

Seltzer, Mark. *Bodies and Machines*. New York: Routledge, 1992.

Tyler, Carole Anne. "Boys will be Girls: The Politics of Gay Drag," in *Inside/ou*, ed. Diana Fuss. (London: Routledge, 1991) 32–70.

Williams, Tennessee. *The Glass Menagerie*. Volume 1 of *Theatre*. New York: New Directions, 1971: 128–237.

Windham, Donald. *Tennessee Williams' Letters to Donald Windham, 1940–1965*. New York: University of Georgia Press, 1996.

Two Transient Plays
A Streetcar Named Desire and *Camino Real*

Frank Bradley

Tennessee Williams chose to introduce the public to *A Streetcar Named Desire* by focusing attention on the "spiritual dislocation" he felt on the heels of his most abrupt and dramatic *coup de théâtre*—his sudden success and notoriety in the wake of *The Glass Menagerie* ("Success" 3). In an article entitled "On a Streetcar Named Success" which appeared in *The New York Times* a few days before *Streetcar*'s opening,[1] Williams described his awkward assumption of a public identity, "an artifice of mirrors," which alienated him from his private and relatively anonymous identity as a literary struggler "clawing and scratching along a sheer surface and holding on with raw fingers" (1). He described himself as:

> [. . .] snatched out of virtual oblivion and thrust into sudden prominence, and from the precarious tenancy of furnished rooms about the country I was removed to a suite in a first-class Manhattan hotel. (1)

It was as if he'd walked across *Camino Real*'s plaza from the skid row Ritz Men Only to the plush Seite Mares. Yet as disorienting as his new accommodations were (his famous destruction of hotel rooms might be seen as a means of resurrecting the spiritual comfort of his clawing and scratching years), the deeper "spiritual dislocation" had more to do with language and relationships than physical environs:

> I soon found myself becoming indifferent to people. A well of cynicism rose in me. Conversations all sounded like they had been recorded years ago and were being played back on a turntable. Sincerity and kindliness seemed to have gone out of my friends' voices. I suspected them of hypocrisy. (3)

Success alienated him. Only when he returned to a state of relative misfortune, hospitalized "in pain and darkness" after one of many serious eye operations, did Williams once again hear "sincere . . . kindly voices with the ring of truth" (9). In order to stabilize his self-image vis-à-vis those of his friends, he had to suffer. Restored through suffering, he then sought a more deliberate experience of dislocation:

> I checked out of the handsome suite at the first-class hotel, packed my papers and a few incidental belongings, and left for Mexico, an elemental country where you can quickly forget the false dignities and conceits imposed by success, a country where vagrants innocent as children curl up to sleep on the pavements and human voices, especially when their language is not familiar to the ear, are soft as birds.' My public self, that artifice of mirrors, did not exist here and so my natural being was resumed. (9)

From the Siete Mares back to the Ritz Men Only—it was here in a Mexican village, a place of soft voices, unfamiliar language, and innocent vagrancy, that Williams found refuge from an alien public self imposed upon him and achieved restoration of a private "natural" one. Here in Mexico, in what he called "a final act of restoration," he resumed work on a play he called *The Poker Night,* which later became *A Streetcar Named Desire.* Sometime between his Mexican restoration and his writing about it he began work on another piece, originally called *Ten Blocks on the Camino Real* (agent Audrey Wood initially cautioned him to put it away, out of sight), which in 1953 became a longer play with a shorter title, set in an imaginative Mexican setting no doubt inspired by his restorative experience (Murphy 64). A transient from a broken home, a seeker of sincerity, and a writer who throughout his professional career sought accommodation to homelessness,[2] Williams attempted in these two plays to dramatize the rescue of a private self from a degraded collection of imposed public identities which, like the posh hotel rooms that he often trashed, repulsed him as they attracted him.

Although "On a Streetcar Named Success" casts Williams's attempted rescue of a private identity in a personal light, of greater significance to a study of Williams's works and of twentieth-century drama is the dramaturgical dimension of his effort. Far from typical examples of bourgeois domestic drama, both *Streetcar* and *Camino Real* nonetheless cannot be analyzed without reference to the bourgeois dramatic tradition of which they, like a number of twentieth-century plays from Chekhov to Miller, signal the collapse. The central figures of both plays—Blanche DuBois, Don Quixote, and Kilroy—are, like Williams, itinerants who seek in their own ways the "sincere . . . kindly voices with the ring of truth," voices which once were the hallmark of bourgeois domestic drama.

Peter Szondi's analysis of an early theorist of domestic drama, Denis Diderot[3], throws light on some of the significant dramaturgical issues with which Williams struggled in *Streetcar* and *Camino Real.* Szondi draws from Diderot the contrasting dramatic principles of *tableau,* roughly defined as a stable, interior family display whose purpose was to express visually and verbally the family members' feelings for one another in a free and protected private space; and the *coup de théâtre,* or the unexpected and often capricious reversal of fortune characteristic of a pre-modern world governed by the fickleness of absolute rulers who had the power to impose motivation from without. Diderot's points were that a new drama for a newly emergent middle-class audience needed to find a way to reflect and express the condition of its audience truthfully, that the principle of the *coup de théâtre* belonged to a dying order, and that the *tableau,* belonging as it did to the private, domestic world of the paterfamilias, "secluded from the public area, and therefore also from the state and from politics in general," was the appropriate dramatic expression of the middle class (Szondi, *Tableau,* 334).

As Szondi points out, Diderot was greatly concerned with the concept of dramatic *vérité,* or "true speech," which might roughly be described as truth, with overtones of sincerity. The point of Szondi's analysis of early bourgeois drama is that, as Diderot recognized, social conditions brought on by the rise of the middle class had changed the dramatic rules by which *vérité* could be manifested on stage from the expression of "great passions" to "the realistic representation of the author's own social surroundings" (*Tableau,* 325). The realistically represented social surrounding was, of course, the middle class interior, governed by rationalism, whose purpose it was to keep at bay the unforeseen capricious events which had governed the earlier drama.

In his *Theory of the Modern Drama,* Szondi analyzes another aspect of dramatic *vérité* in a changing social and dramatic landscape. He refers to the Drama[4] as a product—born in the Renaissance and perfected in the domestic dramas of the eighteenth century—of "a newly self-conscious being who . . . sought to create an artistic reality within which he could fix and mirror himself on the basis of interpersonal relationships alone" (7). To Szondi, the Drama is absolute, "conscious of nothing outside itself," distinguished by "[t]he absolute dominance of dialogue," which "reflects the fact that the Drama consists only of the reproduction of interpersonal relations" (8). The domestic Drama orients its characters, and its spectators, according to a dialogic bond which forms a community built upon a family model. Dramatic *vérité* is produced and reinforced via the mutual interaction of the domestic *tableau,* whose demands of realistic detail and accuracy grew throughout the Drama's period of ascendancy, and the intersubjective dialogic bond of characters whose private space, the space for such dialogue, is protected by the walls of the home.

That Diderot and Williams represent the alpha and omega of domestic drama is nowhere more clearly seen than in the common search for *vérité*—for Williams the "sincere . . . kindly voices with the ring of truth"—amid widely differing conditions. A product of a broken home whose life was marked by transience, Williams sought a means of expressing truth and sincerity on a stage in which the home, the site of dialogic bonding, had virtually collapsed. His project, then, was the same as Diderot's—how to express dramatic *vérité* in a transitional period, when old forms had collapsed and new ones had not yet defined themselves.

In the distant background of *A Streetcar Named Desire* can be seen a home which produced the *vérité* of Diderot's drama. Since Stella's departure from Belle

Reve, the Du Bois family home in Mississippi, life there under Blanche's steward-ship had undergone a series of degradations, from the "long parade to the grave-yard," (261) to the "epic fornications" (284) for which inheritance was exchanged. Despite the fact that Blanche herself had participated in the latter (in recent years Belle Reve was declared "out of bounds" to a nearby army camp) (361), the ances-tral family home remained the site of one of the few periods in Blanche's life when she was—as a child—more "tender and trusting" than anyone (376). But this brief reference stands as a mere precursor to a recent history of degradation which has pushed Blanche out of the home onto a series of conveyances, from Laurel to New Orleans, from the streetcar named Desire to the one called Cemeteries, and finally to Elysian Fields[5]. Her search for companionship, in the person of the least sexual-ly identified man in the play, Mitch, a level-headed fellow from a stable home, devoted to his mother, merges together all of the elements missing from her recent history, elements once displayed in Diderot's domestic *tableau*—stability, intersub-jectivity, and a cessation of the capricious reversals of the *coup de théâtre*. If Blanche's libido at times turns her into "Dame Blanche," whose "intimacies with strangers" set her adrift, her value system remains essentially that of a daughter seeking the pro-tection of the family bond and its domestic walls (386). As she says, rather desper-ately, to her sister, "I want to *rest*! I want to breathe quietly again!" (335).

As the title suggests, *Streetcar* embraces the metaphor of movement, or more specifically, public transit, in order to engage the question of dramatic *vérité* in a world in which private relations have become problematic. The companionship which Blanche seeks must find a means of expression and enactment in a stage envi-ronment which has shaken the home's foundation and thereby blurred distinctions between private and public.

Although the home in *Streetcar*—the Kowalski apartment—still stands, it does so largely in the character of an environmental antagonist to Blanche. Her chief problem in the dirty, crowded, and oppressive apartment is that she is subject to too many personal disclosures at the hands of too many strangers, and on terms not her own. The apartment crowds a number of people into a very small space, and is itself surrounded by other spaces of intrusive activity which condition it. The location of the Hubbel apartment upstairs, the flimsiness of walls, and the necessity of open windows to combat the New Orleans heat and humidity guarantee that the Kowalskis and the Hubbels will never be free from each other. As if this weren't enough, Williams adds the device of making the back wall of the apartment trans-parent at times so that we might be reminded of the conditioning of the action with-in by a larger outside context, as he describes during the scene which immediately precedes the inevitable "date" that Blanche and Stanley have "had with each other since the beginning":

> *Through the back wall of the rooms, which have become transparent, can be seen the sidewalk. A prostitute has rolled a drunkard. He pursues her along the walk, overtakes her and there is a struggle. A policeman's whistle breaks it up. The figures disappear.* (399)

Voices and sounds from the outside keep intruding on attempted "private" dialogues: Blanche asks Stella if she may "speak—*plainly*" her opinions of Stanley's brutishness, at which point the loud sound of a train approaching temporarily makes hearing her impossible (322).

Inside the apartment there are no doors between rooms, and there are only two rooms. Its inhabitants must undress in view of each other. Nothing is safe from another person's scrutiny in such a space. It is significant that Stanley's first penetration of Blanche's privacy happens largely as a result of space and proximity: because there is literally no place for Blanche's trunk to be stored, it must remain throughout the play in a high-traffic area in Stanley and Stella's bedroom, vulnerable to Stanley's rough dissection as he hurls about the room the remaining vestiges of her private life—her dresses, furs, jewelry, and love letters (273–274). That Blanche's bed is in the most public place of all—a kitchen, where Stanley and his friends play poker—serves as a constant reminder of her all-too-public past while at the same time it visually reinforces the problem of her present lack of privacy. To lack privacy is to be exposed to multiple and often conflicting outside influences. To be public is to be impure, and every space in this setting is impure. Even the home's most private space, the bathroom, does uncomfortable double duty: Blanche's periodic rejuvenating baths occur in the same space where Stanley and his friends urinate.

As was the case in Diderot's time, the domicile in Williams's world reinforces the value system of its paterfamilias. Stanley's explanation of the Napoleonic code suggests that everything in the apartment bears his mark. By this principle alone he appears far better accommodated to living in crowded conditions which blur the distinction between private and public. He is a man of the present, well-adjusted to an instrumental world which has no time for Blanche's ornate literary discourse, but insists on laying his cards on the table (279). But if the environment of Elysian Fields antagonizes Blanche, her mere presence antagonizes Stanley. He feels the pressure of having his space violated by a stranger, as he complains to Stella:

> God, honey, it's gonna be sweet when we can make noise in the night
> the way that we used to and get the colored lights going with nobody's
> sister behind the curtains to hear us! (373)

To lack privacy in this broken home is to lack the ability to speak purely (even if, in Stanley's case, speaking purely means nothing more than making noise), to disclose oneself with completeness and sincerity, and on one's own terms. Speech is inevitably compromised in this instrumental space; the search for *vérité*, the "sincere kindly voices with the ring of truth," takes place on grounds that make its achievement virtually impossible to enact.

Compromised language, no longer capable of manifesting the intersubjective bond that Blanche desires, becomes in *Streetcar* as menacing and disorienting as the alien environment in which she wanders. A literary figure (she was an English teacher) set loose in a brutal and instrumental world, Blanche bears witness to a trail of broken meanings which intensify her fragmentation. Her arrival at the Kowalski apartment in the opening scene betrays a naïve faith in words to mean what they say in a crude world governed by insincere relations. She stands bewildered that the reality of her destination, Elysian Fields, contradicts the literary image of paradise that she had heretofore accepted; she uncomprehendingly mutters to the stranger Eunice that "[t]hey mustn't have—understood—what number I wanted" (246). As one who spent a teaching career trying to "instill a bunch of bobby-soxers and drugstore Romeos with a reverence for Hawthorne and Whitman and Poe" (302), Blanche relies upon the literary reference in order to help stabilize her in disorienting surroundings, as she describes her reaction to Elysian Fields to Stella:

> Never, never, never in my worst dreams could I picture—Only Poe! Only Mr. Edgar Allan Poe!—could do it justice! Out there I suppose is the ghoul-haunted woodland of Weir! (20)

Yet as much as Blanche relies upon the literary reference to give orientation, such reference has itself become degraded in her world. Her life in Laurel was characterized by linguistic disjunctions, between the name of "Belle Reve" and its "epic fornications" and "long parade to the graveyard," between "English Teacher" and "spinster," "Flamingo" and "Tarantula Arms," "Sister Blanche" and "Dame Blanche, "lover" and "degenerate," to name but a few. Little wonder then, that the object of her search is a cessation of what has become a long journey of dislocations. A "restful" bond with Mitch, who carries with him as a memento of a former romance a cigarette case with Blanche's "favorite sonnet by Mrs. Browning" might, in Blanche's mind, resurrect the power of language to keep an unstable, possessive, and libidinous world at bay, as it no doubt would have in Diderot's day (297). But Blanche's past, which buried the private identity she seeks to restore, that of the daughter of the family more "tender and trusting" than anyone, under the public mask of a profligate, becomes a means by which Stanley can banish what he perceives as her ornate pretensions and return to his household its pure language, a language of ecstatic shrieks and violent shouts, a language to which his wife, unlike her sister, seems well accustomed.

If *Streetcar*'s broken *interieur* gives rise to a powerful dramatic experience that crushes its heroine's attempt to resurrect a domestic *tableau,* it does so by recognizing that at the core of the play's conflict is a conflict of language. The language of *vérité* which Williams found in the Kowalski house was a language of brutal directness, "lay[ing] . . . cards on the table" and adding one's shrieks to the noisy public atmosphere of the French Quarter, where everyone seems within sight and earshot of everyone else (279). By abandoning the interior altogether in *Camino Real,* Williams carried his search for *vérité* more directly into the public sphere. As he did with *Streetcar,* Williams took the opportunity prior to *Camino Real*'s premiere to draw a connection between his private struggle for expression and the pubic outcome of such expression. His *New York Times* article of March 15, 1953[6] focuses his search for dramatic *vérité* on the problem of how to communicate theatrically the private vision of one who, having squeezed the remaining dramatic potential from a broken home, had reached a more confident accommodation to homelessness, and was endeavoring to discover a new, post-domestic theatrical language. He wanted to share his "sensation of release" with audiences he knew would be challenged by the experimental language of *Camino Real* (419). He wrote that the play seemed, more than any other work he had written, "like the construction of another world, a separate existence" (419). He suspected that this "separate existence" would be a bit hard to swallow for spectators who might not wish to leave the familiarity of the home and its conventional languages, spectators whom he accused of being "a little domesticated in their theatrical tastes":

> A cage represents security as well as confinement to a bird that has grown used to being in it; and when a theatrical work kicks over the traces with such apparent insouciance, security seems challenged and, instead of participating in its sense of freedom, one out of a certain number of playgoers will rush back out to the more accustomed implausibility of the street he lives on. (422)

Williams surely had in mind here a suburban American street nothing like the one he gives us in *Camino Real*. The play's setting is a transitional space, a "port of entry and departure" with "no permanent guests" (503). It reflects Williams's own itinerancy, *en route* between various points of reference—the Siete Mares and the Ritz Men Only; the known and the unknown (the *terra incognita* beyond the back wall of the plaza); and life and death, the latter made present by ever hovering Streetcleaners, whose job it is to collect corpses for scientific dissection. The plaza is distinguished by its absolute proscription of private relations. Serious conversations are forbidden, and every encounter is public, from the exhausted conversations of Marguerite Gautier and Jacques Casanova to the pickups of the Baron de Charlus (469). The presence of Gutman as a menacing authority figure whose role doubles as epic narrator continually reminds denizens of the plaza and the spectators of the play that everything in this place has an audience. Kilroy's occasional escapes into the auditorium similarly remind spectators of the public nature of the play.

As is the case with *Streetcar*, *Camino Real* casts a glance back to an abandoned home which was once capable of producing intersubjective meaning. When Don Quixote, a transient like Blanche, arrives in the plaza, he refers back to a more fulfilling time in his past, drawing attention to the bit of faded blue ribbon on the tip of his lance, which he keeps as a remembrance of vérité:

QUIXOTE: It . . . reminds an old knight of that green country he lived in which was the youth of his heart, before such singing words as Truth!
SANCHO: [panting] —Truth
QUIXOTE: Valor!
SANCHO: —Valor
QUIXOTE: [elevating his lance] Devoir!

SANCHO: —Devoir . . .
QUIXOTE: —turned into the meaningless mumble of some old
monk hunched over cold mutton at supper! (433–434)

Soon after this exchange Sancho leaves Quixote, setting in motion the play's
theme of a search for companionship. Quixote falls asleep in order to dream:

> . . . a pageant, a masque in which old meanings will be remembered
> and possibly new ones discovered, and when I wake from this sleep and
> this disturbing pageant of a dream, I'll choose one among its shadows
> to take along with me in the place of Sancho . . . (437)

The quest for companionship is related to the quest for meaning which here,
unlike in *Streetcar,* holds out the possibility for something new. Given the abandonment of the home and the possibility of private relations, there is in fact some pressure for "new meanings" to provide a basis for the companionship which Don
Quixote seeks. Williams wrote *Camino Real* in order to discover what these new
meanings, the new basis for dramatic *vérité,* might be.

The new companion with whom Quixote bonds at the end of the play is an
archetypal character, the all-American boxer Kilroy, who, like Quixote, is a drifter
who has left a once fulfilling home. Kilroy hit the road because of a bad heart, "as
big as the head of a baby," which compelled him to leave his "real true wornan;" he
became scared that "a real hard kiss would kill me!" (456). In Quixote's dream,
which constitutes the play-within-the-play, Kilroy learns from the exiled Jacques
Casanova that "the exchange of serious questions and ideas . . . is regarded unfavor-
ably here" (472); is forced to put on a clown wig and play the role of patsy for
Gutman; wins an evening with Esmerelda, a prostitute whose virginity is restored
with each new moon (532); undergoes a ritual murder at the hands of the
Streetcleaners (577); and finally, after having his solid-gold heart pulled from his
chest in an autopsy, is pronounced the only sincere "Chosen Hero" of the Camino
Real (583). Declared sincere, Kilroy joins the awakened Quixote and walks with
him out of the plaza into the "terra incognita" visible beyond the upstage wall (591).
If at the play's conclusion Williams give us a sign that a sincere, bonding relationship has been accomplished, we are left to figure out what its conditions are and
what has made it possible.

Recalling Williams's own post-*Glass Menagerie* Mexican restoration which
revived his private self with the soft sound of an unfamiliar language, and taking a
cue from Quixote's nostalgia for a time and place when companionship was stable
and words meant something, it can be inferred that the new theatrical language of
vérité which Williams sought to express in *Camino Real* must both embrace the
strange and overcome it. The play embraces the strange by reasserting, boldly, the
force of the *coup de théâtre*—the sudden, capricious reversal of fortune which the
domestic *interieur* helped protect against. *Camino Real* is punctuated by sudden
reversals by which Williams was able to "give . . . audiences my own sense of some-

thing wild and unrestricted that ran like water in the mountains" *(Camino Real,* 420). The world of *Camino Real* is governed by caprice; but if the *coup de théâtre* of classical drama reflected the arbitrary power of an absolute ruler, that in *Camino Real* reflects nothing more than the playwright's sense that life is a "wild and unrestricted" ride, the source of which is obscure. The most striking example of this is the "Fugitivo," a "non-scheduled" flight which appears on "orders from someone higher up" (500). The Fugitivo is a means of escape which is offered as a hope, but it cannot be controlled or bought, as we learn from Marguerite's futile efforts to bribe the pilot. A fanciful *coup de théâtre,* the Fugitivo arrives without warning (even Gutman, who seems in control of most of what goes on, is irate that he isn't told of its immanent arrival [512]), creates havoc by turning people against each other in a mad rush for its doors, and reinforces the status of the play's characters as helpless objects of some outside agency. In its own way, the Fugitivo is as brutal a theatrical agent as Stanley Kowalski; by disrupting the *tableau,* it reinforces the victimization of those who would engage it.

Williams was clearly attracted to this kind of theatrical communication, as attested by his writings during the 1940s and early 1950s on the need for a new "plastic theatre" to replace the "exhausted theatre of realistic conventions," a theatre of "unconventional techniques" which might find "a more penetrating and vivid expression of things as they are" (Adler 28). Writing specifically about *Camino Real,* Williams celebrated the theatrical power of the visual symbol, which he called "nothing but the natural speech of drama," able "to say a thing more directly and simply and beautifully than it could be said in words" (421). Here, it seems, the poet in Williams who sought a restoration of verbal sincerity ran into conflict with the stage manipulator impatient with the theatrical inefficiency of words. "Symbols," he wrote in reference to *Camino Real,* "are the purest language of plays" (422). As an example, he described the battered portmanteau full of Jacques Casanova's "fragile mementoes" which, when hurled from the balcony of the Siete Mares, signals his eviction:

> I suppose that is a symbol, at least it is an object used to express as directly and vividly as possible certain things which could be said in pages and pages of dull talk. (422)

Symbols and objects are vivid and penetrating; talk is dull. Tzvetan Todorov, in discussing Friedrich Creuzer's description of the symbol, noted the power of the symbol to have an effect of "lightning that in one stroke illuminates the somber night," and "a ray that falls straight from the obscure depth of being and thought into our eyes, and that traverses our whole nature" (217). The *vérité* of the symbol strikes with the power of the *coup de théâtre.* Despite the efforts of Williams, Blanche, and Don Quixote to resurrect the restful companionship of the past built on intersubjective dialogue, greater sincerity on Williams' stage, whether in Stanley's home or on the plaza of *Camino Real,* speaks the language of an instrumental world. The scene which precedes the Fugitivo, that which culminates with Lord Byron's exit into *terra incognita,* puts the question of theatrical language into stark relief.

Byron is the literary center of the play-within-the-play. A poet who, like Williams, is concerned with his own powers of expression, he has been living for some time at the Siete Mares, where he has lost his inspiration: "The luxuries of this place have made me soft. The metal point's gone from my pen, there's nothing left but the feather" (503). He speaks of an "old devotion" to something which he doesn't name (504), and then proceeds to tell the story of the burning of Shelley's corpse on the beach at Viareggio. As he describes Shelley's heart being removed from his body, "snatched out—as a baker would a biscuit," the gross materiality of it all strikes him like a *coup*:

> I thought it was a disgusting thing to do, to snatch a man's heart from
> his body! What can one man do with another man's heart? (506)

At this point Jacques, in another moment which exploits the power of the visual symbol to communicate efficiently, twists, crushes, and stamps on a loaf of bread, exclaiming, "He can do this with it!" (506). Byron then counters this demonstration with a speech which pays homage to the poet's vocation:

> [. . .] to influence the heart in a gentler fashion than you have made
> your mark on that loaf of bread. He ought to purify it and lift it above
> its ordinary level. For what is the heart but a sort of [. . .] instrument!—
> that translates noise into music, chaos into—order [. . .]—a mysterious
> order! (507)

Byron goes on to note how his poet's vocation had become obscured by the vulgar materiality of the world, its wealth, "baroque facades," and "corrupting flesh," which he attributes to a "passion for declivity" in the world (507–508). He now plans to leave this corrupting place, to set sail for Athens, where he hopes to revive within himself "the old pure music" of the poet (508). He will depart "from my present self to myself as I used to be" by first crossing *terra incognita* (503).

Byron is an example for Don Quixote and Kilroy, whose departure at the play's conclusion signals an achievement of companionship while avoiding answering the question of what makes companionship possible and dramatically representable. Given the suffering that Kilroy must still undergo after Byron's departure—his near escape from the Streetcleaners in Block Eleven; his encounter with Esmerelda in Block Twelve that mocks the very idea of conversation and intercourse, climaxed by a chanted repetition of "I am sincere" as he lifts Esmerelda's veil (562); his capture and dissection by the medical students, one of whom holds aloft his solid gold heart (581); and finally, his having a slop jar dumped on him (587)—it seems clear that the signs of companionship that Williams wishes to dramatize consist in a mutual recognition of one's victimization at the hands of manipulative, "rugged" forces which, like the experience of life in *Camino Real*, cannot be controlled. Given this state of things, companionship cannot be intersubjectively represented; it can only be referred to, much like the hope of recovering lost meanings. What binds Don

Quixote and Kilroy is the common recognition that one goes on, with a tolerant smile, in the face of inevitable suffering in a world in which actions speak louder than words (589).

If Byron, Quixote, and Kilroy hold out the promise of "new meanings," we are no closer to finding out what these meanings may be at the end of the play than at the beginning. This is the continuing romantic quest carried by a literary figure identified with persistence in the face of lost causes. The final line of the Esmerelda's bedtime prayer, "let there be something to mean the word *honor* again," echoes Quixote's nostalgic reminiscence about the "green country" of the youth of his heart when words like "truth," and "valor," meant something (586). Williams is still searching for what that may be in a stage which, like the Mexican town to which he retreated after *The Glass Menagerie,* has none of the familiar reference points provided by the home. The only things he seems confident of are that these meanings existed in the past, that we were better off when they existed, and that the only way to find them again is to traverse an open landscape that is as empty as a desert. In the meantime, his embrace of the language of the "plastic" theatre ensures that the quest for new/old meanings will be nothing but quixotic. If Williams's Mexican restoration resurrected a sense of private integrity in the face of an insincere world, it did so by reaching an accommodation to a stage on which the representation of private meaning, and private life, became impossible.

NOTES

1. Also reprinted in the Signet New American Library edition of *Streetcar Named Desire.*

2. See, for example, Leverich, or Williams's own *Memoirs.*

3. "*Tableau* and *Coup de Théâtre*: On the Social Psychology of Diderot's Bourgeois Tragedy (with Excursus on Lessing)."

4. Szondi capitalizes the term.

5. Thomas P. Adler has denoted the fluid structure of *Streeetcar,* signified by Blanche's line "I'm only passing through:"

> Blanche's opening line about disembarking from a series of . . . conveyances introduces the notion of a journey. Virtually her last line in the play, "I'm only passing through (. . .)," concludes the metaphor and confirms the spectators' sense that Williams builds his action around the image of an alienated, isolated wanderer seeking some kind of human connection. (20)

6. Reprinted in the New Directions edition of *Camino Real.*

WORKS CITED

Adler, Thomas P. A. *A Streetcar Named Desire: The Moth and the Lantern.* Boston: Twayne, 1990.

Leverich, Lyle. *Tom: The Unknown Tennessee Williams.* New York: Crown, 1995.

Murphy, Brenda. *Tennessee Williams and Elia Kazan: A Collaboration in the Theatre.*

Cambridge: Cambridge University Press, 1992.

Szondi, Peter. *"Tableau* and *Coup de Théâtre:* On the Social Psychology of Diderot's Bourgeois Tragedy." Trans. Harvey Mendelsohn. *New Literary History* 92 (1980): 323–43.

———. *The Theory of the Modern Drama.* Trans. Michael Hays. Minneapolis: University of Minnesota Press, 1987.

Todorov, Tzvetan. *Theories of the Symbol.* Trans. Catherine Porter. Ithaca: Cornell University Press, 1982.

Williams, Tennessee. *Camino Real.* Volume 2 of *Theatre.* New York: New Directions, 1971: 417–591.

———. *Memoirs.* New York: Doubleday, 1972.

———."On a Streetcar Named Success." *A Streetcar Named Desire. New York Times* Nov. 30, 1947, sec. 2: 1, 3.

———. *A Streetcar Named Desire.* Volume 1 of *Theatre..* New York: New Directions, 1971: 239–419.

On *The Rose Tattoo*

John L. Gronbeck-Tedesco

"On" is a sure tip-off to the genre of this piece—or if you like—to the range of permissions I claim for myself as a writer. What you have before you is an essay in the traditional sense of the term. You will find little effort to use methodology in what has become its more or less typical role within the cultural humanities: that is, to triangulate the authorial "me" and the subject "it" by means of some third voice or cluster of voices ("he" "she," "they"). No "alienation effect" here, at least not intentionally. Judge my assumptions as you will. These you shall find elusive sometimes and as instrumental in constructing the "I" I want to occupy as you read as they are in creating a particular version of sense. In addition, I have granted myself the prerogative of wide generalization, at least in discussions of background information. Finally, my essay is a perspective on the play rather than an analysis of it. Or, perhaps more specifically, it is a retrospective. For, I'm writing at the turn of the millennium, forty-eight years after the play's Broadway production, after the obsessions of the post-war period, after the publication of Williams's memoirs, after his death, after the first wave of the AIDS epidemic, and after all the other victories and defeats of the twentieth century. (Which, incidentally, seem to change places depending on the congregations to which you swear your fidelity.[1]) I am writing after everything that has impelled the catabolic phase of this century's optimism. Not that optimism run down and ground under can lead only to pessimism. A certain skeptical hope is also possible. And, it is precisely this oxymoron that I want to open up here on the verge of the play's golden anniversary.

Upon the next millennium, I think it is good to remember *The Rose Tattoo,* where Williams reasserts the classical version of the comic mystery: "although individuals always die, the collectivity somehow survives—at least, so far." Williams earned the right to his own skeptical hope because he himself was so thoroughly terrorized by the contradictions of mid-century America. In any case, *The Rose Tattoo* engages those very contradictions and does so in ways that speak both about the century that is ending and the millennium that is about to begin.

I have granted myself a rather large swash of latitude, I know. To those who are still resistant, I appeal on grounds of charm. Imagine my wizened yet still cherubic face smiling over an attractive tie. Maybe style makes the discourse.

The Revolutionary Contract

In their biography of Tennessee Williams, Dakin Williams, the author's brother, and Shepherd Mead view *The Rose Tattoo* as an attempt to bring Italy, which so often served as a sunny refuge for the playwright, back home to the United States (171). I find this characterization provocative, because it frames the play as an instance of expatriate writing and thereby links Williams to American writers of the preceding generation who used a European sojourn to gain a critical vantage on the status of the American project. Hemingway, Stein, Fitzgerald, Richard Wright and others troubled the democratic experiment in a variety of ways. One of their most frequent tropes portrayed an America that violated its own Revolutionary Contract[2] with its citizens. That contract, derived from Enlightenment principles and enunciated in the nation's founding discourses, promised to link social justice and individual liberty. The former the obligation of the community, and the latter the right of any citizen who participated actively in the construction of a just comity. In many of the novels and essays of the American Risorgimento, America was portrayed as a nation full of promise but also busy sacrificing this promise to a naive opportunism that viewed wealth as the way to autonomy and confused self-interest with social justice.[3] For many authors, Europe took on a complex, ironic status. For it was both a world of historical origins, where the principles of American democracy first had emerged, and a world that, through various forms of opposition including war, pushed the American experiment toward specific self-definition.[4]

What I propose for the next few pages is to view *The Rose Tattoo* as a continuation of the Lost Generation's critical project. It is, of course, a continuation with differences. Williams's sojourn occurred in fits and starts through more than a decade. Whereas his predecessors became foreigners and strangers, he chose the roles of tourist and nomad. And, whereas they wrote in the aftermath of World War I, he wrote in the swamp of influences following World War II. Specifically, I shall view the play as yet another trope on the cumbersome tension between America's Revolutionary Contract and daily governance: the subject of periodic memorialization and reinvention; the second ongoing, practical and often at odds with the ideals of the former. What I find in Williams's depiction of Italian characters is a reinterpretation of America's violations in governance against its own fundamental commitment to protect the dynamism between personal freedom and participatory social justice.[5] Produced in 1951, *The Rose Tattoo* assaults the politics of the New Normalcy[6] that defined so much of American culture immediately after the Second World War and supported the Cold War in the context of national security.

What motivated Williams to pit Italy against the post-war return to normalcy? I think the answer comes in the dedication printed on the play book: "To Frankie in Return for Sicily." Williams referred to *The Rose Tattoo* as his "love-play to the world . . . permeated with the happy young love" for Frank Merlo, a first-generation Italian who took Williams to his homeland (*Memoirs* 162). In acknowledging his relationship to Merlo, Williams underscores the position of their Italian holiday as a watershed that renewed his realization of the extent to which he had to exist "outside of conventional society while contriving somewhat precariously to remain in contact with it" (162). If memory is the surrogate for absence (Roach), it is also the grounds of desire. The memory of Italy instilled in Williams a longing for a relationship with Frank Merlo that could be as publicly open and transparent as it had been in Italy. Williams regarded the Italians with whom he socialized as more accepting, less condemning and therefore more permissive than their American counterparts.[7] In part, it is in memory of and longing for his Italian experience that Williams bequeathed such a strongly stated and combustive sexuality on the play's protagonists, Alvaro Mangiacavallo and Serafina delle Rose, whom I take to be both surrogates for and parodies of Frankie and Tenn, and at the same time, embodiments of what Williams found so significant in his Italian experience: "the total freedom of life" that seemed "a golden dream"(*Memoirs,* 144). The sexual freedom Williams so closely associated with Italy was liberating enough to permit a sense of comedy to accompany his nostalgia: "In Rome you rarely see a young man on the street who does not have a slight erection. Often they walk along the Veneto with hand in pocket, caressing their genitals quite unconsciously. . . . They are raised without any of our puritanical reserves about sex" (*Memoirs,* 141).

In part, *The Rose Tattoo* is a comic trope on a tomb rite, complete with goats, a village as much Old Country as it is American, religious figures—a priest and a witch—and a chorus of old women. The play enacts a memory at the very scene of its death. That memory is of the Italian portion of the playwright's relationship to Frank Merlo; the scene of death is America where sexuality in general and homosexuality in particular were under assault by the politics of the moment. The comedy is classical: Dionysian rejuvenation—one of the themes Williams himself designates for the play (*Vogue,* 96)—overtakes and transforms the characters, albeit amidst the dark encroachments of their American milieu. In *The Rose Tattoo,* Williams uses Italy and Italians to displace the very world that has displaced him. He finds the dominant culture wanting for the same reasons that it has found him wanton—for a perverted view of human sexuality. To Williams, the politics of normalcy was nothing more than yet another acting out of the national anxiety over sex and gender, only this time in the name of national security and social stability.

The Politics of Normalcy

To remember the '50s is to recall the great store set in ordinariness. The culturally proposed sameness of everyday life was supposed to be a source of calm for the ex-G.I.s and their families who were trying to forget a time when the future was profoundly uncertain. I was four in 1951, and 'someone named John Tedesco was living my life, and I knew— as I no longer do—exactly who he was.'[8] It was not until much later that I could fathom the price that some had to pay for the ideology I called home.

The post-war obsession with normalcy was the scene of two major agendas: (1) the restoration of men to their previous positions in the American social system (both inside and outside the family) and (2) the commitment to winning the Cold War. Each gave rise to a different cultural rhetoric: the rhetoric of domesticity and the rhetoric of cultural dominance. Both provide a vantage for reviewing Williams's play and so bear some discussion. [9]

In the decade following the war, the American bedroom was a scene of anxiety (*Streetcar Named Desire*)—the place where the war visited the dreams and impulses of former soldiers whose status as victors was incompatible with the post-traumatic reactions that could not be named until much later (Gronbeck-Tedesco 1993). The rhetoric of domesticity provided absences and images that occluded any insight into the demons that remained hard-wired into the Stanleys, Mitches, and Pacos that won the war. For instance, early television pictured families that were complete and supportive with parents that treated one another with warm politeness but never as lovers. In the calm living rooms and kitchens of the afternoon and evening sitcoms, sex and sexuality had no place.[10] Yet the baby boom was nonetheless evident. But where did Rick and Dave, Wally and the Beaver, Babs and Junior, Joyce and Jackie come from? All of these kids just appeared, cute visitors from central casting with no roots in any kind of sexual agency. They were somehow procreated without being conceived.

While popular culture often ratifies the status quo, it can also allude to cultural anxieties. It is the ellipses around sexuality that gesture to the terror and repression which Williams opens up in so many of his plays written during the decade following the war. The fact secreted behind the laugh tracks is that Ozzie, Ward, Riley, Stu and their friends were former G.I.s (or allusions to former G.I.s) in recovery. Their wives were their nurses. Harriet Nelson, June Cleaver, Peg Riley, and June Erwin were responsible for preserving their men from excitement of any kind. Sex and sensuality had no place in their treatment. On network television, the American domicile became a nursing home where Dad was a successful patient in whom there was no longer any sign of the violence that brought him through the war safely and victoriously.

The Cold War provided further legitimation for the ideology of normalcy that imposed strict constraints on human sexuality. Against the Russian-American competition for world dominance, non-normative sexual relationships of any kind were seen as destabilizing. Heterosexuality, outside the narrow confines of traditional marriage, threatened the family, the very cornerstone of social stability. Homosexuality was even more intensely proscribed. At the outset of McCarthyism and the Cold War, the 81st Congress officially declared homosexuals to be perverts (D'Emilio, 41–44). The arguments advanced by the Republican floor leader, Kenneth Wherry, and Governor Thomas Dewey of New York were a tangle of tortured enthymemes. Homosexuals were deviants and perverts. Accordingly, they were lacking in emotional stability. This in turn was a symptom and cause of weakened moral resolve making homosexuals unfit for most kinds of national service.

It was on the issue of national security that heterosexual and homosexual violations came together. Because both were deemed such serious moral transgressions, they had the power to ruin reputations and careers in the public sphere. Therefore, blackmail could become the easy route by which foreign agents might inveigle support and secrets from government workers who wished to keep their sexual trespasses secret. In the high-pitched concern over national security, conformity to sexual constraints became the sign of a country that had girded its loins on behalf of a militant return to normalcy against the Soviet Union and its toxic ideology, communism. In tune with de Toqueville's prophecy that America would be great as long as America was good, the dominant political culture of the early '50s turned sexual repression into a strategy of national defense and the very equivalent of moral virtue.

The Politics of Comedy

For Williams, the normalcy that spoke in the forked tongues of domesticity and national security was persecutory. As an allegory heated by the discovery and loss of a liberating Italian scene for sexual freedom, *The Rose Tattoo* undermined the cultural equations of the post-war period. The threat to liberty came not from an external foreign power or from too enthusiastic a practice of personal freedoms but from an assault on social justice and individual liberty by the very political structures charged with their maintenance and renewal. From his predecessors of the Risorgimento, Williams took up Puritan motifs as metonymies and analogues for the larger theme of political persecution against which his comedy comes to life.

The Puritan allusions in *The Rose Tattoo* cut in several directions. At the beginning of the play, Serafina delle Rose is doing precisely what Hester Prynne does after taking up the scarlet letter: both women sew (Weldon). But Hester's work is associated with her own spiritual development. Sewing for her neighbors becomes a tranquil act whereby she sutures herself back into the community, despite those who had intended to break her communal bond and to destroy her equanimity. But Serafina's sewing is an all out assault on the peace of her own Gulf Coast village. Although recognized for the quality of her work, she often refuses to complete the commissions she receives. On the very day of high school graduation, Serafina has not finished the formal dresses she has been making. When the chorus of mothers asks for them, Serafina issues *"a long, animal howl of misery . . ."* (297).

In addition, whereas Hester has made her own scarlet insignia as the acknowledgment of a cooperative comity with her peers who have sentenced her to wear it, Serafina's tattoo, usually a sewn object, is in her case a mystical apparition she did not make and cannot control. The tattoo appears only after passionate conception. Her first account is the most explicit:

> [. . .] I knew that I had conceived on the very night of conception [. . .]
> That night I woke up with a burning pain on me, here on my left
> breast! A pain like a needle, quick, quick, hot little stitches. [. . .] On
> it I saw the rose tattoo of my husband! (277)

Early in the play, before Alvaro Mangiacavallo enters her life, Serafina is living in abstinence much as Hester does immediately after her sentence. Hester's vow is the result of the community's explicit injunction. Serafina's is a self-imposed flight from passion in memory of a dead husband who must be perpetually idealized so that she can preserve herself from the shame that too real an account of history might bring. Serafina's vow is misguided because her husband, Rosario, was a philanderer and a racketeer who died in the negative double for World War II, a gangland battle.

What makes for the most drastic differences between Prynne and Serafina is the way Williams uses them in concert to trouble the notions of community, nation and heritage. Hawthorne draws Hester as a member of one of America's original Puritan communities, who transforms the sentence of her peers into something redemptive for herself, her lover, and even for the community that has judged her. But as evoked and defined through Serafina, Hester becomes Williams's "fau Puritan"—a literary pawn in his play of passion and rejuvenation, who appears more like a character in a horror movie. Like so many women characters from that genre, her condition is one of abjection and victimization.[11] Multiple images of Hester remain always on stage. These are the sewing dummies—without heads or limbs—that flank Serafina in her makeshift studio and haunt her every move. And, ghosts of the past are exactly what the dummies and Hester are. Right out of the Puritan woods, they turn the anti-puritanical sensibilities of the American Risorgimento toward the grotesque. The first edition of the script calls for *"seven of these life-size mannequins, in various shapes and attitudes. . . . Principal among them are a widow and a bride who face each other in violent attitudes as though having a shrill argument, in a parlor"* (270). The genealogy of the mannequins reaches beyond North American shores. They are part of the early modernist preoccupation with automata that often symbolize mechanization without heart or passion, and they emerge again, even earlier, in Dickens's *Great Expectations* where mannequins are the cadaverous "guest" at Miss Haversham's unconsummated wedding celebration. Serafina too suffers for her participation in Williams's parody. The member of a diasporic Italian community flung upon the Gulf Coast, she is humorously unequal to the task of serving as Hester's post-colonial surrogate. Serafina's vow of celibacy drives her and her community crazy. A Puritan she ain't, a fact that Williams wants us all to celebrate.

Hester as a dummy, dismembered of passion and sense? Not fair: neither to Hester nor to Hawthorne; even less so to the generations of interpreters who have seen so much complexity in Hester's Puritan conscience.[12] But all is fair in love and war. And, *The Rose* is both a love letter to Frankie Merlo and a battle with the post-war forces that keep Frankie and Tenn off the stage and out of their own play. By means of Italy-come-to-America, Williams issues his counterpoint to the repressive politics which were supposed to help restore and keep the nation. Serafina and Mangiacavallo displace and reverse a major convention in earlier American theatre, that of using homegrown comic characters like Jonathan, Solomon Swop and Mose the Bowery B'hoy to stand as paragons of nature and common sense against Europeans and European imitators who revel in artificiality and pretentious social norms. In *The Rose Tattoo,* it is the European characters who are the figures of passionate life against the ground of deadly rigidification brought to the play by the American characters who have lost any vivifying connection with their European origins. Williams marks these Americans with a disfigurement in the form of a hypocritical and exploitative view of sexuality and gender signified, in part, by their costumes and clownish behavior. Flora and Bessie, for example, are man-hungry floozies who view sex as "part sport and part escape" (Durham and Gronbeck-Tedesco 1998). They are ridiculed by the play even as they ridicule Serafina:

> BESSIE: I'm a-scared of these Wops.
> FLORA: I'm not afraid of nobody! [. . .] *But both of the clowns are in retreat to the door.* [. . .] *Serafina rushes at them with the broom.* [. . .] *Bessie, outside, screams for the police.* [...] *The high school band is playing "The Stars and Stripes Forever."* (314–15)

Both women invoke the grotesque mannequins, which surround them, and so perform yet another distortion on the figure of Hester as they insult Serafina for once again failing to complete a sewing assignment.

In Williams's modernist universe, Italy, Serafina, and her eventual lover Mangiacavallo are the wellspring of a sexuality that is irrepressibly natural and wholesome against Hester, and the 81st Congress, committed to what is unnatural, hypocritical and so thoroughly perverted. Prynne and her Congressmen are ancestor and progeny of a whole line of mythic frontier characters—Jackson, Boone, Crockett, Cody, and others—who took possession of themselves in the forests of the New Land and thereby took possession of the New Land itself (Bank, 59–74). Serafina and Mangiacavallo have little of these frontiersmen in them. Unlike Prynne and her children who suffer from the anti-historical amnesia that goes with the role of an American "original," the mad lovers from the Gulf Coast have not forgotten their transoceanic history, nor sought a new identity in a new topography. Serafina assumes a comic arrogance early in the play based, in part, on her deceased husband's upper-crust Sicilian origins: "My folks was peasants, contadini, but he—he come from *land*owners! *Signorile,* my husband—At night I sit here and I'm satisfied to remember, because I had the best" (311). And Mangiacavallo remembers too: " . . . Mangiacavallo has nothing. In fact, he is the grandson of the village idiot of Ribera . . . [N]o joke!— Davero!—He chased my grandmother in a flooded rice field. She slip on a wet rock.—Ecco! Here I am." (366). Their identities still reside in these memories, however double-edged, and in their connection to a heritage that America has not yet erased or assimilated. Serafina and Mangiacavallo are completely and comically unself-possessed and therefore more easily commanded by "the Dionysian element in human life, its mystery, its beauty, its significance" (Williams, "Interview," 96).

Moreover, in the first Broadway production and the film, the Old Country marked the bodies and speech of Serafina and Mangiacavallo. These immediate bodily signs of Italy and the Italian also embodied the Dionysian eroticism Williams aimed against Puritan constraint and the agendas of normalcy. In order to create these bodies, Williams and Daniel Mann (who directed the Broadway production) resorted to a style that was close at hand, American primitivism. It was primitivism—a troublesome discourse within modernism—that both completed and complicated the play's satiric binary conflict: "Italy, sex and freedom" against "America, normalcy and repression." And, it is to this style that I now turn.

The Politics of Primitivism

As Robert Goldwater suggested in his seminal study, "primitivism" is a protean term with a peculiarly nimble response to the politics of culture.[13] By the turn of the century, the term had come under the particular influence of the French critic, Guillaume Apollinaire who used "primitivism" as an ironic term in a counter- hegemonic discourse against the colonialist attitudes of nineteenth-century Western Europe. In cahoots with Picasso, Picabia and Duchamp, Apollinaire insisted that the booty of conquest arrayed in the Trocadero Museum be regarded as art works rather than non-western artifacts of purely ethnographic value.[14] For the early modernists, primitivism became the scene of a return to the first principles of design where the *nature* and *essence* of art could be reasserted against the mimetic rules of the academy. Accordingly, in the early twentieth century, primitivism became an important path to abstraction. French artists of the avant-garde cited objects from the Trocadero in their own work,[15] and used African and Asian art to expand notions of beauty beyond customary European prejudice: "[T]he new artists are searching for an ideal beauty that will no longer be merely the prideful expression of the species, but the expression of the universe" (Apollinaire quoted by Samaltanos, 26). The works of Egyptian and Dahomean artists, like those of ancient Greece and Italy, were examples of what was allegedly "innate," "instinctual," wholesomely "childlike," "primordial," "sublime," and "mystical," in artistic expression. All of these attributes of what was natural and essential to art were proclaimed the products of powerful imagination unencumbered by academic reason (Connelly, 10).

The close association between primitivism and modernism produced troubling paradoxes. Even as it contributed to the modernist focus on universal values that allegedly transcended social mores, European primitivism remained a discourse dedicated to capturing what was considered foreign. Consequently, what got essentialized and naturalized on the primitivist canvas were constructions of otherness, understood in terms of race, gender, nationality, and ethnicity. Synecdoche was the dominant figure. Gesture, color, facial expression, anatomy—all shaped by supposedly innate and inherited artistic impulses—were used to create marks that signified (and also typified) non-Western, foreign or ancient peoples. Moreover, primitivism was a thoroughly Western discourse directed at accumulating influences that would rejuvenate Western art and the assumptions on which it rested.

Modern dance placed primitivism on the American stage. Ted Shawn, Ruth St. Denis, Doris Humphries, Pearl Primus, Martha Graham, Katherine Dunham, José Limon and other major dancers and choreographers staged dances based, in part, on rituals and daily celebrations of pre-industrialized, non-Western communities or of the ancient forebears of Western communities.

Dance-gone-primitive inherited the contradictions apparent in painting and sculpture but with some variations in emphases. Modern dance, no less than modern art, attempted a level of abstraction that was supposed to separate dance from politics. Yet, while opening up avenues of abstraction, primitivism in dance also undermined the modernist urge toward formal purity by foregrounding narrative and character (Burt, 132). The former often involved the portrayal of specific ceremonial activities within the context of a sacred space in a "native land." These narrative features often produced a sense of a fictional world in which there were social roles inhabited (i.e. portrayed) by dancers. Primitivism created a physical vocabulary for "natural impulses" acquired through something called heritage, understood as the physical, emotional, and spiritual legacy of a particular race, nationality or ethnicity. Because modern dance often included dynamic ensembles, the impact of primitivism turned heritage into a kind of generalizing force that imposed a strong group identity readable within the standard categories of difference. The bodies of the dancers became *essentially* African, Asian, Malaysian, African-American, Polynesian, etc. In this way, primitivism joined modern dance to the larger political discourses of the day without always challenging the most basic assumptions of those discourses (Martin, 1–3). But in fairness to primitivism, the human body—however typified and generalized—was on a counter-hegemonic mission. Within the aesthetics of high modernism, the primitive, dancing body, was always beautiful. From a more contemporary perspective, the powerful modern technique martialed by primitivism seemed always dedicated to the *beauty of otherness,* and so imbued the dancing body with a variety of questionable qualities: exoticism, fascination, eroticism, and strangeness, each of which collided with one another to create an enormously rich and politically ambiguous style, and one that was a major part of Williams's immediate milieu.

The primitivist turn is crucial in Williams's attempt to satirize the politics of normalcy, for it allows him to construct "Italian" as unconstructed; that is, as a group of identifying qualities that actually exist in nature and are therefore ontological, albeit always embodied. In *The Rose Tattoo,* "Italian" becomes a distinctive, foreign identity, the product of heritage (in the sense noted above) rather than of personal choice or cultural circumstance. The reason why Serafina delle Rose cannot conform to the Puritan ideal is because of her "primitive" Italian nature which has been reconfirmed and reignited by another Italian whose name is all impulse and desire, Mangiacavallo means "Eat a horse," just as Serafina means "a fine night."

But on stage, nature and essential identity can be inferred only from particular physical attributes—the meaning from the code. For the Broadway performance, Williams had wanted Anna Magnani in the role of Serafina. When she declined, he coached Maureen Stapleton for her callbacks, based on what he had admired in Magnani. On stage and in the film (for which Magnani won the Oscar), the acting strategies were a blend of body shapes and gestures allusive to the Commedia and to the Manneristic figures of the late Italian Renaissance (Gronbeck-Tedesco 1995). Burt Lancaster, Anna Magnani, Eli Wallach, and Maureen Stapleton played the comic scenes with strong up and down movements, often breaking at the waist, with gestures that placed the elbows in prominent angular positions. Photographs and the film show Stapleton, Wallach, Lancaster and Magnani in *contrapposto* postures with the latter playing several of Serafina's more intense moments with diagonal gestures and body alignments. Through these physical frameworks, the actors performed Italians that were spontaneous, visceral, honest in their desire, emotionally mercurial, sexy, comedic and often in motion.

In performance, Mangiacavallo and Serafina are immigrants whose heritage is always in the foreground of performance. Both suffer the impositions of the dominant Anglo-American culture, which is crass, vulgar and terrifying, made up of people who have been cut off from their heritage and so are no longer shaped by it spiritually or physically. For example, the salesman who beats up Mangiacavallo tries to sell Serafina an unspecified trinket that eventually "explodes in [her] face" (349). Like the floozies mentioned earlier, he is a clown figure adjusted to a satiric purpose: *"His face is beet-red and great moons of sweat have soaked through the armpits of his jacket. His shirt is laven-der, and his tie, pale blue with great yellow polka dots, is a butterfly bow. His entrance is accompanied by a brief, satiric strain of music"* (347). He, Bessie and Flora are American characters who come out of nowhere and return to locales that remain unnamed and unspecific via a highway that is occasionally heard but never seen.

Gloss

While on the East Coast Frankie and Tenn were waiting in the wings to come out on the frontispiece of the published script, a very different kind of coming out was under way on the West Coast. Harry Hay and a group of chiefly middle class gay men were forming an organization they would call the Mattachine Society (also known as the Society of Fools). Together they would dedicate themselves to a mis-sion that later became known generally as gay liberation. The cause Hay champi-oned was slow to enter the traditional lists of civil rights activism. So too, his potential for shaping interpretations of Williams has gone unexplored. Hay's early work opens up *The Rose Tattoo* anew—late in the twentieth century and late in this paper— forcing another into an already long sequence of subtitles. Kept waiting by historians and critics, and therefore admitted late to the show, Hay provides an interesting lens through which to review the play's legacy to the century.

Hay was an expatriate, too, but unlike Williams, Hay's outside perspective came from his immersion in indigenous cultures, beginning with the Native Populations of Nevada and California and continuing in New Mexico through the later stages of his life. Under Hay's leadership, the Mattachines tried to free homosexuality from its customary association with criminality, disease and perversion. Hay and his col-leagues used a modernist rhetoric, in some ways similar to Williams's, to restage homosexuality as a thoroughly natural variation on human sexuality and therefore essential to their identities. "We say that homosexuality is a perfectly natural state, a fact, a way of life. . . . We believe that homosexuals can best serve themselves by accepting the total naturalness of their homosexuality" (Hay, 177). Also like Williams, Hay went on to primitivize homosexuality in order to free it from the atti-tudes of the straight majority. He reiterated and interpreted the anthropological work of Morgan, Boas, Benedict, Densmore, and Herskovitz (94) in order to argue the positive and accepted role of homosexuals among the Iroquois, Native Hawaiians, ancient Egyptians, Babylonians, and Persians. Part of Hay's agenda was a call to aggressive citizenship: "The Homosexual must once again set as his goal the winning of the complete trust and faith of his fellow citizens" (115). More pointed-ly, the First Mattachine was committed to "fight against, and eliminate, police brutality, political and judicial shakedown, and civic blackmail" of homosexuals on the streets of urban America (67).

Although they shared the primitivist turn, Hay and Williams came from different ground. Hay, publicly out on the West Coast, argued in direct address to the establishment. His rhetorical strategies were deliberative and forensic, focussed on case-making. He and early contingents of the Mattachine performed a traditional rationalism that linked evidence to arguments and conclusions: category reversals, enthymemes, epichiremes, syllogisms, social studies and history. Williams, still not quite public, deferred direct address to an epideictic rhetoric informed by the poetics of moral satire—metonymy, synecdoche, analogy, prosopopeia, aporia, ellipsis, and drama—which, in turn, implemented webs of surrogacy, displacement, substitutions and allusions. Hay, in the persona of scholar, attacked unconstitutional prejudices in daily governance and the injustices of political exclusion. Williams, as the fatally flawed genius-poet, satirized the perversion of the revolutionary mandate by the politics of normalcy.

But read side-by-side, *The Rose Tattoo* and the formative papers of the Mattachine Society create a complex view of one another. Hay and Williams play a framing game that creates a critical effect not unlike Marcel Duchamp's "ready mades." When Duchamp placed urinals and other everyday objects in formal frames, he exposed the label of "art" to questions about the term's authority and prerogatives. The latter day framing of Hay by Williams and Williams by Hay works a similar effect. When framed by Hay's formal use of evidence, argument and scholarly authority, Serafina and Mangiacavallo (stand-ins for Frankie and Tenn) seem to embody—however ironically—the shamanic identities Hay discerned for homosexuals in the non-western societies he studied so assiduously. On this analysis, the audience (understood in one modernist scheme as a microcosm of the human community) becomes the target of an uproarious exorcism from the very sexual repression perpetrated by the post-war political agenda. Yet, on another level, there is a critique. Hay exposes the way Williams's strategies appeal by invoking chains of ambiguous equivalencies and deferrals that the audience may interpret in a variety of ways or ignore altogether. In 1951—the year of *The Rose Tattoo*'s premiere—Frankie and Tenn never made the entrance that would have permitted them to address the audience, and Williams's play never closed on its signified date. Conversely, when Serafina and Mangiacavallo are allowed to frame Hay's anthropology and history, they highlight the directness and rationality of his discourse on gay liberation. But here too there is a critical edge. By their own purposeful irrationality, these characters expose the power game at work in Hay's reliance on the academy to help him link Edenic foreign communities to his own progressive social values. Williams's comedy parodies this linkage, using some of the same primitivist turns that Hay uses to establish the connection.

Tattoos

Nearly fifty years after *The Rose Tattoo* opened at the Martin Beck, I have become restive before the primitivist modernism of Hay and Williams. I was born in the same year as Stanley Kowalski's son. We both grew to disillusionment in the days of Viet Nam, at a time when we finally began to recognize the sanity of his aunt Blanche and the insanity of his father (Gronbeck-Tedesco, 1993). I have acquired the altogether fashionable suspicion of fundamental terms—being, nature, essence—for, throughout the twentieth century, these have served not only the interests of liberation but also those of prejudice and persecution (Hutcheon, Berman).

Natalie, Indexa, Marie, Leslie and Sasha are the co-owners of Black and Blue Tattoo at 483 14th Street near the corner of Guerrero in the Mission District of San Francisco. Their web site (at http://www.black-n-blue- tattoo.com/) provides autobiographical material, short mission statements and pictures of their work. The site also records commendations from local print media. For example, Betty and Pansey's *Severe Queer Review of San Francisco* notes that the parlor is "dyke owned and operated." All five of the owners regard themselves as artists. Together their backgrounds encompass anthropology, publishing, sculpture, murals, collage, performance art, photography, metal art and figure drawing. They view the "skin as a canvas" and the tattooed body as "living, breathing art." Multiple tattoos can blend "different identities on the surface of the body [and create] a tangible means to view oneself." There's something familiar about the vocabulary: the residues of modernism attach to signs of the contemporary. I want these women to be more . . . less; . . . oh, I don't know—more bodacious, less wrapped in a familiar groove? At least, that's what I want from my own safe vantage in Kansas, 1,500 miles away from the Mission District. Yet, for their part, they accept me and my kind unseen. Betty and Pansy report that "[Y]ou don't have to be a lezzie either. These chiquitas would love to take thousands of high speed needles to boy flesh as well." In part, Natalie, Indexa, Marie, Leslie and Sasha see themselves in a thoroughly modernist vein, as a "community of the medium" (Williams, 92). Their needles and ink bestow identity marks on the body. In the year 2000, as gender, sexuality and even ethnicity become "performances" to be chosen or not, what about tattoos? More popular than ever, are they signs of a nostalgia for something stable and ineluctable? Are tattoos part of a performance of permanence or at least of continuity (here today here tomorrow)?

Barb is the young woman at Milton's who pours cappuccino each morning for dazed and grateful customers. Her wedding band is a tattoo that surrounds her upper arm with the words "bone of my bone" (her husband's reads "flesh of my flesh"). In the post-new view, Barb and the rest of us are always changing, not according to any geometric metaphor linear or circular, but more like the surface of a pond under random raindrops. Yet, the tattoo declaring the center and touchstone of Barb's life resists definitive change. Only authoritative, technical intervention can radically alter or erase the marks intended to capture commitment. Will her husband always be grafted to her center, and she to his? Are their tattoos an attempt to make hope indelible?

Hope

I began with mention of skeptical hope, expatriation and the anxious relationship between governance and revolution that some have found recurrent in American letters. I came to a close—or maybe only a halt—by placing three revolutionary texts together. Each comes from an outsider's perspective on the American project, and each links the Enlightenment concepts of individual liberty and social justice to the disquieting rhetoric of modernism. Yet, taken together, they produce a cautiously optimistic view of human agency at the millennium—a view filled with my own desire for indelible hope.

I

We hold these truths to be self-evident: That all men are created equal; that they are endowed by their Creator with certain unalienable rights; that among these are life, liberty, and the pursuit of happiness; that, to secure these rights, governments are instituted among men, deriving their just powers from the consent of the governed; that whenever any form of governmnent becomes destructive of these ends, it is the right of the people to alter or to abolish it. —*The Declaration of Independence*

II

With full realization that encroaching American Fascism, like unto previous impacts of International Fascism, seeks to bend unorganized and unpopular minorities into isolated fragments of social and emotional instability; . . . With the full realization that a GUILT BY ASSOCIATION charge requires that the victim prove himself innocent against undisclosed charges (and is, therefore, impossible), . . . We aim to integrate ourselves into the constructive social progress of society, on the side of peace, for the program of the four freedoms of the Atlantic Charter, and in the spirit and letter of the United Nations Charter, by providing a collective outlet for political, cultural, and social expression to some ten percent of the world's population, in which the collective force of their vote and voice may have substance and value. (Hay, 63, 64, 67)

III

ALVARO: Scusatemi, Baronessa! [. . .] For me it is winter, because I don't have in my life the sweet warmth of a lady. I live with my hands in my pocket! [*He stuffs his hands violently into his pants' pockets, then jerks them out again. A small cellophane-wrapped disk falls on the floor, escaping his notice, but not Serafina's.*]
SERAFINA [*Ominously*]: I like the poetry good. Is that a piece of the poetry that you dropped out of your pocket? [*He looks down.*]—No, no, right by your foot!
ALVARO: [*aghast as he realizes what it is that she has seen*]: Oh, that's—that's nothing! [*He kicks it under the sofa.*] [. . .] [*in a small voice*]: Baronessa?
SERAFINA: I told you good night. Here is no casa privata. Io, non sono puttana!
ALVARO: Understanding is—very—necessary. (385–86)

NOTES

1. I owe this notion of audiences as congregations to Bruce E. Gronbeck, *Paradigms of Speech Communication*.

2. I have fashioned the term "Revolutionary Contract" based on several sources, most notably Donald E. Pease; Dennis Welland's "The Language of American Fiction Between the Wars" and Malcolm Bradbury's "The American Risorgimento: The United States and the Coming of the New Arts" both in Marcus Cunliffe, *American Literature Since 1900*, and D. H. Lawrence, *Studies in Classic American Literature* .

3. F. Scott Fitzgerald's *The Great Gatsby* exemplifies this theme directly. So too, perhaps, does the Alfred Steiglitz photograph, *The Steerage*.

4. This last paragraph is based on Donald E. Pease's first chapter.

5. My take on Williams's project owes inspiration and method to Pease's reading of D. H. Lawrence's *Studies in Classic American Literature,* cited in note 2.

6. I label the period the "New Normalcy" to distinguish it from the period immediately following World War I, often referred to as the "Return to Normalcy."

7. Some of this sense of freedom Williams owed to the milieu in which he circulated while in Italy. This included, among others, Anna Magnani, Luchino Visconti, Franco Zeffirelli and Gore Vidal.

8. A somewhat different version of this phrase is attributed to Luigi Pirandello who inscribed it on a plaque that he kept hanging on the wall above his desk.

9. I owe much of the historical information in this section to Ronald Oakely, *God's Country*.

10. By way of contrast, some of the sit-coms of late '50s, '60s and '70s often indicated a sexual relationship between parents, although usually in a comic or circumspect manner. For example, Danny Thomas and Marjorie Lord portrayed a cheerful sexual interest in one another in *The Danny Thomas* Show and so did Dick Van Dyke and Mary Tyler Moore in *The Dick Van Dyke Show.*

11. Cynthia Freeland critiques the notion of abjection in horror films but goes on to recover the term in a more precise and limited capacity. See her "Feminist Frameworks for Horror Films."

12. See, for example, the remarks in Chapter Two of Donald Pease's book.

13. See particularly the last chapter of Goldwater.

14. For a clear discussion of the role of primitivism among the French avant-garde of the early twentieth century, see Samaltanos.

15. In this regard, Picasso's *Les Demoiselles d'Avignon* (1907) is an early example.

WORKS CITED

Albright, Ann Cooper. *Choreographing Difference: The Body and Identity in Contemporary Dance.* Hanover: Wesleyan University Press, 1997.

Bank, Rosemarie K. *Theatre Culture in America, 1825–1860.* Cambridge: Cambridge University Press, 1997.

Berman, Art. *Preface to Modernism.* Chicago: University of Illinois Press, 1994.

Burt, Ramsay. *The Male Dancer.* New York: Routledge, 1995.

Connelly, Frances S. *The Sleep of Reason: Primitivism in Modern European Art and Aesthetics, 1725–1907.* University Park: Pennsylvania State University Press, 1995.

Cunliffe, Marcus, ed. *American Literature since 1900.* New York: Peter Bedrick Books, 1987.

D'Emilio, John. *Sexual Politics, Sexual Communities.* Chicago: University of Chicago Press, 1998.

Durham, Leslie Atkins and John Gronbeck-Tedesco. "The Rose Tattoo." in *Tennessee Williams: A Guide to Research and Performance,* edited by. Philip C. Kolin. Westport: Greenwood, 1998.

Freeland, Cynthia A. "Feminist Frameworks for Horror Films," in *Post Theory: Reconstructing Film Studies,* edited by David Bordwell and Noel Carroll. Madison: University of Wisconsin Press, 1996.

Goldwater, Robert J. *Primitivism in Modern Art.* New York: Harper and Bros., 1938.

Gronbeck, Bruce E. *Paradigms of Speech Communication Studies: Looking Back Toward the Future.* Boston: Allyn and Bacon, 1998.

Gronbeck-Tedesco, John L. "Absence and the Actor's Body: Marlon Brando's Performance in *A Streetcar Named Desire." Studies in American Drama, 1945–Present.* 8.2 (1993): 115–126.

———. "Ambiguity and Performance in the Plays of Tennessee Williams." *The Mississippi Quarterly* XLVIII.4 (Fall 1995): 735–49.

———. "Everything's Comin' Up Roses: Rainer Marie Rilke Reads Tennessee Williams and Vice Versa." *Publications of the Mississippi Philological Association,* (1998): 7–12.

Hay, Harry. *Radically Gay: Gay Liberation in the Words of its Founder,* edited by Will Roscoe. Boston: Beacon, 1996.

Hutcheon, Linda. *A Poetics of Postmodernism: History, Theory, Fiction.* London: Routledge, 1988.

Lawrence, D. H. *Studies in American Literature.* New York: Viking, 1923.

Martin, Randy. *Critical Moves: Dance Studies in Theory and Politics.* Durham: Duke University Press, 1998.

Oakley, J. Ronald. *God's Country: America in the Fifties.* New York: Dember Books, 1986.

Pease, Donald E. *Visionary Compacts: American Renaissance Writings in Cultural Context.* Madison: University of Wisconsin Press, 1987.

Roach, Joseph. *Cities of the Dead.* New York: Columbia University Press, 1996.

Samaltanos, Katia. *Apollinaire Catalyst for Primitivism, Picasso, Picabia and Duchamp.* Ann Arbor: University of Michigan Research Press, 1984.

Weldon, Roberta F. "*Rose Tattoo:*A Modern Version of *The Scarlet Letter." Interpretations* 15.1 (Fall 1983): 70–77.

Williams, Dakin, and Shepherd Mead. *Tennessee Williams: An Intimate Biography.* New York: Arbor, 1983.

Williams, Raymond. "The Metropolis and the Emergence of Modernism," in *Modernism/Postmodernism,* edited by Peter Brooker. New York: Longman, 1992.

Williams, Tennessee. "Interview." *Vogue,* 15 March 1951, 96.
————. *Memoirs.* New York: Doubleday, 1983.
————. *The Rose Tattoo.* Volume 3 of *Theatre.* New York: New Directions, 1971:
    257–415.

The Politics of Sexual Ambiguity in *Sweet Bird of Youth*

Ann Wilson

Sweet Bird of Youth is a play which, by Williams's own admission, is flawed. In an interview with C. Robert Jennings, he recalled that "when we were first reading *Sweet Bird*, I jumped up and said, 'Stop it at once. It's dreadfully overwritten.' . . . My greatest weaknesses are structural" (250). In this essay, I want to consider what Williams termed as "structural" flaws as part of a pattern of disruptions which are thematic and structural. Certainly, if thematic and structural coherence is a standard of dramatic excellence, *Sweet Bird of Youth* is flawed. In this essay, I am not concerned with evaluative judgements of the play, but rather with the ideological significance of disruption.

I offer two related propositions: first, that the disruptions refuse the possibility of coherence and so, create a theatrical space in which the exchanges and substitutions are not only obvious, but obviously amount to inexact equivalences; secondly, the consequence of the first proposition is the question: what is at stake in the exchanges within the play? My argument is that the play's stylistic jumble and the slippages in the economies of exchange create fissures and silences which announce the repressed homosexuality which drives *Sweet Bird of Youth*. In its expression of ideologies of sexuality, *Sweet Bird of Youth* is both troubled and troubling. It is troubled because Williams can't find a way of expressing his homosexuality, and troubling because the homoerotic impulses which drive the play depend on female characters who are described in images of death. Or, they are "excessively" feminine—to the degree of being parodies of femininity—as if the case of the "Princess Kosmonopolis" and Thomas J. ("Boss") Finley's mistress, Lucy. Both renderings of femininity in terms of death "hyperfemininity" evacuate female subjectivity. The evacuation, or absence (which means, effectively that all women are equated with death) meet the needs of what, in the course of this essay, I discuss the terms of

Williams's sense of homosexuality which depends on a troubled representation of women that is not a consequence of personal pathology—although that aspect of Williams is well-documented—but socially produced by the ideological forces of the moment in which he was writing.

To begin, a brief reminder of the narrative of *Sweet Bird of Youth* is useful. The play opens in a hotel room which Chance Wayne occupies with an aging movie queen travelling under the pseudonym "The Princess Kosmonopolis." Chance has returned to his home town, St. Cloud, on the Gulf coast of Florida, to renew his relationship with Heavenly, his first love. She is the daughter of the area's leading political boss called, appropriately enough, Boss Finley. Boss Finley loathes Chance because he blames him for causing his daughter to incur a condition requiring an operation which rendered her sterile. Boss Finley, ashamed and angered by the defilement of his daughter, wants Chance castrated. The plot seemingly circulates around Finley's seeking of a grotesque mode of revenge. I say "seemingly" because the demand for revenge isn't expressed until well into the play—and after Williams has established the curious relationship between Chance and the Princess.

Williams, through his description of the hotel in St. Cloud "*resembling one of those 'Grand Hotels' around Sorrento or Monte Carlo*" in a style that is "*vaguely Moorish*," carefully establishes the setting for the relationship between Chance and the Princess. For those familiar with Edward Said's *Orientalism*, a pioneering work on the West's imagining of "exotic" locales as arousing sexual dissidence, the implications of the setting of *Sweet Bird of Youth* are resonant. "Moorishness" suggests that this is a "hot" climate and, for those with even a passing conversance with literature, hot climates in English literature of the West are normally not simply a measure of climate, but indicate sexual desire which is so overheated that it is dangerous. Or, put another way, climatic conditions tend to correlate with libidinal energies—the hotter the climate, the more sexual the citizenry—and the excessive sexuality never amounts to anything good. Williams's setting is a signal that this is a play about excess, sexualities churning in a dangerous way.

Thematically, the return of Chance Wayne, the central character, to his hometown of St. Cloud on Florida's West Coast disrupts the town because the citizenry seems aware that Boss Finley wants to avenge Chance's sexual "wronging" of his daughter. This "wrong" leads to Finley's declaration of a messianic mission (106) to protect "something that we hold sacred: our purity of our own blood" (107). By the point at which Finley makes his declaration, spurred by Finley's earlier declarations of his vision (at a rally which is antecedent to the action of the play, but mentioned in the narrative), a group of men have selected "a nigger at random and castrated the bastard to show they mean business about white women's protection in this state" (90). At political rallies, including the one staged in *Sweet Bird of Youth*, a heckler disrupts Boss Finley's speech to demand clarification about the operation performed on Boss Finley's daughter Heavenly. "How about the operation your daughter had done on her at Thomas J. Finley Hospital here in St. Cloud?" (108). The heckler's question is meant to disrupt the ruse of Finley's railing against miscegenation, by exposing it as a tactic which diverts attention from his daughter's operation publicly described as removing her appendix (108), but in reality, removing her uterus (71).

The theme of disruption is mirrored in the structure of the play which swings uneasily between styles. There are campy scenes between Chance Wayne and his travelling companion, the screen star Alexandra del Lago. The introduction of Heavenly seems indebted to expressionism; and the scenes in which Chance engages with the town's people seem to conform to conventions of theatrical realism. Indeed, the play ends with a scene in which Finley's henches are about to take Chance away to face Finley's revenge. As if to remind the audience about the importance of disruption to this theatrical project, the illusion of the fourth wall is broken by the final speech in the play, Chance's direct address to the audience in which he pleads "Just for your recognition of me in you, and the enemy, time, in us all" (124).

From one vantage, the plot of *Sweet Bird of Youth*, Heavenly is central to the play. She and Chance were high school sweethearts who performed at a national drama contest in "The Valiant," a one act play written and directed by Chance. The play took fourth place in the competition, disappointing the dreams of Chance (if not Heavenly.) On that "sad, homegoing train," Chance bribed the Pullman conductor for an empty compartment where he and Heavenly made love:

> When she undressed, I saw that her body was just then, barely, begin-
> ning to be a woman's and [. . .] I said, oh, Heavenly, no, but she said
> yes, and I cried in her arms that night, and didn't know that what I was
> crying for was—youth, that would go. (81–82)

It is worth noting that, in Chance's account, he makes the arrangements with the conductor that will facilitate the tryst, but it is Heavenly who instigates their love making, even when Chance seems reluctant.

This memory of Heavenly contrasts with the woman whom the audience finally sees, well into the second scene. She doesn't appear until the audience's expectations have been set up by the comments of male characters. Before she enters, her father asks her brother "Where's your sister?" Tom Junior replies that "She's lyin' out on the beach like a dead body washed up on it" (59). When Heavenly finally enters, her father asks to speak with her, but she refuses to be engaged and begins to wander off (66). Her refusal coincides with the entrance of the "*old coloured manservant*" which "*marks a formal division in the scene*" that shifts stylistically to become expressionistic: "*The sea wind sings.* HEAVENLY *lifts her face to it.* [. . .] HEAVENLY *is always looking out that way, toward the Gulf, so that the light from Point Lookout catches her face with its repeated soft stroke of clarity*" (66). Cast in light which makes her seem not just removed from the concerns of this world, but almost otherworldly, Williams indicates that Boss Finley looks at his daughter and is revived. In a curious stage description, the playwright calls for Boss Finley to approach Heavenly "like an aged courtier comes deferentially up to a crown princess or infanta" (66–67). He adds:

> *it's important not to think of his attitude toward her in terms of a crudely
> incestuous feeling, but just in the natural terms of almost any aging father's*

feeling for a beautiful young daughter who reminds him of a dead wife
that he desired intensely when she was the age of his daughter. (67)

In citing at length this stage direction which shifts the style of the play, disrupting the realism of the scene, I want to draw attention not only to the ethereal
quality of Heavenly (signalled with no subtlety by her name), but to the fact that
Williams intends the moment to inscribe complex erotic economy in which the
daughter stands for her mother, who is dead, a substitution that licenses what
Williams feels is a father's "natural" sexualized response to a daughter.

Whatever a reader might make of Williams's depiction of sexuality within families, the point which I want to emphasize is that Heavenly stands for her dead
mother, a substitution that associates her with death, and reinforces her brother's
earlier comment that she looks like a "dead body." Heavenly herself pushes the association with death to a more explicit level. When the expressionistic moment breaks,
Boss comments to Heavenly that she is "still a beautiful girl. . . . Lookin' at you
nobody could guess that—" Heavenly breaks in and completes her father's sentence,
"The embalmers must have done a good job on me, Papa . . ." (67). The implica-
tion is that Heavenly is not merely *associated* with death but is, figuratively, dead.
She is devoid of any engagement with life, including her sexuality.

Heavenly "dies" when she has a hysterectomy to cure her of a venereal disease
which her father alleges that she contracted from Chance Wayne. Act Two opens with
Boss Finley telling Dr. Scudder (the head of the hospital named for Boss Finley, the
physician who performed Heavenly's hysterectomy and is now engaged to marry her)
that Chance Wayne "had" his daughter when she was fifteen and took pictures of her
which seem now to be in circulation (56, 57). It is not until later in the play—Act
Two, scene 2—that the audience learns of the terms by which Heavenly contracted a
venereal disease that led to the operation. Says Tom Junior, "My little sister, Heavenly,
didn't know about the disease and operations of whores, till she had to be cleaned and
cured—I mean spayed like a dawg by Dr. George Scudder's knife" (103).

What is worth noting is that before Chance learns of Heavenly's fate, he says to
Tom Junior, "[. . .] but I swear I never hurt Heavenly in my life," a claim he never
retracts (102). Heavenly herself, who speaks little in the play, never provides a clue
about how she became infected. Her youthful sexual curiosity and confidence which,
at least by Chance's account of their tryst, opens the possibility that she had other lovers.
It is clear that her father and brother believe that Chance is the source of the infection
and, indeed, Tom Junior goes to some length to explain the route of transmission. He
accuses Chance of being a gigolo to a rich Texas woman, Minnie, saying that:

> she slept with any goddam gigolo bastard she could pick up on
> Bourbon Street or the docks, and then you would go on sleeping again
> with my sister. And sometime, during that time, you got something
> besides your gigolo fee from Minnie and passed it onto my sister, my
> little sister that had hardly even heard of a thing like that, and didn't
> know what it was till it had gone on too long and— (102)

Given the array of amphetamines that Chance ingests in the course of the play, it is not unreasonable to suggest that the action of *Sweet Bird of Youth*, in the absence of notes specifying the period in which it is set, is contemporary to when it was written—the mid-1950s. Given that by this point, antibiotics were commercially available, it is curious that Dr. Scudder resorted to the drastic measure of a hysterectomy, rather than a course of antibiotics, to deal with venereal disease. But plays are not medical tracts and playwrights aren't bound by medical practice. Clearly the hysterectomy serves a dramatic purpose, allowing Heavenly's father, as if heeding the Old Testament adage of "an eye for an eye," to mete out his revenge for her loss of fertility by imposing an equivalent punishment on Chance by castrating him.

Further, the description of Heavenly's situation becomes a transaction between men: believing that Heavenly has been wronged by Chance, seeking recourse for the wrong does not fall to her, but to her father and his surrogate, Tom Junior. Williams's representation of the incident fuels his scheme of substitutions which is key to the play. As I indicated earlier, to deflect attention from his daughter, Boss Finley—who speaks as the "Voice of God"—deploys the white sexual panic about Afro-American men as dangerously oversexed and threatening to white women. Thus, Finley can claim being seeking the protection of "something that we hold sacred: our purity of our own blood" (107), a call which resulted in the lynching and castration of an Afro-American man, chosen at random.

Panic over sexuality underlies *Sweet Bird of Youth*. Boss Finley's invocation of the Southern fear of miscegenation diverts attention not only from his daughter, but from his own sexual philandering and the fact that he has a mistress, the overblown Lucy, a working class woman whom Finley "keeps." Given that the story detailing the transmission of Heavenly's venereal disease locates its source in Minnie's casual pickups on Bourbon St. and the docks, Finley's fear is not racial, but a fear of the working class as overly sexual and diseased. Given his relationship with Lucy, Finley is drawn to the very sexuality he reviles. His behavior mirrors Minnie's—legitimized only because he is a man—and opens a reading that his aggressive protection of his daughter is not simply a display of patriarchy at its most overbearing, but a sign of his own anxiety over his sexuality.

Such a reading would be more credible if any character in *Sweet Bird of Youth* were more complexly realized. Boss Finley, finally, is a caricature of a Southern politico whom Williams offers with insufficient depth to support, uncontested, the reading of his behaviour which I have offered. But, as I suggested, sexual panic underlies *Sweet Bird of Youth*. The anxiety isn't restricted to heterosexuality. The story of transmission which Tom Junior offers is credible within the terms of the play because it rehearses Chance's relationship with Alexandra del Lago; as Tom claims that Chance was Minnie's gigolo, so he is Alexandra del Lago's, just as Lucy is Boss Finley's mistress. It is important to note, however, that there is little in the text to indicate that "Princess Kosmonopolis" and Chance are having sex; indeed, given how stoned and drunk both are, it would seem that consummation is unlikely. The apparent absence of sexual intimacy between Chance and the Princess might be read as a consequence of fading youth, which preoccupies both characters, except for Chance's reluctance, on seeing Heavenly's naked body, to consummate that relationship: he said, "no" and she said, "yes." This reluctance I read as an indication of Chance's ambivalence about his sexual orientation. The ambivalence of the character is heightened by the campiness of the opening scene of the play which has Alexandra del Lago flailing in the throes of a nightmare and Chance presented to the audience in an eroticized manner.

Sweet Bird of Youth opens in a room in a "grand hotel" of fading splendour. The audience sees a woman, lying in bed, whom we later discover is the fading Hollywood star, Alexandra de Lago. She is escaping her recent failures on stage by drinking heavily, by taking drugs, and by keeping company with Chance Wayne. This scene sets the stage for the sexual ambiguity which is key to the play. Chance, sits on the edge of the bed and lighting "*his first cigarette of the day*" (13). He rises and "*pauses a moment at a mirror in the fourth wall*"; in other words, he stands, facing the audience. The man whom we see is:

> in his late twenties but his face looks older than that; you might describe it
> as a "ravaged young face" and yet it is still exceptionally good-looking. His
> body shows no decline, yet it's the kind of body that white silk pajamas are,
> or ought to be, made for. (14)

Whether or not a director has an actor whose physique actually realizes Williams's imagined possibilities of "*the kind of body that white silk pajamas are, or ought to be, made for*" is unimportant; the stage directions make clear that the playwright wanted to eroticize Chance for the audience. Given that the playwright directs Chance to face the audience, pretending to comb his hair, an action which surely involves the possibility of those silk pajama bottoms slipping off his hips, the thorny question is: for whom is Chance being presented as a object of desire? Given that Paul Newman played Chance in the Broadway production (and in the subsequent film version), straight women might well experience a tingle of desire; but so, too, might gay men.

The homoerotic energy is also evident in Williams's depiction of the Princess Kosmonopolis, beginning with the question of the inspiration for the character. Donald Spoto, in his biography of Williams, claims that Williams's friend, Lilla van Saher boasted, "'The curtain rises, and I am there, in bed with my trade! Is (sic) very clear a play about me!'" (207). Spoto offers a corrective that Tallulah Bankhead was the source of inspiration, given her accusations against her former secretary Evyleen R. Cronyn of forging cheques worth more than four thousand dollars. Cronyn countered that the star was too drunk to sign the cheques to pay for her liquor, drugs and sex (207). Spoto, in an unacknowledged reference, quotes Bankhead as responding, "Of course I drink, but nobody has to forge my checks to buy liquor. And if I had been getting dope, do you think I'd pay for it by *check*? And God knows I never had to *buy* sex!" (207).

In the *Playboy* interview Williams speaks about Tallulah Bankhead playing Blanche DuBois in a revival of *Streetcar Named Desire*. Bankhead was apologetic for her rendering of Blanche, which Williams claims to have told her was the "worst" he'd seen. But he adds:

> All the drag queens were out there screaming; she was a riot. But she did quite an amazing job of controlling the faggots; whenever there were lines they'd scream at, she'd drag herself up and try to shut them off. Being naturally camp, it was difficult for her to cut down on it, but she did try. (243)

The details which Williams offers in his depiction of Alexandra del Lago corresponds closely enough to the tiff between Bankhead and Cronyn to suggest that Bankhead was, as is widely acknowledged in the criticism of the play, the inspiration for Princess Kosmonopolis. What interests me is Williams's location of Bankhead within gay culture, as an actor who drew a gay audience and whose persona invited the identification of drag queens with her. As Williams said, Bankhead was camp.

Susan Sontag, in her essay, "Notes on 'Camp'" suggests that it is "not a natural mode of sensibility, if there be any such. Indeed, the essence of Camp is its love of the unnatural: of artifice and exaggeration. And Camp is esoteric—something of a private code, a badge of identity even, among small urban cliques" (275). The terms of Sontag's description of camp deserve close scrutiny, but for the moment I want to focus on the notion of camp as involving "artifice" and "exaggeration." Williams's description of Bankhead suggests that he saw her as a campy exaggeration of femininity to the degree that she is a figure with whom drag queens identify. That Bankhead was biologically female seems less important to her persona than her performance of femininity, which was so artificial that even men can perform "Bankhead."

In a play which is filled with disruptions and exchanges so that in her father's eyes, Heavenly stands for her dead mother, the campy Bankhead is key to another crucial scheme of substitutions. Alexandra del Lago, in her persona of the aging movie queen "Princess Kosmonopolis," is histrionic. Our first glimpse of her is in the opening moments of the play, when she is sleeping with her face "*partly covered by an eyeless satin domino to protect her from morning glare. She breathes and tosses on the bed as if in the grip of a nightmare*" (13) That opening image of del Lago, thrashing in her disrupted sleep, sets the stage for del Lago's waking scenes which begin with her "*struggling out of her nightmare*" and sitting up "*gasping and staring wild-eyed about her*" (20). She then demands oxygen before taking an assortment of pills and alcohol and ordering Chance not use her real name but to refer to her under her assumed name, "Princess Kosmonopolis." Given that Bankhead, the icon of drag culture, seems to have been the inspiration for the character of Alexandra del Lago/Princess Kosmonopolis, there is a hint that the relationship between Chance and Alexandra del Lago may not be one between a man and a woman; rather, it is a relationship between a man and a persona of such exaggerated femininity that the Princess Kosmonopolis could as easily be a man in drag as a woman.

Carole-Anne Tyler, in "Boys Will Be Girls: The Politics of Gay Drag" offers a useful reminder that the view of femininity as masquerade has been adopted by some theorists as way of reading gender as performances which meet the needs of the dominant social ideologies, including positioning heterosexuality as the normative sexuality (32). She continues to remind her readers that this theoretical turn has allowed male drag to be recuperated from earlier views which saw it as a cruelly misogynistic parody of womanliness and now allow it to be read as a radically dissident exposure of all sexualities, however naturalized within the terms of dominant ideologies, as performed roles (33). Drag becomes the ally of feminism in its project of exposing the terms under which sexuality, and its oppression of women— straight or lesbian or permutations thereof—and gay men. Taylor remarks that "the controversy over the meaning of camp reveals as much about the fears and desires of theorists of drag as it does about the fears and desires of impersonators themselves" (33). Her point is that the celebration of drag, as a performative destabilization of socially produced normative sexuality, tends to foreclose the complexity of drag by celebrating it as simply emancipatory.

My reference to the opening moves of Taylor's essay is to signal that my project is not one of "queering" *Sweet Bird of Youth* and suggesting that underneath the play's veneer lies its true, gay meaning. Homosexual energies drive *Sweet Bird of Youth*, but those energies are shaped by the times in which Williams lived and wrote. Sexuality and gender are categories of social identity which are ideological, part of a complex weave of ideologies which create regulation and order that characterize the social sphere.

In my discussion of Heavenly and of Alexandra del Lago, I have tried to indicate that neither character is a realistic representation of a woman. Heavenly, as I have indicated, is a cipher, the figure of a woman who represents death; she doesn't view herself as alive, and in terms of the staging is mainly relegated to the background. If death is a form of silence, Williams's decision to have the male characters tell Heavenly's story, rendering her voiceless, is another indication of her being associated with death. Miss Lucy, like Heavenly, is a figure of death. The audience first sees her *"dressed in a ball gown, elaborately ruffled and very bouffant like an antebellum Southern belle's. A single blonde curl is arranged to switch girlishly at one side of her sharp terrier face"* (74). Miss Lucy stands for death, decked as she is in the attire of a culture which no longer has currency. Her anachronistic quality is heightened by the fact that she is ridiculously overdressed for the location, a cocktail lounge of the hotel. Clearly, the excess of Miss Lucy's attire is similar to the excesses of the Princess Kosmonopolis. Thus, Miss Lucy's staging of her femininity is both a sign of death and a sign of drag.

Tellingly, the relation between drag-like representations of women and death has been signalled earlier in the play by Princess Kosmonopolis when she tells of her retreat from Hollywood. Speaking to Chance, but as the stage directions indicate, facing the audience, she recalls that she "was an artist, not just a star whose career depended on youth. But I knew in my heart that the legend of Alexandra del Lago couldn't be separated from an appearance of youth . . ." (33). Her humiliation occurred when she attended the premiere of a movie that was to mark her return to the screen. There was a close-up which revealed her as an aging actor:

in the frame of the picture with a light blazing on it and all your terrible history screams while you smile . . . after that close-up they gasped . . . People gasped . . . I heard them whisper, their shocked whispers. Is that her? Is that her? (34)

Alexandra del Lago retreats from the theatre, tripping over her elaborate gown. She leaves Hollywood and her identity, creating a persona for herself as "The Princess Kosmonopolis." Chance Wayne becomes her attendant, ostensibly because the fading Hollywood star will provide him with an entrance into the film world. They travel, never settling, as if the aging screen legend is intent on avoiding the fact that her beauty and currency within Hollywood have waned. Her need for an attendant is occasioned by her spending the aftermath of confronting her face on screen ingesting copious quantities of alcohol and hashish to stave off attacks of panic.

Alexandra del Lago/Princess Kosmonopolis can be understood as a response to Oscar Wilde's *The Picture of Dorian Gray*. Dorian Gray lived, publicly maintaining youthful beauty while his portrait, hidden in the attic, assumes the wears and tears of his life. Like Dorian Gray, del Lago's social currency depends on youthful beauty; unlike Gray's, del Lago's image "lives" only through movies while in retirement, the actress grows old. When she presents herself as she is, in the movie meant to be her return to the screen, the audience gasps in shock and the actress, rejected for no longer being young, retreats from Hollywood, creating a persona which, in its campy elements, make her seem like a drag queen—and not a princess.

The fascination with youth and beauty in *Sweet Bird of Youth* as well as my reference to *The Picture of Dorian Gray* suggests what Jeff Nunokawa has described as the fatality which underlies *The Picture of Dorian Gray* and feeds social understandings of homosexuality as death-driven. The persona of the Princess makes it seems as if Alexandra del Lago is self-consciously performing femininity rather like a drag queen might; her constant need to escape through being endlessly on the move, stoned and drunk, if not death-driven, certainly refuses life and hence fits neatly with representations of homosexuality as death-driven, the contagion which is imagined to threaten life-affirming heterosexuality.

Having suggested that the ideological force of seeing homosexuality as death-driven and heterosexuality as life-affirming, *Sweet Bird of Youth* is clearly uneasy about heterosexuality, as is evident in its presentation of Boss Finley as the unpleasant caricature of The Father, of patriarchy and the law—both civil through his political position and religious through his invocation of God; through its campy offerings of Miss Lucy and Alexandra del Lago as the Princess Kosmonopolis; and through the sexual ambiguity of Chance Wayne who is clearly staged by Williams in a manner which invites the worst elements of an audience's voyeurism. In Chance's nostalgia for the youthful Heavenly, there is a sense of Williams's investment in notions of heterosexuality and the coupling of a young man and woman as potentially procreative. Significantly, the register of heterosexuality is only evident as a fuzzy nostalgia; it is not clear whether Chance actually wanted to sleep with Heavenly or felt that that was the sexual logic of young manhood. And, certainly none of the representations of women present them as figures of life whose bodies are fertile. Mainly, they are represented as figures of death; Miss Lucy and the Princess are so hyperbolic that they don't necessarily read as women.

The play's relationship to homosexuality is no less troubling because reading the play as queer depends on addressing the play's problematic renderings of women and race. Can a celebrator politic of gay identity be built for this play which insistently evacuates women of life and deploys them as figures of death? Can a gay politics be built when the narrative depends on the audience knowing that an Afro-American man has been castrated because, by virtue of his race, he stands for excessive sexuality which, in this play, seems to permeate readings of all sexuality? As I suggested in my opening, the play is troubling.

And, as I suggested, it is troubled. I want to return to my earlier reference to Susan Sontag's understanding of camp, offered in an essay written in 1964. In her suggestion that camp is "not a natural mode of sensibility, if there be any such." Sontag queries the category of "natural"; nevertheless, the category still stands for her, even if to be only to be cast under scrutiny. Further, "camp" is clearly represented as an oddity, "esoteric—something of a private code, a badge of identity even, among small urban cliques"; and camp is located as a subculture of the urban. My point is not to debate the merits of her definition, but rather to insist on a historicization of it. Sontag isn't suggesting that "camp" is part of an emancipatory project of renegotiating sexual politics; rather it is something of an oddity, restricted (she believes) to the urban, and even then accessible only to a few. Given Sontag's cautious location of camp, Williams's public outing is a useful index of homosexuality, historically situated.

In his interview with C. Robert Jennings, Tennessee Williams commented that until David Frost, in an 1970 interview asked him "point-blank" if he "were a homosexual," he had never talked publicly about his sexual orientation. Williams continued, "I was very embarrassed. I said, 'I cover the waterfront'" (232). Later, in the same interview, he tells Jennings that ". . . I'm only attracted to androgynous males, like Garbo" (229). I make reference to this comment because of its syntactical ambiguity: was Williams, like Garbo, attracted to androgynous males? Or, was Williams confiding that he was attracted to men who somehow reminded him of Garbo? And, why does Garbo, a movie star, figure in his sexual imaginary?

Williams continued to tell Jennings that he found:

> women much more interesting than men, but I'm afraid to fuck men now. I find *sexual excitement* in women, but I can't act with them. By completing the act I don't mean oral copulation. I'm just as anxious to feel a woman's ass and embrace and kiss her and enter her as I am a boy. . . . With a boy who has the androgynous quality in spirit, like a poet, the thing is more spiritual. I need that. And the other, too; I always want my member to enter the body of the sexual partner. I'm an aggressive person, I want to give, and I think it should be reciprocal. It's wonderful when they do and you do—let's face it. (229)

Williams's assessment of the terms of his desire is from an interview in the early 1970s, almost fifteen years after *Sweet Bird of Youth* premiered on Broadway. Proponents of gay history might feel inclined to reclaim Williams as a gay playwright whose sense of his own sexuality, like that of many gay men of his generation, was constrained by dominant codes. To a degree, my imagined cultural historian of gay sexuality would be right: growing up in the South, with all of its social strictures, and feeling sexual inclinations towards men in an age in which these desires are both pathologized and criminalized, provides cues about why Williams professes a conditional attraction to women.

In moving toward the conclusion of this essay with a long rehearsal of Williams's self-definition of his sexuality, I don't want to suggest recourse to a hoary critical strategy of mapping the autobiographical onto the literary as a means of interpreting the work. Rather, I want to suggest that Frost's question is not surprising in light of plays like *A Streetcar Named Desire* and *Suddenly Last Summer* which deal with homosexuality as thematic concerns, and in light of Williams' own life which, by the early '70s, was that of a man whose homosexuality was not a great secret. Yet, Williams had not spoken of his homosexuality publicly and his response of "embarrassment" at Frost's question serves as a telling index of his uneasiness of having his private erotic life part of the public record. There is no doubt that Williams was a homosexual, a man who was attracted sexually to other men. But, as his comments suggest, his negotiation of that desire is fraught, depending on repeated assertions that he is attracted sexually to women (to some degree) and through an elaborate public articulation of his desire for boys as transcending mere carnality and leading to a heightened spirituality. The issue isn't the veracity of the claims, whether Williams was attracted to women and whether acts of sexual intimacy enhanced his spiritual life; rather it is his need to provide public justification of the terms of his sexuality. His comments speak to the powerful force of heterosexuality being positioned socially as the normative sexuality and the degree to which this imperative was internalized by Williams, forcing him to feel the need to justify his desire which not only society, but he, saw a dissident.

Sweet Bird of Youth, as I argued, isn't a very "straight" play. Its insistent theme of disruption and formal disruptions which rupture stylistic coherence render problematic neat, formulaic readings of the play. The incoherence of the play can be read symptomatically as the force of a homosexual erotic which drives the dramaturgical project. But, as I have suggested, Williams's sense of homosexuality, read through his comments about his own sexuality, make this a troubled project. I offer cautions about the terms of a celebrator recuperation of the play as queer, suggesting that the representations of women and Afro-American men make this project problematic. Sexuality, as a modality of identity is part of the social and hence subject to the force of history. As Jeffery Weeks work suggests, homosexuality (like heterosexuality) is shaped by the social and by the specificity of history. Williams was a homosexual; *Sweet Bird of Youth* seems dramaturgically driven by a homoerotic energy; but crucially, the terms of Williams's homosexuality, and of the energy which drives *Sweet Bird of Youth*, are historically situated. Reading *Sweet Bird of Youth* does not reveal an essential queerness which transcends history.

NOTE
   1. This essay owes much to the work of Robert F. Gross, and a particular debt to his paper "Dressing Up and Falling Flat: Williams, Ludlam and a Queer Aesthetics of Failure" which he gave at the University of Guelph on 25 March 1999.

WORKS CITED
Hayman, Ronald. *Everyone Else is an Audience*. New York: Yale University Press, 1993.
Nunokawa, Jeff. "'All the Sad Young Men': AIDS and the Work of Mourning," in *inside/out: Lesbian Theories, Gay Theorie,* ed. Diana Fuss (New York: Routledge, 1991), 311–23.
Said, Edward. *Orientalism*. New York: Random House, 1978.
Sontag, Susan. "Notes on 'Camp,'" in *Against Interpretation*. (New York: Dell, 1966). 275–92.
Spoto, Donald. *The Kindness of Strangers: The Life of Tennessee Williams*. London: Methuen, 1985.
Tyler, Carole-Anne. "Boys Will Be Girls: The Politics of Gay Drag," in *inside/out: Lesbian Theories, Gay Theories*, ed. Diana Fuss, (New York: Routledge, 1991), 32–70.
Weeks, Jeffery. *Coming out: Homosexual Politics in Britain from the Nineteenth Century to the Present*. London: Quartet Books, 1990.
Williams, Tennessee. "Playboy Interview: Tennessee Williams," in *Conversations with Tennessee Williams*, ed. Albert Devlin. (Jackson: University Press of Mississippi, 1986), 224–50.
———. *Sweet Bird of Youth*. Volume 4 of *Theatre*. New York: New Directions, 1972: 1–124.

Tracing Lines of Flight in *Summer and Smoke* and *The Milk Train Doesn't Stop Here Anymore*

Robert F. Gross

> But the wonderfullest trick of all was the coffin trick. We nailed him
> into a coffin and he got out of the coffin without removing one nail.
>
> (Williams, *The Glass Menagerie*, 167)

I. Williams, Deleuze and Guattari—Escape Artists

Tennessee Williams is the great American artist of the escape act, and his plays show-case aspiring Houdinis in their struggles. To cite only a few notable examples: in *Cat on a Hot Tin Roof*, Maggie throws Brick's crutch out the window and refuses to set him free until he has sex with her; in *The Night of the Iguana*, the Reverend Shannon finds himself trussed up in a hammock, and recognizes a kindred creature in the iguana held captive beneath the porch, and in *The Red Devil Battery Sign*, the Woman Downtown struggles desperately to free herself from illegal house arrest in a Dallas hotel. From Port Tyler in *Spring Storm* and the prison in *Not About Nightingales* in the early years of his career, to the locked theatre of *Out Cry* and the mental hospital of *Clothes for a Summer Hotel* in his final years, Williams's landscape is marked with sites of captivity, and his plays repeatedly dramatize efforts at escape.

It is not surprising, then, to find an affinity between Williams and those two late twentieth century proponents of "nomadic thought," Gilles Deleuze and Félix Guattari. Best known for their provocative and brilliantly imaginative companion volumes *Anti-Oedipus* and *A Thousand Plateaus* (together comprising *Capitalism and Schizophrenia*), Deleuze and Guattari chart movements of capture and escape that echo Williams's.

This is not to argue for influence running in either direction. *Capitalism and Schizophrenia* never directly cites Williams, and Williams's artistic vision took its shape long before the appearance of any work by the two French mavericks. Rather, the three authors inhabit a common moment in Western culture, as modernist revolt, proclaiming a discourse of desire, begins to affect a transition to the post-modern—a moment they inhabit with such otherwise varied thinkers as Herbert Marcuse, Norman O. Brown, Roland Barthes and Michel Foucault, and a equally wide range of artists, including Jean Genet, Marguerite Duras, Francis Bacon, Jess Collins, Rainer Werner Fassbinder, Luis Buñuel and Pier Paolo Pasolini. For all their substantial differences, they tend to share a common interest in the opposition between bourgeois life, especially in its most fascistic manifestations, on the one hand, and individual desire on the other. Although influenced by Freud, they often take exception to what they see as his bourgeois tendencies and the use of his insights in social technologies that impede desire. They are often drawn to outsider artists and thinkers who proclaim desire's primacy: for Deleuze and Guattari, Heinrich von Kleist, Antonin Artaud and Henry Miller; for Williams, Arthur Rimbaud, Hart Crane and William Blake. Deleuze, Guattari and Williams all give a special place to D. H. Lawrence as a prophet of desire.[1]

In *Capitalism and Schizophrenia*, Deleuze and Guattari contrast the larger forms of the *molar*, best represented in binary thinking with the smaller, *molecular,* play of difference, which exists beneath the threshold of the molar and even escapes it, fleetingly. The official works of State philosophy and art try to rigidify binaries in an attempt to contain desire into dialectical oppositions that efface the freer play of difference. In Western drama, the binary is most frequently expressed through the agonic conflict between protagonist and antagonist. But regardless of the State's efforts to keep binaries intact, the system continually springs leaks, allowing lines of flight to develop. For Deleuze and Guattari, as for Williams, the basic social scenario exists in the tension between molar forms and molecular movements.

The molar is, above all, the expression of fixity, rigidity and stasis. It finds its fullest expression in the concept of masculinity. "There is no becoming-man because man is the molar entity par excellence, whereas becomings are molecular" (*Thousand Plateaus,* 292). Molecular lines of flight from molarity repudiate molar masculinity in favor of less normative currents of desire:

> From the viewpoint of micropolitics, a society is defined by its lines of flight, which are molecular. There is always something that flows or flees, that escapes the binary organizations, the resonance apparatus, and the overcoding machine: things are attributed to a "change in values," the youth, the women, the mad, etc.
>
> (*Thousand Plateaus,* 216)

To this short list of possible fugitive becomings, all of which are exemplified in Williams, we might add becoming-addict (Brick in *Cat on a Hot Tin Roof,* Alexandra in *Sweet Bird of Youth*), becoming-queer (Sebastian in *Suddenly Last Summer,* Lot in *Kingdom of Earth*), becoming-sick (Jane in *Vieux Carré,* Kip in *Something Cloudy, Something Clear*), becoming-animal (Wolf in *The Red Devil Battery Sign, The*

Gnädiges Fräulein), becoming-space alien (Ben and the Girl in *Stairs to the Roof*) and becoming-artist (Val in *Orpheus Descending* and Mark in *In the Bar in a Tokyo Hotel*).

I could easily continue to sketch lines of flight across Williams's corpus, but I find it more revealing to examine in some detail the tension between molar and molecular elements, and their dramaturgical implications, in just two plays: one early, *Summer and Smoke*, and the other at the beginning of the final phase, *The Milk Train Doesn't Stop Here Anymore*. Through this examination, it becomes clear that Williams was caught between an aesthetics of the molar that has tended to dominate Western dramaturgy from the Renaissance to the present (most clearly codified in the mechanics of the well-made play), and a more elusive dramaturgy of the molecular.

II. Summer and Smoke: Escaping the Binaries of Glorious Hill

At first, *Summer and Smoke* seems a poor choice for my investigation. No play by Williams appears more strenuously symmetrical in its plotting and binary in its thematics. It is structured around the opposition of Alma Winemiller and John Buchanan as soul and body, respectively, and its neat reversal of their apparent positions by the play's end gives the overall trajectory of the action a chaistic form reminiscent of August Strindberg's *Miss Julie*, but with the gender opposition mapped onto an opposition of philosophical positions, rather than class. The heroine Alma, "Spanish for soul" (202), as we are reminded in a moment of sledgehammer-subtle allegorizing, moves from her rarefied world of genteel art, idealism and hysteria, to a less idealized world of drugs and assignations with travelling salesmen. At the same time, John moves in the opposite direction, from dissipation in the violent shadows of the Moon Lake Casino to a career of hard work, heroic medicine and cloying domesticity. The plot structure's strong thematic opposition is further underscored by the setting's division into the Winemiller and Buchanan households. Indeed, the structure is so symmetrical that it can appear overly pat; a *Gift of the Magi* with allegorical pretensions.

And, on the heels of the charge of schematic structure follows the charge of naivete. Isn't this body-soul allegorizing slightly simpleminded, a sort of bargain basement dualism that hardly seemed fresh when the play premiered, and today seems quaint at best and silly at worst? A cursory view of *Summer and Smoke* reinforces the dominant view of Williams as an evocative poetic realist who lacked the capacity for deep thought; wonderful at stage images, inspired at histrionic displays, but clumsy at handling ideas.

But there is another way of approaching this play, one that focuses on the moments that escape binarization. I propose that we take the John/Alma opposition, which is displayed horizontally across the stage by the Buchanan/Winemiller households, and see it in relation to a more complex arrangement of images and ideas—one that suggests lines of flight away from the dominant, molar oppositions.

To begin, rather than looking at the opposition of the two households, let us examine their commonality. Both are, first and foremost, middle-class households. Each is presided over by a patriarch whose profession gives the household its place in the play's allegorical binary—the medical profession for the Buchanans and the ministry for the Winemillers. Both households are marked by feminine lines of flight from the patriarchal: John's mother has died, Alma's has retreated into a malicious and manipulative eccentricity. Both households contain children who are unable or unwilling to conform to their fathers' orders, and, as a result, are condemned as undisciplined. Both Alma and John have energies that are stifled at home: John's release is in dissipation; Alma's, in artistic expression and hysterical outbursts. Although the two houses tacitly claim to divide the world between them as care of the body and the soul, they are both common expressions of a bourgeois ethic that attempts to contain potentially disruptive energies. In short, despite their opposition, both households share a common adherence to a white, bourgeois, patriarchal order, in which both body and soul are pressured to submit to a rigorous discipline of hygiene. The molar opposition of the households claims to divide the world in two, while conspiring together to uphold a common bourgeois order.

But, if we read with an eye that tracks molecular flows of desire, the Buchanan/Winemiller binary is only one level of the play, and does not succeed in creating a closed and totaling system. Considering the play from the vantage point provided by Deleuze and Guattari's observation that a system is defined by what escapes it (*Thousand Plateaus,* 216), we can begin to see movements in the play that escape its overt symmetries. The bourgeois order of Glorious Hill, Mississippi is far from hermetically sealed.

Glorious Hill is bounded on one side by the realm of immensity and on the other by the realm of the minute. The statue of Eternity that stands midstage testifies to that which escapes domestic discipline by its very resistance to representation. As a statue it is simply the figure of a woman—and, as such, assimilable to bourgeois discipline. But its name, the word at the base of the statue so worn that it cannot be read, but only deciphered by touch—"Eternity"—gives the statue its sublime aura. Standing between the two houses, and given special focus at the opening and conclusion of *Summer and Smoke*, the statue suggests a dimension beyond bourgeois discipline. It reverberates with Immanuel Kant's famous example of the sublime—the inscription at the entrance of the Temple of Isis. Kant muses:

> Perhaps nothing more sublime was ever said and no sublimer thought ever expressed than the famous inscription on the Temple of Isis (Mother Nature): "I am all that is and that was and that shall be, and no mortal hath lifted my veil." (160)

For Kant, the sublime is a category of experience elicited by whatever, in its magnitude or power, overwhelms the human observer, who cannot comprehend its totality in a single instant. Similarly, Williams's Eternity overwhelms its subject as an expression of boundlessness—an incomprehensibly immense unity which defies division into dichotomies.

Bounding Glorious Hill on the other side is the world of the microscopic, a teeming world of minute beings. It is a "mysterious" realm that is, as John Buchanan tells us, "part anarchy—part order" (141). We never learn what the principles of this realm are; in its own way, it remains every bit as mysterious as Eternity. But, rather than being vast and unified, it is minuscule and multifarious—an image of molecularity. Neither of John's terms—anarchy and order—can be applied to Glorious Hill's Eternity or Immanuel Kant's Isis, for each is only one thing, and can therefore be neither orderly or disorderly. The stony stasis of the statue has nothing in common with microscopic motions.

Although the opposition of microbe and statue could easily be read as a reiteration of the binary of the households, with the microbe as the physical at its most primitive, and the statue the spiritual at its most ineffable, such an approach would take potential lines of flight and recuperate them back into the molar, leaving no differences apart from binary opposition. It is more emancipatory to see how the inextricable mixture of anarchy and order that John contemplates on his microscope slide (a realm, Alma suggests, perhaps even "more religious" than the realm of the minister [141]), permeates *Summer and Smoke*, and makes the world of the play one of molecularity, as well as molar opposition.

Molecularity is seen not merely in the opposition between John and Alma but in the differences between them, differences that resist any facile division into boundaries. Why the attraction between John and Alma? What is the impulse that makes John lecture Nellie's mother, as if he were a minister? Why Alma's attraction to William Blake? Or to Oscar Wilde? The notion of a *Doppelgänger*, or second self, that John uses to diagnose Alma's hysteria, may indicate a binary opposition, but it also introduces the notion that we ourselves are split and splitting. In the word of the *Doppelgänger*, the subject is not unified, like the statue of Eternity, but is divided and alien to itself. Like the microscope slide, it reveals a world part order and part chaos.

For what are the principles in this play that bring one body, one bundle of desires, into contact with another? How does John take a wrong turn while looking for the bathroom and come upon Nellie's bedroom? What keeps him there, talking to her? And what is the strange impact of time and circumstance upon those unstable bundles of desire (our protagonists) that make John eager to have sex with Alma at Moon Lake Casino one night, and determined to reject her when she, months later, approaches him with sexual desire? What is the mysterious process that Alma discovers in William Blake's poem, "Love's Secret," and which is reinscribed in the action of the play:

> No sooner had he gone from me
> Than a stranger passing by,
> Silently, invisibly,
> Took him with a sigh? (175)

John recoils from Alma, only to wind up mysteriously, perhaps even grotesquely, in the calculating and social-climbing clutches of Nellie Ewell, while Alma retreats from John, winding up in the hands of the nervously guffawing Archie Kramer. For Alma and John, as for so many of Williams's characters, libido is sparked by chance and even improbable encounters, the whims of a certain time and place, a certain inexplicable vulnerability of the subject. If the standard Broadway play or Hollywood movie of mid-century America put desire under the fateful rule of Necessity, bringing hero and heroine together through a heterosexually monogamous destiny, Williams puts his characters under the sign of Chance. For him, desire is errant, self-contradictory, unstable, destabilizing, and unpredictable in its duration.

All of the disorderly, discontinuous and volatile impulses that thrive in the Moon Lake Casino—drugs, violence, rooms that rent for brief assignations—thrive in a realm of the ephemeral and instantaneous. The moon, stock symbol of change and inconstancy, is linked with the fluidity of the lake, and the rule of chance at the Casino. It is a world of molecularity, and one that Williams's description of the set has trouble accommodating. In his introductory remarks, he describes at length the Buchanan and Winemiller houses, the statue of Eternity and the starry sky, but defers, even dismisses, the setting of the Moon Lake Casino. "There is one more set, a very small exterior representing an arbor, which we will describe when we reach it" (121). What a nervous parenthesis this sentence is, as if eager to deemphasize the world that sets itself apart from the bourgeois order of the self-disciplined subject, of compulsory heterosexual monogamy and concern with reputation! But, despite Williams's marginalizing stage direction, Moon Lake Casino exerts a powerful influence on the play. It provides the scandal that envelops John and fascinates the gossips of Glorious Hill. It is the world of Mrs. Ewell, and the world that her daughter learns to sanitize to land her doctor and claim him for bourgeois domesticity. It is the world that collides with Dr. Buchanan and brings about his death. And, most importantly, it is the world that finally claims Alma. In this context, Williams's dismissive account of the Moon Lake Casino at the play's beginning, and his refusal to grant it any but the slightest presence in the *mise-en-scène* reads as a guilty disclaimer, an editorial statement that denies and distorts the real story that the playwright then proceeds to tell.

But the liquid molecularity of Moon Lake Casino refuses to be contained, either by the domestic boxes of Williams's set, or by his slighting initial reference to it. The play abounds in presences that refuse to solidify: the microbes swarm beneath the microscope's lens; fireworks explode and fade away; clouds and constellations drift across the cyclorama; Alma's prescription medicine makes her feel like "a water lily on a Chinese lagoon" (255). Alma cannot help but produce her *Doppelgänger*, and her awareness of her own inner division causes her to drift out of the house late at night, not knowing who she is, or where she is going. She tells her father to let inquisitive people know "I've changed and you're waiting to see in what way" (225). She at first fears this change will kill her, but comes to understand that fear was naive. "But now the Gulf has blown that feeling away," she tells John, "and I know now I'm not dying, that it isn't going to turn out to be that simple" (241). No longer do her hands freeze up and solidify in panic. Now she drifts like a water lily on a Chinese lagoon, without purpose, without productivity, and without a unified sense of self. The 'smoke' of the title that asphyxiates Alma after her crisis seems not to leave a corpse behind, but a smoke-like creature of mysteriousness and flux.

For *Summer and Smoke* both works to create and dissolve its own binaries. The dissolution begins as early as the play's Prologue, in which young Alma and John consider the statue of Eternity. While Kant imagined us intuiting the sublime by reading the inscription above the doorway of Isis's temple, Williams denies his characters any comfortable ocular distance from the sublime. The word at the base of the statue is worn and can no longer be read. For Williams, the sublime is intuited by touch, the most immediate and sexual of all the senses. Only by moving one's fingers across the base—"You have to read it with your fingers," Alma explains to John, "I read it and it gave me the cold shivers! [. . .] Go on!" she urges, "Read it with your fingers!" (128). In one of the play's most subtle ironies, it is the juvenile Alma who introduces John to the physical pleasures of tactile understanding, in which the "cold shivers" become youthful intimations of the tremors of sexual pleasure. What transforms the statue from a genteel piece of public statuary, at home in Glorious Hill, to a sublime object, is only found by encountering it tactilely. Even at this early point in the play, Williams suggests that the way we encounter the boundlessness of the sublime is not by repudiating sexuality, but by accepting it; not by a flight *from* the present moment of physical sensation, but by immersion *in* it. For even the most solid and monumental object in the play, the statue of Eternity, is a conduit for fluidity—the water it holds in its hands. Through this image, the world of the immense and the minute meet, and the sensual tracing of fingers against worn stone lead to an intimation of Eternity, which in turn, causes the momentary play of shivers across the body.

But the world of fluidity, of Moon Lake and its instabilities, is not without its dangers. Rosa Gonzalez has lived there, and is as disgusted by it in her own way as Alma is. It is violent, as the cock fights and the shooting of Dr. Buchanan illustrate. The denizens of Moon Lake—Nellie, Rosa and her father—yearn to move into the homes of the bourgeoisie, or even beyond them. "The sky is the limit" boasts Mr. Gonzalez, with overtones of exploding fireworks and titanic ambitions (216). The forces of Moon Lake Casino can be very threatening, unless one is assiduously educated, sanitized, cosmeticized and white—like Nellie. Indeed, when these forces erupt into the sedate neighborhoods of Glorious Hill, Williams seems almost as desperate to banish them as Alma is. Look how rapidly the characters shift, as the play almost vaults to its conclusion after the crisis. The Gonzaleses vanish, John has an offstage conversion, Nellie fastforwards into pseudo-maturity and Alma undergoes symbolic death. After the leisurely pace of the first two-thirds of the play, the last third contains more shifts in plot and character than the play can comfortably accommodate. Later evidence reinforces the suspicion that Williams himself was uncomfortable with what he had done here. He later extensively revised the material under the title *The Eccentricities of a Nightingale*, and expressed his preference for the later play, finding its predecessor, he observed, too "conventional and melodramatic" (7).

Indeed, there is much that is conventional in the conclusion of *Summer and Smoke*. As it speeds to its conclusion, it reverts to sketching out a Freudian scenario, recuperating John's energies in the service of molarity. John, having rebelled against patriarchy, suddenly finds his patricidal impulses become reality with his father's death. After this, John assumes the patriarchal position and becomes the good doctor, husband and model citizen who repudiates Alma's advances. In the final scenes, John's story becomes the most stock aspect of *Summer and Smoke*, leading me to wonder if the frequent performance of the play on college campuses has not been in large part due to its easy assimilation to a narrative of moral improvement and social integration into a bourgeois order; John becomes patriarch to Alma's fallen woman and must spurn her, however gently, to achieve true bourgeois masculine respectability. Following this line of interpretation, Alma becomes the waste product of John's maturational process—the molecular flow that must be repudiated in favor of molar masculinity. Facing the catastrophe of Moon Lake Casino erupting into Glorious Hill, Williams takes refuge in an Oedipal form, which "secretes ideology according to the dominant codes" (Deleuze and Guattari, *Anti-Oedipus*, 133).

Summer and Smoke gives us a powerfully melodramatic structure built on binary opposition—the houses of body and spirit—and contains a strong drive to affirm both the binary and the hierarchy it holds in place. But it also questions the binary, pokes at it, folds it back in on itself and dissolves it. The play is sustained by a binary which is almost painfully simplistic at times, but it is also animated through subtle moments that repeatedly refuse to be reduced to a binary—fireworks that "burst into a million stars" (149), the immensities of a curved, Einsteinian space, the floating of a lily on the water, the fantastical entrance of Rosa Gonzalez in the park, and the countless subtle movements that Alma and John make within themselves and between each other that defy the very opposition they so vociferously insist on. The play strains to move beyond the dichotomies of its stage setting, perhaps more subversively than Williams himself was quite comfortable with, even as it rushes toward some sort of socially acceptable closure.

But how absolute is that closure? The last image of John shows him kissing his fiancee with "*his eyes tight with a look of torment*" (250). The last image of Alma shows her saluting the statue and us. As we approach closure, the protagonists withdraw, becoming more opaque and mysterious. Do John's tightly closed eyes suggest that his assimilation to patriarchy is incomplete, that the project of molar masculinity has not yet obliterated molecular lines of flight? Does Alma's decision to visit Moon Lake Casino mean loneliness or lust, a triumph over hysteria or self-destruction? (Becoming-opaque is another line of flight.) Subordinated to the plot, John and Alma are captives to the binaries of Glorious Hill, but simultaneously, beneath its molar structure, they suggest myriad lines of flight.

Despite these evocative resistances to molarity, however, *Summer and Smoke* shows Williams having trouble meeting the challenge of creating a dramaturgy of flight. The combination of strongly binary mechanisms of plot and setting, along with the climactic confrontation of Alma and John before the anatomical chart, all tend to overpower the moments of molecularity, both in reading and mainstream production. At this point in his career, Williams had not yet moved far enough from the assumptions of well-made, realistic drama to keep the binaries from recuperating most lines of flight. The playwright had not yet quite succeeded in escaping the binaries of Glorious Hill.

III. The Milk Train Doesn't Stop Here Anymore:

Flight and Catastrophe
Unlike Alma Winemiller, Flora Goforth, the protagonist of *The Milk Train*

Doesn't Stop Here Anymore, left her small-town Southern roots behind her in the dust decades ago. A youthful inhabitant of One Street, Georgia, Flora found her line of flight as a striptease dancer who adorned her performances with bawdy commentary. She moved from hick town stripper to Broadway entertainer in the *Follies*, married repeatedly for wealth and status and once for intense sexual pleasure, and now finds herself wealthy, famous and working on her memoirs in a mountain villa above the Mediterranean Sea.

Although Flora's luxurious villa is far from One Street, it is far from being an idyllic realm of freedom. Guarded by wild dogs and a sadistic, uniformed guard named Rudi, it is as much a site of demonic incarceration as a place of refuge. When the mysterious visitor, Chris Flanders, comes to visit Flora, he is attacked by the dogs, beaten by Rudi, deprived of food, stripped of his possessions, and threatened with death when he considers escaping. He is installed as a potential sexual plaything for Flora, just as the female employees seem vulnerable to the unwanted sexual aggressiveness of Rudi.

Around the villa monsters proliferate, alive with the mysterious interplay of logic and anarchy that distinguish Doctor John's microbes. (Becoming-monster can be added to Williams's lines of flight.) "The sea is full of Medusas" we are told (44), and although they are merely stinging jellyfish, they share the name of the mythical monster, part-human and part-viperous. Flora, we are told, is a griffin—part lion, part eagle, and, at the same time, entirely human (7). Less aggressive but no less hybrid is the host of *"painted and carved cupids"* (30) that decorate Flora's guest bedroom.

More significant than these monstrous bestial hybrids, however, are the monsters that transgress the most fundamental binary, that of the living and the dead. The Witch of Capri, who lives off blood transfusions, has become a vampire, a *pipistrella* (45). Chris has been christened "The Angel of Death," because of his repeated proximity to dying socialites (49). At first sight, Flora is struck by Chris's uncanny resemblance to her fourth husband, Black identifies herself as a wraith—"I'm not dead but not living!" she asserts. Gilbert Debusscher is right to note that the coming of the "Angel of Death" to Flora echoes the summoning of Everyman in the morality play (399), but this messenger arrives on a scene already permeated with death, and the messenger is aware that even he is growing older.

Flight does not lead to liberation in *Milk Train*, for lines of flight are not secure trajectories that lead from captivity to freedom. They have nothing to do with liberal projects of maturation, in which the individual becomes more autonomous, like Ibsen's Nora in *A Doll's House*. For not only does flight always run the risk of recuperation back into the molar, but the very impulse that impels the fugitive can easily lead to self-destruction, fascism and death. Free of the molar, the molecular can be threatened by itself:

> instead of connecting with other lines and each time augmenting its valence, *turning to destruction, abolition pure and simple, the passion of abolition*. Like Kleist's line of flight, and the strange war he wages; like suicide, like double suicide, a way out turns the line of flight into a line of death. (*Thousand Plateaus*, 229)

In *Milk Train* there is no longer a home (or home town) to escape from. The characters inhabit a mere stopping place for jet-setting nomads who wander pointlessly from one chic address to another. The escape from molarity has not led to fulfillment, but to meaningless movement:

> the thing people feel when they go from room to room for no reason, and then they go back from room to room for no reason, and then they go out for no reason and come back in for no reason—
>
> (90)

Chris is ostensibly speaking of Sissy's restless wandering in her villa, but he might as well be describing himself. His peregrinations among the geriatric jet set reveal no purpose, but inscribe a line of flight that encounters death at every turn.

In world of aimless wandering, all encounters become chance. Chris arrives at Flora's, bearing a mobile he has made for her. Entitled "The Earth is a Wheel in a Great Big Gambling Casino" (31), it is a paradoxical object. A work of human artifice and choice, it nevertheless testifies to the sovereignty of chance. The aleatoric realm of Moon Lake Casino resurfaces here, but now expanded to the cosmic level. No longer awkwardly shoehorned in among the realms of bourgeois discipline, it has come to include, not only the onstage space, but the entire universe.

But these wanderings and chance encounters are not the products of ennui, but of unfocused and floundering desperation. *Milk Train* shows a desperation that erupts in delirium. Dictating night and day over a loudspeaker system, Flora produces a chaos of disjointed memory texts, leaving her secretary Blackie the impossible task of imposing some order on them in time for publication, even if Flora were to live long enough to actually cover the major events of her life in this rambling, sometimes hallucinated, manner. Mortally ill, feverish and desperate, Flora seems to subsist on a diet of black coffee, mineral water, cigarettes, codeine, empirin and booze as she works to complete the telling of her life. Even in her few hours of drugged sleep, she does not find repose, but is prey to nightmares. In her sleep, a dream can suddenly trigger memory and memory a new passage in her memoirs, one that can become so vivid as to become a horrifying present. She wakes to remember the death of her first husband, narrating her response to the event on her terrace, only for the experience of Harlon Goforth's terrified mortality to become her own (58–59). Chris, for his part, confesses to fears of losing his "sense of reality" (110), is attacked by wild dogs and Rudi, and has nothing to sustain him but black coffee. Blackie works frantically around the clock, while suffering from Flora's caprices and accusations. All the major characters are on edge and easily given to strong outbursts of emotion and aggression.

This delirium ruptures the bounds of realism, making the play delirious as well. In *Summer and Smoke*, Williams gave great attention to the construction of a constraining, realistic milieu that his characters could attempt to escape from. In *Milk Train* realistic milieu has been replaced by clusters of theatrical gestures, molecular flows which, like the stars and microbes of the earlier play, do not lend themselves to the conflict between character and setting so prevalent in realistic drama. Whereas *Summer and Smoke* is predominantly realistic, *Milk Train* is predominantly *catastrophic*.

For Deleuze and Guattari, catastrophe is that which subverts systematic thinking and representation. While the lines of flight chart movements away from the binary in molecular flows, the catastrophic momentarily undoes the binary, rupturing it into flows of desire.

Certainly catastrophic events are represented in Williams's plays from the start of his career: storm and suicide in *Spring Storm*, torture and violent death in *Not About Nightingales*, lynching in *Battle of Angels*, rape in *27 Wagons Full of Cotton* and *A Streetcar Named Desire*, to list only a few. But those catastrophes are safely contained within the conventions of realism, and therefore do not provoke crises of realistic representation. In the plays from *Milk Train* to the end of his career, however, there is a pronounced tendency to rupture realism and concretize catastrophe in both dramatic structure and *mise-en-scène*. Catastrophe is no longer represented as a discrete event contained within a predominantly realistic drama, but the drama itself is presented as the site of catastrophic forces.

This aesthetic development in Williams's work is similar to a development that Deleuze and Guattari identify in the paintings of J. M. W. Turner. In his earlier work, Turner depicts catastrophic events such as storms and avalanches. In his late work, however, the painting is no longer a representation of a catastrophic event, but *becomes* the catastrophe itself:

> The canvas turns in on itself, it is pierced by a hole, a lake, a flame, a tornado, an explosion. The themes of the preceding paintings are to be found again here, their meaning changed. The canvas is truly broken, sundered by what penetrates it. All that remains is a background of gold and fog, intense, intensive, transversed in depth by what has just sundered its breadth: the schiz. Everything becomes mixed and confused, and it is here that the breakthrough—not the breakdown—occurs.
>
> (*Anti-Oedipus*, 132)[2]

In catastrophic art, gestures are deterritorialized, that is, freed from hierarchies of subordination. When, for example, Amanda in *The Glass Menagerie* enters in the dress she wore to receive her gentlemen callers, it is a realistically probable moment. When Flora enters in her kabuki costume, however, it is a purely theatrical flourish. Though she later explains that she once wore it for a benefit (43), the costume's place in Flora's past is minor, even arbitrary, and tells us nothing about her. The kabuki costume more clearly links to other sartorial gestures in the play, such as her deceased husband's Japanese robe, and the Witch of Capri's exotic garb. which gives her the appearance of a *"creature out of a sophisticated fairy tale"* (42). (Is becoming-masquerade yet another line of flight?) The costume, momentarily sprung loose from the constraints of realism, presents itself as an instant of pure performance, which then hovers in an ever-shifting constellation of theatrical gestures.

Similarly, both characters and their interactions are liberated from coherence. Although Flora and Chris dominate *Milk Train* as thoroughly as Alma and John do *Summer and Smoke*, it is far more difficult, if not impossible, to understand their relationship. In part, this is because they are less characters in the traditional sense than heterogeneous assemblages of qualities. Chris may be the "Angel of Death" and the avatar of Flora's favorite husband, and certainly those attributions resonate throughout the play. But he is also an aging hanger-on to the wealthy, a burnt-out poet, a builder of mobiles, a man bearing the weight of a notorious reputation, a mystic, a man who worries he may be losing his mind, a man who once helped an old man drown himself, and quite possibly a cheat, a liar, a thief and a murderer. A similar list could be assembled for Flora.

Such multiple roles render character relationships unstable. Rather than trying to ground them in relationship to plot, character or theme, the play postulates a varied series of possible relationships between the two leading figures. For example, consider all of the following statements about Flora's relationship to Chris: she is attracted to him as the return of her dead and much-desired husband; she fears him as the notorious "Angel of Death"; she has contempt for him as a social parasite who is little better than a gigolo; she sees him as a counterculture figure with no respect for her wealth and power who must be brought to heel; she wants to use him sexually, as she uses her drugs, to mute her terror of impending death. The histrionic power of the play resides in the exploration of all these impulses (and others), rather than in the reduction to a single Method superobjective. The relationship between two characters in Williams's catastrophic dramas is not a fixed equation, but a field of possibilities. Although *Milk Train* is shares a superficial resemblance to *Summer and Smoke* in its construction around a series of encounters between a female protagonist and her male foil, the encounters are more easily recuperated to dominant structural binaries in the latter play, and more molecular and free-floating in the former.

The opposition of Flora and Chris does not reinforce gender binaries, but subverts them. Sissy is wealthy, powerful and brutal. She is sexually aggressive and casts Chris in the role of the object of her desire. She is the one compared to a legendary Greek explorer. Chris, by comparison, is passive. He is vulnerable and the object of desire, first appearing onstage with his *lederhosen* half torn from his body. He is never identified as anyone's sexual partner, and withdraws from Flora's advances. As binaries weaken and prove less able to hold things in place, man becomes-woman and woman becomes-monster. Binaries of gender give way in favor of molecular becomings, and all attributes become liable to dispersal.

As *Milk Train* moves to its conclusion, not only do characterological binaries disperse, but the very landscape dissolves into a final lack of differentiation that seems a reversion to a sublime primal chaos, with sky and sea "dissolving into each other. Wine-dark sea and wine-dark sky" (106). The dramatic space is depopulated: Sissy dies, her household staff scatters, taking her valuables along with them, and Chris contemplates his own disappearing flight into Flora's small shack near the shore, which is called " 'The Oubliette'—from the French verb *'oublier'* which means to forget" (81). (Becoming-forgotten, becoming-unseen, are also lines of flight.) In the fugitive space of the unseen and the forgotten, Chris plans the creation of a catastrophic artifact. After the sound of powerful waves striking the rocks beneath the villa, Chris's mobile will be named "Boom," but the title does not provide an explication. "It says 'Boom' and that's what it means. No translation, no explanation, just 'Boom.'" (120) he says. Another becoming-opaque, but in this case it is a moment of metadramatic commentary that reflects back on the entire play, wrapping all of it in a layer of resistance to interpretation.

While earlier plays, such as *A Streetcar Named Desire* and *Summer and Smoke*, depicted fugitive characters, *Milk Train's* catastrophism impels the play itself along a line of flight. Fleeing the constraints of commercial writing (at the same time that Williams, unfortunately, continued to hope for success on Broadway), *Milk Train* is as much a fugitive from domestic realism as any Williams character is from home. Mixing realistic business, expressionistic devices, presentational conventions, literary references, allegorical gestures, social satire and camp repartee, the play is, as Gilbert Debusscher so rightly observed, as much monstrosity as Flora's griffin (406). No longer like the human figuration of *Summer and Smoke's* statue, it is like Chris's mobile, it is a response to a disjointed and aleatoric cosmos. Like "Boom," it is a Duchampian assemblage that works to resist recuperation through interpretation.

In many ways, *Milk Train* initiates the final phase of Williams's career, one in which the molar structure of binaries dissolves, leaving plays that chart the molecular flows of desires and images. But the more the molecular dominates, the less audiences and critics have been inclined to accept the plays. The tenacious canard that underlies most Western drama tells us that "drama is conflict," and depends on the molar opposition of protagonist and antagonist, structured in movements of agonic confrontation.

But in his repudiation of molar dramaturgy, Williams becomes a forerunner of some of the most exciting theatre in America today. When Richard Foreman describes his drama as "an amorphous cloud of molecular particles" (27) that refuses to be subsumed into larger, molar, dramaturgical shapes, he is offering a description that might lend itself to *Milk Train*, and suggests a fruitful directorial approach. When JoAnne Akalaitis observes that "chaos, not conflict, is the essence of drama" (quoted in Saivetz, 151), she shows an affinity to Williams at his most daring. Rather than thinking of poetic realists like Paul Zindel and Lanford Wilson as the only creative heirs of Williams, it might be more apt to consider Foreman, Akalaitis, the Wooster Group, the Lake Ivan Performing Group and other important experimental theatre practitioners as artists who have spun out some of the implications of Williams's later style. More than any other American playwright of the mid-twentieth century, Tennessee Williams's career inscribes a general movement from a traditional dramaturgy based on binary conflict toward an experimental dramaturgy of catastrophe.

IV. Postscript: Flight without Freedom

Like Chris Flanders, Tennessee Williams's dramaturgical lines of flight are always shadowed by mortality. In the passage from *The Glass Menagerie* that serves as the epigraph to this paper, a frustrated Tom Wingfield wonders at a magic act in which a man escapes from a coffin, calling it "the wonderfullest trick of all" (167).

Although it is clear that Tom sees the coffin as a metaphor for his current death-in-life of monotonous work and domestic frustration, it is also important to note that escape configures as a flight from mortality. In *Summer and Smoke*, young John Buchanan's rebelliousness is rooted in a similar impulse. He confesses to being repulsed by the sight of his mother on her deathbed, and explains that he does not want to be a doctor because it means having "to go in a room and watch people dying!" (130). Like Tom's coffin image, John's protest is simultaneously a rebellion against domestic expectations and a flight from death. In *Milk Train* the flights from death proliferate. One Street is far away, but Chris's death-haunted wanderings, Flora's drugged and desperate deliriums, and the Witch of Capri's blood transfusions are all signs of an anxious and losing battle with death. Both *Summer and Smoke* and *Milk Train*, and, by extension, much of Williams's other works, show the line of flight becoming nothing more than self-destructive failure. One escapes the coffin only to become a specter; in Deleuzean terms, the line of flight becomes a line of death.

Why does Williams's work so often chronicle the failure of differentiation from the molar order? Why are the alternatives so often the death-in-life of a brutal collective, and the self-destruction of radical individualism?

First of all, Williams's ideology is ultimately individualistic. He only rarely conceives of a benign and sustaining collectivity that can transcend individuality and provide consolation in the face of death, as in *The Night of the Iguana*. Usually, flight is identified with the individual's desire, and does not seek alliances that go beyond itself. As a liberal individualist, Williams is "attaching a higher moral value to the individual than to society or any collective group" (Arblaster, 15). With flight solely as the trajectory of the subject's individual desire, the subject is always hounded by the knowledge of its inevitable extinction, leaving it with a dramaturgical appointment in Samarra, in which the flight from death becomes a headlong flight into it.

For the line of flight in Williams rarely achieves emancipation. It always bears the scar of separation from the molar system, impelling the fugitive to return, whether in fact (*Sweet Bird of Youth*) or memory (*Something Cloudy, Something Clear*). Flora's disjointed memoirs are a surrender to a chaos of recollection in which present and future are obliterated in a desperately mortal solipsism. "It's really all memory, Connie, except for each passing moment," she observes (46). And, while lost in reminiscence, she brutalizes her staff and guests in a prison-like villa. Chris Flanders is equally prey to memories, for, despite his wanderings, his repeated encounters with death make it his vocation, and his own aging and inability to write testify to his own mortality. In *Milk Train*, we flee only to find that we are still imprisoned; flight holds only an illusory promise of liberation.

Tom flees from Amanda, John revolts against the demand that he relives the sight of his mother's death, and Chris averts his eyes from the desiring body of a dying woman. In all three cases, the mortal body that initiates flight is maternal. But this must not be reduced to a Kristevan variant of family romance. The molar body of domestic control is a decaying body, springing leaks and precipitating flight. The domestic body is always on the verge of erupting into catastrophic disarray. The primary line of flight in Williams's work is from a decaying body that proves to be at once maternal and one's own.

One must look elsewhere for alternatives to Williams's vision of self-destructive flight. Herbert Marcuse's sage observation, "Men can die without anxiety if they know that what they love is protected from misery and oblivion" (216) provides one alternative to Williams's desperate and defeated lines of flight. Deleuze and Guattari provide another—"Life must answer the answer of death, not by fleeing, but by making flight act and create" (*Thousand Plateaus,* 110). Williams's personal acts of creation are both eloquent answering statements and seriously flawed models of action for how we might meet our common mortality. As author, Williams performs creative acts of flight, leaving behind works that suggest utopian visions (Savran, 164–174). The characters he presents and the stories he tells, however, often fall prey to solipsism and self-destruction. His experimental techniques are often more emancipatory than the plots he contrives.

NOTES

1. For a useful, though ultimately negative, history of desire as a major term in contemporary thought, see Goodheart. For an erudite consideration of Williams in the light of New Left thought and politics, see Savran, 144–74.

2. For a further exploration of catastrophism and its implications for painting and philosophy, see James Williams.

WORKS CITED

Arblaster, Anthony. *The Rise and Decline of Western Liberalism.* Oxford: Basil Blackwell, 1984.

Debusscher, Gilbert. "French Stowaways on an American Milk Train: Williams, Cocteau and Peyrefitte." *Modern Drama* 25.3 (1982): 399-408.

Deleuze, Gilles and Félix Guattari. *Anti-Oedipus: Capitalism and Schizophrenia.* Trans. Brian Massumi. Minneapolis: University of Minnesota Press, 1987.

_____. *A Thousand Plateaus: Capitalism and Schizophrenia.* Trans. Brian Massumi. Minneapolis: University of Minnesota Press, 1987.

Foreman, Richard. *Unbalancing Acts: Foundations for a Theatre.* New York: Pantheon, 1992.

Goodheart, Eugene. "Desire and Its Discontents." *Partisan Review* 55.3 (1988): 387–403.

Kant, Immanuel. *Critique of Judgment.* Trans. J. H. Bernard. New York: Hafner, 1951.

Marcuse, Herbert. *Eros and Civilization: A Philosophical Inquiry into Freud.* New York: Vintage Books, 1962.

Saivetz, Deborah. "An Event in Space: The Integration of Acting and Design in the Theatre of JoAnne Akalaitis." *TDR* 42.2 (1998), 132–56.

Savran, David. *Cowboys, Communists and Queers: The Politics of Macsculinity in the Work of Arthur Miller and Tennessee Williams.* Minneapolis: University of Minnesota Press, 1992.

Williams, James. "Deleuze on J. M. W. Turner: Catastrophism in Philosophy?"

Deleuze and Philosophy: The Difference Engineer. London: Routledge, 1997: 233–46.

Williams, Tennessee. *The Glass Menagerie*. Volume 1 of *Theatre*. New York: New Directions, 1971: 128–237.

_____. *The Milk Train Doesn't Stop Here Anymore*. Volume 5. New York: New Directions, 1976: 1–20.

_____. *Summer and Smoke*. Volume 2 of *Theatre*. New York: New Directions, 1971: 113-256.

The Hungry Women of Tennessee Williams's Fiction

Michael R. Schiavi

Throughout his "secondary" career as a fiction writer, Tennessee Williams repeatedly staged dramas of female appetite. This theme also anchors some of his seminal stage-work: *A Streetcar Named Desire* (1947), *Summer and Smoke* (1948), *The Rose Tattoo* (1951), and *Kingdom of Earth* (1968) all pivot upon women's sexual needs and satis-factions. In short stories, however, Williams proved far more adept at tracing multiple female desires as they transfix and baffle observation. Free from Broadway's narrow conception of stageworthy bodies, Williams the storywriter spent nearly fifty years dis-playing women in open gratification of various hungers. Indeed, in his fiction, female characters' appetites constitute their very narrativity and make them worthy of the dra-matic venue often denied them. With highly noticeable physical proportions and expression, these women manifest theatrically to bewildered spectators who, in strug-gling to name and interpret the aberration before them, become negligible forces with-in their own dramas. By no coincidence, these spectators are typically males who, over the years of Williams's career, become inversely less active against the consuming women who devour figurative "stage space."

Before discussing the stories, it is necessary to address a staple of Williams crit-icism: that the playwright venomously travesties female representation for the male homosexuality he cannot stage openly.[1] As a mid-century gay man, Williams had great personal stake in the risks of gratifying a proscribed appetite,[2] and, like many of his female characters, knew well the dangers of putting his desires on public dis-play. At the same time, it is reductive to assume that Williams conflated the differ-ent experiences of abject women and gay men. Gay men appear on their own terms throughout the body of Williams's fiction in such stories as "In Memory of an Aristocrat" (c. 1940), "The Mysteries of the Joy Rio" (1941), "The Angel in the Alcove" (1943), "The Malediction" (1945), "The Interval" (1945), "Something

About Him" (1946), "The Night of the Iguana" (1948), "Hard Candy" (1949-1953), "Two on a Party" (1953), "Mama's Old Stucco House" (1965), "The Killer Chicken and the Closet Queen" (1977), and "The Negative" (1982). By treating gay themes and characters ever more explicitly in stories—a more tolerant venue than Broadway—Williams had no need to use female characters as camp "beards."

Indeed, most of Williams's women experience a vulnerability unknown to his fiction's gay men. In his stories, Williams generally keeps gay sex hidden, whether behind the wall Miss Jelkes shares with an amorous male couple in "Iguana," or in the shadows of the Joy Rio balcony. Effeminacy, which American culture continues to read as infallible (homo)sexual marker, remains conspicuously absent throughout his stories (and his plays, until Quentin in *Small Craft Warnings* [1972]). Without such displays, the gay men of Williams's fiction generally address their hungers without excessive notice or risk. Such is not the case for the overweight and sexually direct women of the stories. These characters cannot hide their passions; their bodies and behavior keep them at high profile. Their satisfaction of appetites meets with a critical scrutiny that seems to elude men.[3] The stories' hungry women thus help Williams to stage a personally familiar war of wills that the theatre of his time did not tolerate.

The Broadway of Williams's career allowed precious few large women to tread the boards. When they did appear, qualified stage directions attempted to defuse the visceral shock of their bodies. In Eugene O'Neill's *A Moon for the Misbegotten* (1946), Josie Hogan is "so oversize for a woman that she is almost a freak," but her largeness comes chiefly from height. She has a "slender" waist and, their strength notwithstanding, reassuringly feminine arms. O'Neill rushes to reassure us that she is "all woman" (301), and Josie herself comes to know that size needn't kill all hope for love. In *Who's Afraid of Virginia Woolf?* (1962), Edward Albee chivalrously describes Martha as "ample, but not fleshy," and her "ample" figure certainly doesn't prevent her offstage seduction of Nick, twenty-two years her junior.

Other large women of the American canon enjoy a reprieve from the judgmental gaze by dint of their age and/or de-sexed maternity. "Short" and "stout," Big Mama in Williams's *Cat on a Hot Tin Roof* (1955) may earn authorial comparison to a "Japanese wrestler," but the noted "sincerity" with which she seeks to unify her family elevates her above ridicule (33). Mama of Lorraine Hansberry's *A Raisin in the Sun* (1959), euphemized in stage directions as "full-bodied," is also described as "beautiful" and possessing enough strength of character to save her family from moral bankruptcy (39). Even the "rather fleshy" Myrtle of Williams's *Kingdom of Earth*, perhaps the most clownish of these women, treats her husband Lot with an ill-deserved maternal delicacy that bespeaks essential kindness (9); Chicken's desire for Myrtle, moreover, deflects interest from her size to their deferred coupling.

While these women exceed the physical boundaries of normative female representation, they do so through motherly and/or sexual channels that steer spectators' attention from their girth. Aside from Josie's potshots at herself, no character criticizes the women's bodies. Never, more importantly, are any of these women described as "fat," a term that stops dramatic plotting in its tracks.[4] Since Susie Orbach's pioneering *Fat Is A Feminist Issue* (1978), self-declared "fat" women have often cited the deadly performativity of their bodies; once named, fat becomes its own visual *raison d'être* and ensures its bearer's inability to participate in other narratives. W. Charisse Goodman, for example, recalls that "anytime I moved my body, people would laugh at me . . . even if I sat still and quietly read a book they would point and laugh." As the neighborhood "fat kid," Goodman considered herself not a self-determined subject, but rather "just an object described by an adjective." She discusses fat in appropriately theatrical terms: ". . . big women are typically trotted onstage solely to amuse and reassure the members of the [thin] ruling class" (x, ix, 5). Charlotte Cooper similarly describes herself and other fat women as "super-visible and vulnerable as targets" and argues that the "fear of fat encourages people to be judgmental" about corporeal deviance, particularly that observed in women (26, 3).[5]

Fat bears a hyperactive semiotic curse. Viewers of non-streamlined chins, breasts, stomachs, buttocks, and legs search passionately for etiology: what has brought a woman to such physical explosion? Poor self-discipline? Wild overindulgence? Indifference to popular image? Such interpretations construe fat as a key symptom of immorality and its public appearance a nervy performance deserving unchecked attack.

Williams realized the dramatic possibilities of conspicuous bodies that resist abjection. He also knew, however, that such bodies would find no greater welcome in theatre than they generally do in public. He thus turned to short stories as the venue in which he could most thoughtfully mount dramas of rebellious mass. From the anonymous scribbling of his twenties through the commissioned work of his late career, his fiction is filled with women whose appetites for food, credibility, and, later, sex, read distinctly on their bodies.[6] Williams exults in dropping such characters into social arenas crawling with critics. He also exults in showing how these women, even when overpowered or banished, govern the thought and speech of their detractors, whom they demote from actor to reactor even within the critics' own stories. Having removed these nominal protagonists from the reader's focus, Williams celebrates women whose evident hungers receive endless public attention.

Literal Hungers

In her openness to attack, Mrs. Meighan of "Twenty-seven Wagons Full of Cotton" (1935) mirrors several of the best-known women in American short fiction. John Steinbeck, Flannery O'Connor, and Joyce Carol Oates have all written tales about isolated women who, thinking themselves invulnerable at home, suffer exploitation by a male interloper. In Steinbeck's "The Chrysanthemums" (1935), mannish Elisa loses all sense of self when a peddler charms her out of her prized flowers only to obtain their copper pot. Haughty Hulga of O'Connor's "Good Country People" (1950) loses her wooden leg—hence her mobility, autonomy, and identity—to a Bible salesman whom she, like Elisa, had treated with initial dismissiveness. In Oates's "Where Are You Going, Where Have You Been?" (1970), teenaged Connie finds herself overpowered by a sinister male visitor who gradually seduces her from her empty family home. Like Elisa and Hulga, Mrs. Meighan attracts notice in physical aberration; like Connie, she faces sexual menace from a demonic male visitor who traps her in her own house. Unlike Steinbeck, O'Connor, and Oates, however, Williams allows his protagonist to maintain narrative sway even as she falls prey to assault. Throughout the tale, both Mrs. Meighan and the "little man," her unnamed visitor, are fixated upon her size. In the story's six pages, the man appreciatively mentions Mrs. Meighan's "bigness" seven times; she herself comments on it three times. The omniscient narrator lingers over Mrs. Meighan's "huge body," its "bulging calves," "lumpy ankles," "tremendous shoulders," the "soft multiple complexities of her chin," and the "mountains of sweating flesh" that comprise her torso (46, 47, 49).[7]

The little man's noticing of Mrs. Meighan's body assumes a sexual rhythm and becomes the story's animating force. The man supplements his intermittent switching of Mrs. Meighan's calves with professed appreciation for her "bigness" until the two acts combine in violent foreplay. By story's end, Mrs. Meighan is badly frightened and stumbling toward escape, her languorous masochism replaced by a realistic fear of being beaten and raped. She becomes "a tremendous, sobbing Persephone" (50) en route to an underworld of sadomasochistic horrors, possibly death. Her Hades masters her not through brute abduction, however, but through incessant invocation of the physical qualities that have led her to deny her beauty (46). In his repetitive flirtations, the little man sexualizes what other men have found freakish, as per Mr. Meighan's calling his wife "the biggest woman in this part of the state" (47). His flirtations also suggest him as the simplest form of spectator/critic, one who bases speech upon the eager pronouncement of difference.

Thus reviewed, Mrs. Meighan is well aware of herself as object of spectatorship, but to her peril, she does not maneuver this heightened objectivity to advantage. Instead, she allows herself to become dulled by consumption. By the time the little man arrives, she has slid into a post-caffeine slump, a casualty of the many sodas she has drunk in the summer sun. Now "utterly numb" (46), she cannot maintain her subjectivity against visual assault. Like the September cotton surrounding her house, she sits in vulnerable, inert abundance, a ripe semiotic system unto herself. Content to parrot the little man's rating of her body, Mrs. Meighan fails to protect herself from attack. Her textual dominance, in other words, does not translate to physical safety.

Williams foreshadows Mrs. Meighan's predicament in her disregard of the little man's power and sexuality. With a longstanding aversion to "little men," she overlooks her inexplicable attraction to her visitor and contemptuously thinks of him as "hardly more than half her size. Why it would be just the same as . . ." (47). Mrs. Meighan's unfinished incestuous thought also occurs to the equally large, unnamed dark woman of "Gift of an Apple" (1936) during her dalliance with a hungry young drifter who is the same age as her son. Throughout their flirtation, the visitor never mentions his hostess's largeness aloud, but the topic overpowers his mind and allows him only a limited mental range. In his observation, the woman is "huge," "big, heavy and dark" with "coarse hairs along her upper lip" and on the "great loose bulge of her bosom," reminding the young man of a sideshow hermaphrodite he'd seen. He watches with some disgust as "her . . . huge jaws . . . munched [an apple] like a horse"; he later imagines her "fat elbows" spread over a table as she devours a "big piece" of "rich, oily meat" (67, 71, 68, 69, 72).

Even as these squalid images crowd the young man's mind, dominating his perception of the woman as well as the sketch's spare text, her size also holds sexual currency for the drifter, who imagines her "big dark female body" spread out at night, waiting for a lover (69). He considers the woman an easy conquest, as vulnerable as the large, bottle-trapped catfish he killed as a boy out of sadistic spectatorship. Wedged in her tiny trailer, this woman seems equally trapped, as pressed into satisfying his appetite as she has her own.

Nevertheless, this guest cannot master his host as Mrs. Meighan's visitor does her. As a hitchhiker, he dreads the weight of an assessing gaze and cannot, therefore, return it with sufficient gravity. Tired and dirty, he has been variously ignored by motorists, viewed with suspicion, and subjected to unwanted caresses from male drivers. The "mental compulsion" (66) he tries to wield over potential hosts on the road proves no more successful than that attempted over the woman, who gives her starving guest but one apple. Sexual aggression, as on the road, also remains out of his hands. The woman follows her open appraisal of his body with a caress and the emasculating assessment, "You got nice skin like a girl's" (71)[8]; before he can take the reins, she abruptly terminates the flirtation upon learning his age. In departing, the young protagonist tries to gain interpretive control by assigning the woman cancer, ironically demonstrating the degree to which even her absent body choreographs his imagination along with the story's plot.

"In Memory of an Aristocrat" similarly opposes young male drifters against a large woman with the ability to dominate spectacle, text, and plot. In the story's first paragraph, the unnamed narrator describes himself and his friend Carl as "hungry" would-be artists dependent on the kindness of Irene, a French Quarter bohemian who "always ha[s] something cooking" and who wishes to "embrace the whole world" (90). Irene satisfies not only her own appetite; others feed off her resources as well. The narrator also feeds imaginatively off Irene's ample body and spirit, aptly characterized as "compulsion to poetry" (85), when he chronicles the epic battle waged between his friend's physical mass and its horrified spectators.

"Aristocrat" features the conspicuous size references familiar from "Twenty-seven Wagons" and "Gift of an Apple," but it also configures its heroine as explicit spectacle. Described as "one of those big, dark girls, everything about her on a monumental scale," Irene had served as an improbable model for New York WPA classes. Despite his qualified appreciation for Irene's beauty, the narrator renders her body in cruel cinematic caricature by "photographing" it "as though the camera had been placed at her feet" in floor-to-ceiling inversion of perspective. From this vantage, the narrator directs our gaze to her "lower part . . . [which] was disproportionately heavy . . . [and] on a larger scale toward the bottom" (85). Irene thus emerges a cinematographer's oddball darling, worthy of funhouse consideration from all angles. In its size, proportion, attire, and public outrageousness, her body becomes an object of spectatorship more imposing than any offered by Williams's Broadway contemporaries.

A perfect Mardi Gras grotesque, Irene appears in self-styled spectacle throughout New Orleans, deliberately spreading her visibility far beyond the attentions of friends and WPA students. Clad only in a grass skirt and "very scanty brassiere," she passes out in a small Quarter bar, overwhelming the space in her sprawl, after "shrieking" through the streets and turning tricks all afternoon (89); clearly, she has given much of downtown New Orleans an unforgettable show. Upon rescue by the narrator, she spends the rest of the night outlining her battered past in between vomiting spells, her body endlessly producing signs of its mythical appetites for food, alcohol, and love.

Prominent even amid the Quarter carnival, Irene assumes Barnum and Bailey stature as she wreaks sideshow vengeance upon the bluebloods who, at their Annual Spring Display, have rejected her submitted paintings. She, in fact, becomes the display, described by one patron as "the floor show" even before targeting the gathering's "too fragile" occupants and accoutrements. Eager "to make a scene," she tears through the room as "Bubonic Plague," befouling the air with obscenities and shattering precious *tchotchkes* in her wake. In unwitting parody of her own maternal expansiveness, Irene falls out of her dress during a toe-stomping, crotch-kicking frenzy that renders her an eminently watchable natural disaster, a hurricane whose energy must exhaust itself before civility can resume. When she collapses, the narrator marvels that "such a *big* girl," who had commandeered mass attention while demolishing her disdainful spectators' own performance space, could dissolve into impotence (92-95). He has become accustomed to Irene's weighty mastery of public view and discourse; even after she disappears from New Orleans, her adopted motto on "the aristocracy of passionate souls" remains scrawled across a wall of her abandoned studio. Her expressive legacy endures.

Cora in "Two on a Party," one of Williams's best-known and most candid stories, is Irene twenty years post—"Aristocrat." The two women share a "monumental kindness" (298), charity to the underdog, hatred of conventional society, and, total public attention. The omniscient narrator drolly refers to Cora as "a noticeable person" (309), a visceral fact that, as in the stories discussed above, determines much of the proceedings. With Billy, her gay friend, Cora wanders aimlessly over the country in search of its most accommodating bars and men, an occupation that pivots on her ability to manipulate common scrutiny to advantage.

For neither character is this an easy task. At nearly thirty-five, Billy is extremely self-conscious about his thinning hair and hearing loss. These disadvantages, however, by no means receive the narrative space allotted Cora's various dissipations. The story begins with Billy's efforts to gauge her obviously advancing age. At their first meeting, he thinks her an "'old bag'" and watches repulsed as she twists her "rather heavy figure . . . into ludicrous positions" while scouting for a lost earring amid "disgusting refuse" on the floor (297). Cora repeatedly refers to herself as a "mess" and laments that she is "so heavy in the hips" and hampered by "big udders," the cumulative effect of which causes her to "shimm[y] fatly" rather than walk (300, 311). Having later exceeded her "saturation point" with nightly ryes, she is left "bloated" and "bloodshot," conditions for which she overcompensates by burying herself in riotous clothing, hair color, and a deafening profusion of charm bracelets (302, 309). If even Billy "thinks she has overdone it a little," she must register at Irene-levels on the world's Richter scale of poor taste.

Indeed, much of Cora's life consists of skirting stares from "bull-like middle-aged couples," the "squares" who regard her drunken, openly sexual antics with contempt (307). While Billy certainly joins her in these escapades, he is protected by male prerogative and the writing career to which Cora believes he will one day return. Cora herself, however, has apparently never had a purpose in life beyond the "party" and cannot imagine what she would do if she got "off" it. Fittingly, even through their inseparable months, Billy learns almost nothing about Cora's past. She remains in his eyes, and ours, a boisterous companion who draws the world's focus to her conspicuous surfaces.

Yet despite her oft-mentioned affronts to public taste, Cora does not behave aggressively; she seeks neither sexual conquest nor social combat. Described, in her passivity, by Billy as a "big piece of seaweed," she seems instead to await friendly notice, allowing it to find her in big-city throngs rather than capitalizing on her natural noticeability (303). Unlike Irene in her rage, Cora attempts to soothe frays with hotel clerks and disgruntled tricks, thereby keeping herself (and Billy) from litigious view. Despite the literal and textual largeness of Cora's persona, her chief influence in the story remains maternal, especially toward Billy, whom she loves and thus supports financially and emotionally without significant return. Williams would spend the rest of his fiction-writing career reprising this figure, assigning her ever greater and more pernicious spectatorial sway.

Other Hungers

As Williams's stagework grew more forthright in its presentation of multiple sexualities, his fiction began to configure "appetite" less literally. Whereas the earlier stories (1935-1953) often conflate women's dietary and sexual desires, later tales (1959-1982) tend to exempt their female protagonists from concerns of literal hunger. Accordingly, these women do not face such constant reading by spectators desperate to catalogue indulgences. Williams replaces the expressly large women discussed above with characters whose public bodies, though aging, remain semiotically uninflected until deferred unmasking. Upon interacting with young, often starving and helpless men, the women manifest with Irene's freakish disregard of presentational etiquette. The men, exaggerated versions of the drifters we have already seen, stumble into the women's lives never on their own initiative, but always by accident or by summons. As the women's exhibitionism brings them ever greater inspection, the men retreat into literal and narrative oblivion. By this point in his writing, therefore, Williams construed "appetite" as an obliterating force, the marshalling of which determined any character's right to be read.

When Jimmy Dobyne reaches the balcony of Flora Goforth's Italian villa in "Man Bring This Up Road" (1959), he encounters an apt symbol for his impending meeting with the owner: a monkey chained in the midday sun, unable to reach water or shade. Stretched like the monkey to the edge of his talents and energies, Jimmy arrives at Mrs. Goforth's after a long succession of visits with wealthy, aging patrons. Like the male protagonists of "Gift of an Apple" and "In Memory of an

Aristocrat," Jimmy is also "ravenously hungry" (370), but unlike those significantly younger characters, he has endured perennial deprivation longer, and, at thirty-five, his chances of finding sympathetic benefactors are waning precipitously.

The story concerns itself with the negligible battle of wills waged between Jimmy and Mrs. Goforth. By no means her match in resources or wit, Jimmy cannot sustain warfare for long, but even his brief efforts illustrate Williams's notion that legible desires, when unsatisfied, prove far more dangerous than their requited counterparts, however outrageous.[9] Immediately upon arrival at the villa, Jimmy lapses into a daylong slumber that intensifies his hunger and vulnerability. As he sleeps, Mrs. Goforth checks his passport, discovers that he is not as young as he pretends, and does some telephone research to build her arsenal against him.

Jimmy thus sits at a factual as well as material disadvantage. Unlike the nameless apple-giver and Irene, Jimmy's hostess makes no gesture to appease his appetite. Dominating discourse as well as resource, Mrs. Goforth holds forth through a rehearsal of her own suspicions and determinations to safeguard herself against fraud. As Jimmy's desperation mounts, he realizes that naked, ungratified hunger rendered him a pariah long before his appearance at Mrs. Goforth's: "Something must be visble in his face that let [old friends] know he had crossed over a certain frontier of. . . . He didn't want to identify that frontier, to give it a name" (372). Jimmy comes to understand that his decipherable cravings for sustenance and contact—inversely proportionate to his hunger for work—have diminished his sphere of influence to non-existence; at his lowest point, he is reduced to begging Mrs. Goforth for sugar in coffee that does nothing to quiet his stomach.

Mrs. Goforth, on the other hand, becomes monstrous in her successful self-gratifications. As she seeks to solidify her power, her gratuitous humiliation of Jimmy lends her a repugnance that Williams literalizes in the misshapen figure she exposes to Jimmy in her colonizing desire for him. Agog at Mrs. Goforth's "Amazonian" hips in their "skin-tight shorts," Jimmy thinks her an "immense fountain [figure]," one "travestied by a sculptor with evil wit" (375). The baldness of her sexual desire, expressed through such a warped medium, proves no more enticing to Jimmy than do his manifold needs to friends and acquaintances. By story's end, Mrs. Goforth has banished him from the villa, where she sits materially bloated and wholly unsympathetic to the reader, yet victorious in the discursive and presentational control she maintains throughout the encounter.

Over twenty years after "Man Bring This Up Road," just a few months before his death, Williams resurrected Jimmy Dobyne as the evacuated protagonist of "The Negative."[10] In the story's corrected manuscript, Jimmy has been renamed Tonio Maresca, yet Tonio retains Jimmy's evaporating youth, impotent artistry, and helplessness before feminine (and effeminate) appetite. Tonio, moreover, becomes the suicide Jimmy might consider as he leaves Mrs. Goforth's villa penniless and starving, overexposed to hungers gone grotesque.

Like Jimmy, Tonio is approaching his mid-thirties in terror over having become "slightly faded" (vii). The tolerated lover of Lord Amberly, a seventy-year-old sybarite, Tonio realizes all too well youth's currency. No longer able to live off his body, Tonio may soon have to live it down, as Lord Amberly himself tries, through ludicrous hair-dyes and sexual incontinence. Tonio, however, lacks the means to fulfill his own appetites and so suppresses them into nonexistence. Recently felled by a stroke, Lord Amberly nonetheless "feeds himself heartily" and cavorts with renters. Half Amberly's age and twice as healthy, Tonio vomits after a failed effort at fellatio and cannot generate sufficient metabolism to spot a bedpan (xiii, ix). The animation and self-assertion required for ingestion seem missing in Tonio, whom others variously describe as "nearly paralyzed," a "non-being," "more of an object than a living being," and someone who "[doesn't] belong in the world" (xvi, xv, xiii, xix).

Thus eviscerated, Tonio can no more credibly write than he himself can be written. His current poem, also titled "The Negative," languishes in incoherence, an inarticulate stab at speaking "the abyss into which his life had descended" (ix). His life a negation of movement, Tonio animates neither his own writing nor Williams's. Lacking even Jimmy's desperation to stay alive, Tonio serves more as narrative device than narrative force. Williams thus hinges Tonio's story on the delayed exposure of Mona, another aged and predatory figure who instigates all significant action in "The Negative" according to her own whim. Williams plots the story by rendering Mona, at first merely an omniscient telephone voice, a disembodied awareness of Tonio's pathetic circumstances, ever more visible to Tonio and to the reader. As with the other stories' women, Williams conjures Mona from her desires, revealing by bits the grasping physicality that delineates her body.

As a telephone presence, Mona emerges in articulate opposition to Tonio's stumbling confusion. Materializing from nowhere, she tears through Tonio's half-hearted queries with blunt acknowledgment of his inertia. She shapes all the written expression he manages in the story by directing him, as one might a barely literate child, to transcribe her street address "in large, clear letters" (xi) that will spell his salvation more effectively than his aimless verses. Following her directions, Tonio finds himself in a lightless hallway where he tries to fend off the clutching hands of a woman he cannot see. When Tonio endures more presumptuous gestures from men, such as Lord Amberly and an examining physician, Williams grants the reader some specificity of action and appearance. Mona, however, only emerges into full sight for one horrifying instant at the story's end after Williams has teased into apoplexy his readers' longing for a look at female appetite.

In order to attain this view, Tonio must escape the citadel of Amberly's house and endure manhandling by a porter, a chauffeur, and a waiter—a painful series of invasions for someone who tries to move through life with minimum physical involvement. His uncharacteristic willingness to withstand such treatment sets impossibly high stakes for Mona's appearance, which, in order to justify all this suspense, must finally manifest at grand Gothic pitch. Williams works this aesthetic by shrouding her in a thick veil and behind sunglasses whose removal prompts a scenario of tightly edited, cinematic revelation. In violent staccato phrases, Tonio rips away her disguise to discover a "lacquered face" aberrant for its lack of "discernible age"; his "terror" grows when he reveals "rapacious" eyes equally slathered in makeup (xx). Flashbulbs and thunderous male voices accentuate the chaos surrounding the pair as Tonio brings to light the inscrutable creature that has consumed his language and attempted to control his physical fate as well.

Williams purposefully reveals his agent of female will and expression with horror-film punch. As with Mrs. Bates in *Psycho* (1960), Regan MacNeil in *The Exorcist* (1973), Eva Galli in *Ghost Story* (1981), and Hedra Carlson in *Single White Female* (1992), Mona assumes complete visibility after long expository delay, at which point she is glimpsed only in flickering narrative bursts that recall the careening light bulb in Mrs. Bates's cellar. Tonio, like many men who view the women named above, does not long survive the sight. His subsequent suicide suggests the enormous power accorded the display of female desire. Williams's application of cinematic techniques to short fiction underscores a wise reluctance to visit such ugliness on theater audiences.

In other late stories, Williams drops aged female protagonists into tableaux of sexual appetite that, outside Rochester's *Sodom* (1664), would seem insane choices for the stage. Sabbatha Veyne Duff-Collick of "Sabbatha and Solitude" (1973) and the Principessa Lisabetta von Hohenzalt-Casalinghi in "The Inventory at Fontana Bella" (1973) emerge through self-framing desires as baroque as their fading names. By story's end, Sabbatha has come to see herself as Cleopatra, who also predicates speech upon imperious demands for constant sex and adoration. Once a poet of some note, Sabbatha has lived through her marshalling of an adoring court. Her social and professional reputation on the wane, she now finds herself satisfying appetites before an "audience of one"; Giovanni, who, like Jimmy and Tonio, a seasoned gigolo whose tenuously bisexual attentions she has purchased for ten years (534).

Williams structures Sabbatha's story around flashbacks in which she remembers her former ability to rivet public interest. At a Vassar lecture, Village restaurant, or interview in Rome, Sabbatha came to realize that her noisy scatological "behavior was leading her into public embarrassment" rather than the paparazzi's homage. This realization, nonetheless, only incites her striptease through St. Peter's Square, where her shrieking display of "rather flat and pendulous breasts" brands her a "*figura bruta*" in the Italian press. Flailing about in the "abandoned posturing of a middle-aged female" (542, 543), Sabbatha has lost all sense of what constitutes engaging spectacle and, accordingly, faces an audience who would consign her to "madhouse" invisibility. Whereas "Aristocrat"'s Irene imposes her body upon critics in heartfelt protest against their dismissal of her work, Sabbatha, validated by an international reputation over which Irene might drool, exposes herself in petulant rebellion against largely imaginary oppression. Her empty signifying leads her to anti-poetic silence and the deadly "solitude" of her story's title.

In "The Inventory at Fontana Bella," Williams slams against the boundaries of tenable female representation that gradually constrain Sabbatha's performances. The Principessa, a Cleopatra figure sixty-five years post-asp, bellows through her solitude as if to command a staff of hundreds. As with Mrs. Goforth, age combined with untempered material and sexual ambition have rendered the Principessa a hideous cartoon whose presence registers insistently even in her absence. Her speech, mere expressionistic "babblings of delirium," discloses only exhaustive lists of her possessions and lewd references to her long-dead fifth husband. This incessant verbal voiding anticipates the actual bowel movement she performs on her open terrace, as well as her masturbation with a live stork's beak, which she imagines to be her husband's penis.

A site of revolting productivity and consumption, the Principessa's body sets final limits on the representation of extreme appetite. Her vaginal suffocation of a watchful stork constitutes a kind of "gaze-rape" that terminates autoeroticism mediated through an "unsuitable"—because "ancient" and incontinent—body. With the Principessa's subsequent death, Williams exorcises from his fiction women whose desires claim lives along with ceaseless attention. His aim here seems far less moralistic than theatrically and narratively expedient. When spectacle becomes so oppressive as to silence, or even destroy, observers, where can it possibly lead? Once it has been remarked as a fascinating abomination, what larger plot function can it serve? Like Mrs. Meighan in "Twenty-seven Wagons," the Principessa becomes far more exhibition than person and thus cannot interact with other characters. At such a point, appetite becomes too visible even for fiction, much less the stage; it must give way to more diegetic hungers if it is to survive as a viable topic for literature.

Williams allegorizes a shift to more presentable appetites in "Miss Coynte of Greene" (1973). The story opens to find its eponymous protagonist the imprisoned caretaker of her grandmother, a despicable crone whose body overwhelms "Miss Coynte," both story and character. Miss Coynte lives in thrall to the "great swollen" creature upstairs, the "massive and immobile body" whose consumptions and productions, like the Principessa's, demand ceaseless ministration (515). Unlike the senile Principessa, however, the grandmother deliberately presses her presence upon observers through her gleeful purges. Intentional incontinence keeps Miss Coynte and Dr. Settle slavishly chained to her bedside, pulled like minor planets into the orbit of her bloated mass. The grandmother excretes sound as wantonly as she does waste: "babbl[ing] all but incessantly" on the telephone, ringing a "loud-mouthed" bell when not actually talking, and finally screaming "like a peacock in heat" (514, 516), she seems less a person than a perpetual venting of sonic toxins.

As with the Principessa, the grandmother's imposition of her appetites on other characters collapses narrative. Prostrate in bed, she becomes a foul monologist presiding over her captive audience. Spending "half [her] time" changing her grandmother's soiled sheets (513), Miss Coynte spends the other half listening to vicious and vapid tales, such as that of Dotty Reagan, an acquaintance whose anecdotal worth depends upon her obesity. While her grandmother lives, Miss Coynte has no opportunity to follow her own animus, thus reducing the story that bears her name a to plotless sideshow.

Following the grandmother's death, "Miss Coynte" redirects appetite into more viable narrative channels. By ridding the house of her grandmother's innumerable acquisitions, Miss Coynte clears the material glut that had held her own life in check; appropriately, she founds an antiques business on the purging of other families' defunct possessions. Having transformed tradition into lucrative kitsch, she can indulge in the sexual adventuring that eventually constitutes both her sense of "mission" and her story's plot (532). Miss Coynte's conquests of various men, all of them young and at least partially black, require little focused analysis here. For the purposes of this discussion, it is sufficient to remark that Miss Coynte comes to control their fates, whether as employer or potential blackmailer, with the power exercised by Flora Goforth over Jimmy, Mona over Tonio, and Sabbatha over Giovanni. Lacking the age and practiced predatory tactics of these women, however, Miss Coynte's body has not yet taken on signs of a grossly satisfied appetite. With her relative youth and "slight but sinewy waist" (522), she escapes the bewildered gaze that thwarts the other women's attempts at seduction along with their successful mixing in public. Via deft "measures of subterfuge" (524), Miss Coynte also avoids the popular scrutiny that would proscribe her "mission" and halt the story. One aborted phone call from a local minister and the sniping comments of a local gossip (whom Williams dispatches in two brief paragraphs) constitute the entire range of public reaction to Miss Coynte's living through appetite.

Williams's obvious delight with Miss Coynte's gratifications prompts a couple of unfortunate indulgences. He ends the story with a broad editorial wink ("'Right on!'") that trivializes the character's own disregard of public approval. More importantly, in his eagerness to anoint Miss Coynte's behavior, he takes no critical stance against her breezy control of either the young black men she dismisses at will, or of Michele Moon, the mulatto daughter whom she acknowledges only as a servant. Such treatment may jibe with Delta racial politics, but it mixes ill with the hero status that the author would accord his protagonist. As Williams treats racial issues much more thoughtfully in other stories,[11] we might attribute this lapse to his triumph over creating a character whose appetites grant her a practicable *modus operandi* along with a reasonably mounted story.

Compared to this rogues' gallery of women, the men of Williams's fiction seem a pretty dull lot. Indeed, in most cases, they serve chiefly as proxies for the theatrical spectators that the women, their hungers like newsprint atop self-satisfied surfaces, never face. Away from the stage, Williams explores through these women the politics of inadvertent physical performance. He returns constantly to the tension between women whose appetites inform their selfpresentation and observers who become so transfixed by female exteriors as to disappear within their own stories. Ultimately, however, Williams needed to reconcile appetite's constitution of narrative with its tendency to become plot-stopping spectacle. The most successful stories discussed here—"Twenty-seven Wagons," "In Memory of an Aristocrat," and "Two on a Party"—explore the hostile fascination that heavy and sexed women receive from impromptu audiences while also freeing observers from impotent spectatorship. Williams thus rehearses in his fiction a theatrical intuition that, of generic necessity, languished unaddressed in his plays.

NOTES

[Unless otherwise indicated, all short stories are quoted from *Collected Stories*.]
    1. See, for example, Taubman, 1 and Kaufmann, 291–94. See also Joe Orton's contemporary determination to cast Fay, the female protagonist of *Loot*, with a "real woman" so as to prevent her seeming like a "Tennessee Williams drag [queen]" (Lahr 257, 247). In the landmark study *From Reverence to Rape* note Haskell's refer-

ence to Williams's female characters as "hothouse, hot-blooded 'earthmothers' and drag queens . . . baroquely transvestized homosexual fantasies. By no stretch can they be called 'real' women . . ." (248–49). It is significant to flag Haskell's verbatim maintenance of this analysis over the thirteen years separating her book's editions. What might have passed for anti-misogynist in 1974 seems blatantly homophobic by 1987.

2. See Williams's *Memoirs*, 123, for an account of his beating by Times Square sailors; see other "dangerous cruising" mentioned in a 1943 journal entry (Leverich, 476). See also Donald Spoto's description of attacks on Williams's person and home.

3. In *Cat on a Hot Tin Roof*, for example, Big Daddy quite openly announces his renewed sexual appetites to Brick, who hardly blinks (93, 96). Later in the play, Big Mama rhapsodizes over her husband's massive consumption of dinner, seeing in it the sign of a "normal appetite" and good health (130–131). No woman in the Williams canon, with the possible exception of Cora in "Two on a Party," hazards such a blasé, or uncriticized, revelation of her own appetites.

4. For critical responses to staged fat, see Jill Dolan's discussion of the vitriol surrounding Kathy Bates's performance of Jessie in Marsha Norman's *'night, Mother*, 30.

5. For other discussions of fat's relations to visibility and interpretivity, see Chernin, Schoenfielder and Wieser, Kano, Bovey, and Thone, all in works cited. For reference to fat as self-determined performance, with possible "coming-out" strategies, see Cooper, 47, and Sedgwick, 72.

6. This legibility stands in marked contrast to such stage protagonists as Blanche DuBois, Alma Winemiller and Serafina Delle Rose, whose various pretensions toward "respectable" behavior mask the sexual passions that govern their behavior.

7. In adapting this story to the one-act play *27 Wagons Full of Cotton* (1945), Williams retained Mrs. Meighan's size while reducing its centrality to the text. Though Jake and Silva mention her girth more than once, it never becomes the focus of her interaction with them. Subtitled "A Delta Comedy," moreover, the quirky *27 Wagons* invites a kind of low-rent gawking unknown to Williams's more substantive dramas. Mrs. Meighan's "tremendous" body fits thematically and presentationally within the carnival milieu that the play's subtitle suggests (11).

Unsurprisingly, though, when Williams brought the story to maximum audience via the screenplay *Baby Doll* (1956), Mrs. Meighan was reduced to a thumb-sucking teenage bride small enough to sleep in a child's crib. The sustained sexual tension that drives the film thus depends on a pedophiliac corruption of innocence, not fetishized girth.

8. In this comment, the woman foreshadows Myrtle's assessment of Lot in *Kingdom of Earth*: "Skin, eyes, hair any girl would be jealous of" (135). In the same exchange, Myrtle admits that her deepest attraction to Lot is "maternal," suggesting her emotional as well as physical authority over him.

9. Williams expanded "Man Bring This Up Road" into the play *The Milk Train Doesn't Stop Here Anymore* in 1963. During the four years between story and play, he had transformed Jimmy Dobyne into Christopher Flanders, an Angel of Death whose presumed power makes him a more formidable adversary for Mrs. Goforth, in the play an old woman trying to sort out her turbulent history as she awaits death.

By assigning Flora a worthier opponent, Williams leaves *Milk Train*'s narrative deck unstacked and explores these dichotomous characters more compellingly than in "Man Bring This Up Road."

10. Unpublished until 1999, when it appeared in *The Tennessee Williams Annual Review* (No. 2).

11. See for example, "Big Black: A Mississippi Idyll" (1932), "The Kingdom of Earth" (1942), "The Mysteries of the Joy Rio" (1941), "Desire and the Black Masseur" (1946), and "Rubio y Morena" (1948).

WORKS CITED

Albee, Edward. *Who's Afraid of Virginia Woolf?* New York: Signet, 1983.

Bovey, Shelley. *The Forbidden Body: Why Being Fat is Not a Sin.* London: Pandora, 1994.

Chernin, Kim. *The Obsession: Reflections on the Tyranny of Slenderness.* New York: Harper and Row, 1981.

Cooper, Charlotte. *Fat and Proud: The Politics of Size.* London: The Women's Press, 1998.

Dolan, Jill. *The Feminist Spectator as Critic.* Ann Arbor: University of Michigan Press. 1988.

Goodman, W. Charisse. *The Invisible Woman: Confronting Weight Prejudice in America.* Carlsbad: Guize Books, 1995.

Hansberry, Lorraine. *A Raisin in the Sun.* New York: Signet, 1988.

Haskell, Molly. *From Reverence to Rape: The Treatment of Women in the Movies.* Chicago: University of Chicago Press, 1987.

Kano, Susan. *Making Peace with Food and Freeing Yourself from the Diet/Weight Obsession.* New York: HarperCollins, 1988.

Lahr, John. *Prick Up Your Ears: The Biography of Joe Orton.* New York: Vintage Books, 1987.

Leverich, Lyle. *Tom: The Unknown Tennessee Williams.* New York: W. W. Norton, 1995.

O'Neill, Eugene. *A Moon for the Misbegotten* in *The Later Plays of Eugene O'Neill*, ed. Travis Bogard. (New York: Modern Library, 1967), 295–409.

Schonfielder, Lisa and Barb Wieser, eds. *Shadow on a Tightrope: Writing by Women on Fat Oppression.* Iowa City: Aunt Lute Books, 1983.

Sedgwick, E. Kosofsky. *Epistemology of the Closet* Berkeley, University of California Press, 1990.

Spoto, Donald. *The Kindness of Strangers: The Life of Tennessee Williams.* New York: Ballantine, 1985.

Thone, Ruth Raymond. *Fat—A Fate Worse Than Death?* New York: Haworth, 1997.

Williams, Tennessee. *Cat on a Hot Tin Roof.* Volume 3 of *Theatre..* New York: New Directions, 1971: 1–215.

———. *Collected Stories.* New York: Ballantine, 1985.

———. *Kingdom of Earth* (*The Seven Descents of Myrtle*). Volume 5 of *Theatre.* New York: New Directions, 1976: 121–214.

———. "The Negative." *The Tennessee Williams Annual Review* 2 (1999): vii–xxi.

———. *27 Wagons Full of Cotton.* Volume 6 of *Theatre.* New York: New Directions, 1981: 3-38.

"Le Jeu Suprême"

Some Mallarmean Echoes in Tennessee Williams's *Out Cry*

Kalliopi Nikolopoulou

I

Tennessee Williams described *Out Cry* as a *cri-de-cœur*, an inner cry that echoes and doubles on a personal level the despair evoked by the title of the play (*Playboy,* 7). The play's failed productions during Williams's lifetime and its continuing obscurity—along with some other of his later works—on both the critical and theatrical stages are only the most obvious reasons for this self-reflexive correspondence between life and text. Faced with the failure of a theatrical experiment, Williams identifies with the cry of his protagonist, Felice, an artist and actor, whose genius also puts him at odds with the institutional world of theater.

Yet there is more to this persistent reference to the cry than the usual biographical explanation according to which the fictional character provides retroactively a cathartic identification for the tormented writer. Upon closer look at the play's title, we see that this cry has already extended from the internal world of emotions toward the outside. Whereas a *cri-de-coeur*—a cry from the heart—stems from our inner selves, the word "outcry" stresses the exterior aspect of this cry, the need to spell out a painful experience and to rid oneself of the despair by crying it out aloud. The title emphasizes this exteriority since it literally breaks outcry into its component parts, namely, the preposition "out" and the noun/verb "cry." One cries out, so to speak, in an attempt to dispel the torment by voicing it, to invoke help, or to protest. This putting-into-view of the inner cry is in fact the very process of theatricalization, of rendering the private into the public, the lyric voice into a collective dithyramb. Whether or not the cry succeeds to reach the outside, theater still promises us the space where our subjective *cri-de-coeur* can be externalized and "worked out."[1]

Williams is aware of the affinities between theater and the lyric expression of suffering when "[he] describes his elemental form as 'personal lyricism'" (quoted. in Jackson, 29). In his preface to *Cat on a Hot Tin Roof*, Williams establishes the cry as the figure that evokes the lyrical moment of his theater: "Personal lyricism is the outcry of prisoner to prisoner from the cell in solitary where each is confined for the duration of his life" (vi).

Such could also be the summary of *Out Cry*, the repeated but ultimately unanswered calls of two characters to each other and to a world that remains inaccessible and hostile to them. The play begins with Felice and Clare, a pair of sibling actors about to perform a play-within-the-play.[2] Bereft of the appropriate props and of the audience that gradually leaves before the curtain opens, brother and sister continue with their performance in order to warm themselves in the cold space of the theater. Felice and Clare are not spared their isolation and pain on either of the play's two dramatic levels. Their acting career as well as their psychological world have both been indelibly marked by a double crime committed by their father, who has killed their mother and then himself. As performers, they are preoccupied by the ultimate solitude of art, which is exacerbated by the roles they assume—roles that uncannily duplicate their personal experiences. Getting into the play as a way of forgetting their familial wounds merely results in them being thrown back into these very wounds, thus necessitating yet another flight into the play, and so on. What is offered as a break and syncopation from the one stage of loneliness serves only as a sinister passage into another.

The passage from the one dramatic level to the next, however, does not operate merely as a clever textual device, namely, as a metatheatrical embellishment that impresses the spectator and complicates the plot. In refusing to establish a clear boundary between the outer and inner frames of the play, Williams presents his characters with an overwhelming confusion that shatters and annuls them both as people and as actors, as persons and as *dramatis personae*. In their attempt to respond to the blows of life, Felice and Clare reduce their art and their act to themselves. The actor's quintessential task, that of embodying someone else's passions and emotions, is turned upon itself, since both performers indulge in mere self-dramatization. Endlessly rehearsing their professional failure in their "real" dialogue, they persistently reenact their subjective trauma in the play-within.

The seamless dissolution between the two dramatic planes thematizes the collapse between reality and representation and weaves a schizophrenic backdrop for the play. Indeed, a telegram sent to Clare and Felice by their managing company on account of their failing tour of *The Two-Character Play* pathologizes them as insane.[3] Granting herself the gift of sanity, Clare displaces the contents of the telegram onto Felice, whom she considers as "not just an eccentric artist but *un peu dérangé*" (18), only to cringe at the sound of the word "confinement" and declare it forbidden. Well aware that confinement best describes their shared condition, Felice exploits his sister's denial in order to give her a lesson on repression: "When a word can't be used, when it's prohibited, its silence increases its size. It gets larger and larger till it's so enormous that no house can hold it" (36). This is why the play demands that the spaces of home, asylum, prison, and theater coincide. "I realize, now, that the house has turned into a prison," says Felice (55). Clare, too, returns to the repressed admitting toward the play's end that "theaters are prisons for players"(68).

As madness proves to be not only a symptom, but the very principle and *raison d'être* of *Out Cry*, it threatens the already fragmented nature of this text on a more structural level, that is, on the level of the plot. The smooth crossover in and out of the internal performance implies that the two dramatic frames can be reversed; that the play can be turned inside out, exposing the fragility of its overall logic. The play-within-the-play turns out to be the main play as Williams's earlier title for the work—*The Two-Character Play*—suggests, and as his return to that original title in a late revision confirms. Read inside out, *Out Cry* reveals its strangest and most terrifying secret: Felice and Clare are not professional actors on tour performing their unfortunate childhood that condemned them to years of isolation in their native New Bethesda; for if we were to believe the radical nature of their isolation, we ought also to logically question how they were ever able to leave their past and pursue the high visibility of theater. What happens, instead, is a tragic and ironic reversal that deceives the spectators into witnessing as "true" a tale of deception: unable to overcome their unbearable past, Felice and Clare have been subsequently coping by performing their life as a theatrical act, transforming each into a psychoanalyst for the other, and attempting a talking cure bound to remain unsuccessful. Having been all along at the same place—their New Bethesda home, which serves as their prison and their stage—neither of them can specify the location of their theater. Clare does not even seem to remember their trip there at all, since it is thoroughly imaginary:

> All I remember about this last trip—I must've had a fever—is that it would be light and then it would be dark and then it would be light or half light again and then dark again, and the country changed from prairies to mountains and then back to prairies again and then back to mountains, and my watch froze to death, and I tell you honestly I don't have any idea or suspicion of where we are now except we seem to be in a huge mausoleum of a theater somewhere that seems like nowhere. (16)

Clare's delirious geography sounds like a hallucinatory trip, or a nightmarish waking, rather than a real journey. At time zero and in the space of a tomb, a terrifying play begins: a game of completely reversing inside and outside, fantasy and reality, dream and waking.

In his fragments on vision and subjectivity, Maurice Merleau-Ponty provides a brilliant image for this moment of inverted perception when he speaks of the finger of a glove turned inside out, leaving intact the one point from which it was turned: "Reversibility: the finger of the glove that is turned inside out. . . . The axis alone given—the end of the finger of the glove is nothingness—but a nothingness one can turn over, and where then one sees *things*" (263–64, emphasis in the original). An infinitely reversible hole, the tip of the glove marks the shared point between inside and outside, anchoring the reciprocity between representation and reality. From this point of nothingness, from the point of the fold, we can see *things* which remain otherwise invisible in our reality and whose privileged site of revelation has been art.

In her study of dramatic mimesis, Anne Fleche astutely points out that in probing the old question of representation, namely, the gap between reality and fiction, Williams did not resort to metatheater: "'Metatheatre' might have been an answer, and in fact Williams's allegorical writing could have accommodated this theory of a theater-about-theater, thus sidestepping its relation to 'reality' or at least putting it off. But Williams doesn't opt for it. He is still interested in what art has to do with 'the real,' even though, or perhaps because [. . .] the distinction itself is part of the illusion" (2). Insofar as Williams explores this dialectic of reality and illusion, he is first and foremost exploring theater's relation to truth. Like the tip of Merleau-Ponty's glove, the reversibility of *Out Cry* points to a truth which is equally a part of reality and illusion, the crux of their symmetry. It is the truth that, in Fleche's words, exposes the distinction between reality and illusion to be itself illusory.

Not only do art and illusion belong to the realm of truth, but more importantly, the real becomes a locus of truth precisely in its relation to art, namely, in its relation to illusion. Whenever juxtaposed to art, the real is illumined by art, revealing itself as "more real" than it already is. "*Art* [. . .] *is the becoming and happening of truth*," Martin Heidegger wrote (183, emphasis in the original), while explaining that for the Greeks, truth (*aletheia*) connotes a movement of concealing and revealing, a pattern through which what withdraws itself from us might at the same time appear under another guise and another light, "present[ing] itself as other than it is" (176). Whether we choose to think of it as deception, dissembling, lie, or withdrawal, concealment bears as legitimate a relation to truth, as does revelation. Theater, as the art of the *hypokrites*,[4] is located precisely in this space between concealment and manifestation, between the truth of the other—which threatens us with dissimulation and misrecognition—and our truth.

More than providing a self-reflexive commentary about theater, or an aesthetic exercise in the modernist trope *mise-en-abîme*, the transport between reality and art in *Out Cry* exposes an existential truth: it reveals that the gap between being and its representation, reality and its idols, vanishes in front of the profound nothingness and loss that mark the experience of being. In other words, the spectrality of representation is no more threatening to Felice and Clare than is the nullity which they feel as they look at their past losses while waiting for their impending death. Immobilized by the trauma of their family history, the two siblings imprison themselves voluntarily in their house, administering to themselves law and punishment at once in their very own penal colony. Even the hope of achieving aesthetic transcendence by acting out their suffering disappears as their performance takes place in an empty theater, a theater with no audience other than themselves. Ironically, the empirical audience of such a play is not spared from having to confront its own potential nullity.

In its embrace of nothingness as our existential truth, *Out Cry* echoes the philosophical concerns of symbolist poetics, whose influence transformed the face of modern theater.[5] The symbolist problematization of drama as a genre addresses the question of truth in theater and, specifically, the ways in which theater's path to truth diverges from that of poetry. Primarily a poetic movement, symbolism advanced a contemplative posture toward the world, one in which the poet conjures forth the innermost reality of things through the use of symbols, and his reliance on the sonorous, orphic elements of language. In contrast to this metaphysical attitude, theater relies much too heavily on presence and embodiment, on the materiality of scenery and of the human body, thus relegating the truth of the written text to the contingencies of the external world. Scenery and performance erect, according to the symbolists, the greatest hurdles on theater's way to truth. Discussing the symbolists' resistance to the exteriority of theater, Maeterlinck's in particular, Frantisek Deak writes:

> The fundamental contradiction between materiality and conceptuality, or between materiality and spirituality, is nowhere more apparent than in the person of the actor. For Maeterlinck, the actor's presence destroys the dream emanating from drama. In reading, he argues, we never see the physical infirmity; there is no material body to interfere with the idea. But regardless of the perfection of the actor, it is ultimately a human presence which is, for Maeterlinck, incompatible with the work of art. The symbol does not allow the ambiguity of the human presence. (24)

In the tradition of Plato's anti-mimetic philosophy, and of Lessing's valorization of poetic ideality over and against imagistic concreteness,[6] the symbolist resistance to theatrical spectacle has offered a productive problematic for the theory of modern theater. It has also been responsible for a corpus of works that consciously address the philosophical contradiction between interiority and exteriority, between the impersonal universal power of the symbol and the personalized expression of performance.

The major formal impetus behind symbolist dramaturgy is the minimal use of theatrical elements to the degree that the plays resemble public soliloquies. Not human characters, but ciphers, ghosts, and puppets are the protagonists, while action and *peripeteia* give way to the contemplation of the favored symbolist *topoi* of nothingness, absence, and death. It is of course noteworthy that, in their aesthetic imperative to write a theater beyond performance, many symbolist plays failed not only as staged productions—after all, that would have been their prerogative—but as aesthetic ones too: symbolist theater proved to be an impossible genre. Such was, for instance, the fate of Mallarmé's *Hérodiade*, *Après-Midi d'un faune*, and *Igitur*, all of which were conceived initially as plays, but returned finally to poetry. The impossibility of this effort to reconcile lyrical interiority with theatrical exteriority is of particular interest to *Out Cry*, since in its similarly stripped-down, reflective structure, as well as its spiritual preoccupation with being and loss, this work inherits the symbolist aspiration of a poetic/metaphysical theater.

The importance of symbolism for Williams has been assessed primarily via his expressionist influences.[7] In response to the realists' depiction of society as the solid framework within which individuals and their relations are constituted and regulated, expressionism wished to reestablish the primacy of the individual with its difference and deviance from this collective fabric. Over and against realism's heroes, who operate within and reflect the societal structures around them, expressionism proposes an unrelenting portrayal of the ambiguity, tension, and fragmentation that mark the modern subject. This emphasis on characterological nuance, in which a particular character refracts rather than reflects the societal norms, aligns Williams with the expressionist project.

However, in my reading of *Out Cry*, I am less interested in the expressionist particularity of subjectivity and more in the impersonal symbolic tropes through which the play approaches the question of our existence, and of our absolute—yet arbitrary—exposure to death. Given Williams's insistence on theatrical lyricism, I explore the symbolist aspects of his play in relation to *Igitur*, Mallarmé's poetic dramatization of the metaphysical outcry toward the absolute. Although Mallarmé is missing from Williams's list of influences, and although *Out Cry* and *Igitur* present us with some obvious textual differences (the replacement of subjectivity by one universal consciousness in Mallarmé is mitigated by two slightly more individuated characters in Williams, while the dense meditations of the former are diffused in the dialogue of the latter), both texts dramatize a similar scene and, thus, demand a similar reading sensibility. In the tradition of the Hamletian desire to understand mortality as the ultimate game of life—the supreme game that Igitur also reenacts—Felice and Clare isolate themselves in the sepulchral space of the theater/home in order to rehearse their existential possibilities.

II

The opening *mise-en-scène* of *Out Cry* already contains within it the structural elements of *Igitur*. With the theater described as a mausoleum and the time frozen at zero, *Out Cry* recalls the space and time of *Igitur*—a dark chamber at midnight where the protagonist awaits for the crucial moment when he must throw the dice, the symbol of chance (*le hasard*), and of death. The downward stairwell leading to the tomb of Igitur's ancestors remains a haunting presence among the stage props of *Out Cry*, now inverted as an upward ladder that leads to nowhere: "These stairs go nowhere, they stop in space" (14), says Clare, recognizing in them neither a heavenly ladder, nor a promise of paradisiacal infinity, but rather a terrifying suspension in nothingness, an opening to a non-world. The rest of the play unfolds as an encounter with psychic, aesthetic, and metaphysical nothingness. Whereas Igitur contemplates with his dice the nature of chance under the ghostly presence of his ancestors, Felice and Clare court death with their father's revolver.

Tempted by the inevitable—albeit inscrutable—moment of death, both Igitur and the pair of siblings play a round of philosophical roulette, whose outcome remains as absurd and indeterminate as the accident they attempt to master through their act. Simply shaking the dice in his hands, Igitur refuses eventually to throw them, since he understands that such an act remains subject to the omnipotence of chance. "The potency of chance is such that it carries within itself its opposite" (Delègue, 103, my translation),[8] namely, the human desire to liberate itself from the domination of chance, thus forming a dialectical spiral through which accident and absolute liberation from it continue to be perpetually reinscribed on one another as polar but interdependent opposites. Even the most willed, controlled, and reasoned of suicides could not liberate the human condition from its determined yet incalculable moment of dying. Maurice Blanchot recognizes this impossibility to meet death on our own terms when he analyzes Dostoyevsky's hero, Kirilov, who wishes to inaugurate through his suicide a noble age for humanity, an age unfettered from the bonds and fear of death: "Even when, with an ideal and heroic resolve, I decide to meet death, isn't it still death that comes to meet me, and when I think I grasp it, does it not grasp me?" (98). Williams upholds this truth as well, since he withdraws from bringing his play to a definite conclusion.

In both plays the futility of any experiment to conquer death, and the resignation that marks such an impossible effort, are framed from the beginning by an inhuman scene. As Igitur prepares to confront the impersonal nature of chance, he himself must be stripped of all the human emotions that might impede the objectivity of his encounter. Devoid "of all meanings but presence itself" (*Igitur*, 9), Igitur occupies the realm of neutrality and indifference that is necessary to make him the universal symbol of the struggle toward the absolute. Without the traces of subjectivity, projected outside of historical time (*hors du temps*) and into the fantastic world of a midnight nightmare, in a physically indistinct location of a tomb chamber, Igitur can dissect himself to embody the two poles of human experience: the human desire—let us say the Hamletian tragic folly—to attain absolute freedom, and the inescapable accident of death which threatens to interrupt this process. It is because of the universality of this drama, because of its impersonal and ontological rather than culturally specific premises, that Mallarmé has resisted the material, spatiotemporal specificity of theater. Elisabeth Howe, for instance, emphasizes Mallarmé's disinterest in staging *Hamlet* as a sixteenth-century costume play, insisting instead on the universality and absoluteness of its meanings which ought not to be constrained by such spatiotemporal specificity (357). Equally, the figure of Igitur cannot be reduced to a particular subjectivity, but must remain a universal and impersonal sign.

Out Cry's stage directions also render this inhumanity explicit: "There should be, at a low level, a number of mechanical sounds suggesting an inhuman quality to the (half underground) vault of a foreign theater" (7). Amidst these machinic voices, Felice discovers another inhuman presence, a cockroach on the floor, at which he exclaims ironically: "A humanizing touch!" (8). Being one "among the last organic survivors" (8) of post-nuclear apocalypse, the cockroach stands for a vision of the world in which humanity has been outstripped by vermin. The earlier version of the play, *The Two-Character Play*, equally stresses this otherworldly dimension, since the setting again "must not only suggest the disordered images of a mind approaching collapse but also, correspondingly, the phantasmagoria of the nightmarish world that all of us live in at present, not just the subjective but the true world with all its dismaying shapes and shadows . . . " (1).

The world of nightmares and of unconscious horrors is symbolized by a gigantic sculpture towering over the scenery, which both siblings find thoroughly inappropriate and attempt to remove. Despite their efforts, this improper presence remains immobile, as if rooted on the stage, both a witness to and a testimony of the psychic horrors Felice and Clare wish to deny. Felice attributes to this monolith the aspect of an "unalterable circumstance" (10), something that cannot be disposed of, a kind of law that is fixed and remains outside of human control. Clare describes it as a "monstrous aberration" (9) and as "obscene" (10)—an object which literally opposes and obstructs the scene, an aberration and a deformation of the image. Such is the disturbance this statue provokes that Clare considers it an inappropriate prop even for *Medea* and *Oedipus Rex* (10). Despite Clare's attempt to dissociate their performance from the horrific nature of this object, her symptomatic reference to these two tragedies exposes the fact that incest, horror, and intra-familial murder constitute the principal themes of *Out Cry* as well.

Indeed, Clare characterizes their play as the "most unusual play in the repertory" (16). According to Felice, it is the only one that they will perform in the future (16), a statement that indicates this play's categorical importance. For Felice, this play signifies not just any theatrical piece, but a game—a supreme game, their version of throwing the dice. The *Two-Character Play* unravels as the human improvisation with death, a confrontation in which these siblings represent two opposing prototypes: Felice, the quixotic artist, proposes that they improvise interminably until they get "both lost in the play" (14). In keeping with the homeopathic aesthetic principle, according to which the artist wounded by art finds in art his only panacea, Felice declares that "if we're not artists, we're nothing" (22). In a down-to-earth fashion, Clare, on the other hand, insists on knowing what she is about to perform, and "especially how a play ends" (15). Although frequently portrayed at the verge of hysterical fits, Clare is injected at critical moments with the forces of rationality, realism, and determination. To her practical insistence on foresight, Felice proposes the mercurial and speculative nature of the artist.

Nowhere else is the antagonism between these two principles expressed better than in an argument the siblings have about necessity and impossibility. Here Williams draws the Hamletian countenance of Felice:

> FELICE: We're going to do *The Two-Character Play* as we've never done it before.
> CLARE: Impossible.
> FELICE: Necessary.
> CLARE: Some necessary things are impossible.
> FELICE: And some impossible things are necessary. (19)

Whereas Clare, the realist, sees no purpose in engaging with the impossible, Felice, the idealist, calls for the necessity of doing so. However, the seemingly clear division between the practical and constrained nature of Clare as opposed to the free and visionary nature of Felice hides an interesting paradox in the dialogue's chiasmatic structure: the less philosophically inclined Clare comes far closer to understanding the demands of the impossible than does Felice, who in his wish to be free beyond any impossibility is forced to subject his very wish to the realm of necessity, and thus of unfreedom. Suspended between the lines of Clare's and Felice's dialogue, between resignation and improvisation, is the place of Igitur: the place of radical abandonment where the best way to understand chance is neither to affirm nor negate it.

In fact, it could be said that Felice and Clare embody the opposite principles that are consolidated in the figure of Igitur. Not surprisingly, this bipolarity is bound up with gender. After citing several etymological analyses of Igitur's name, Robert Greer Cohn links the typographical form of this name to a symbolic representation of the masculine and feminine principles: "*i*, the Hebrew *iod*, as is universally recognized in occult tradition, is the phallic letter par excellence, male, vertical; *u*, with its trough or womb shape, a receptacle, is female" (27). Cohn adds that, "the central thread of *Igitur* is this kind of dialectic between male idea and female unconscious (a light-dark polarity symbolized by candle and darkness of varying sorts; also an up-down polarity, etc.), and the 'narrative' to a large extent is the extrapolation of the paradoxical reversals of one into the other" (27). Completing each other's sentences throughout their dialogue, Felice and Clare similarly move into each other's psychic territory, reversing whatever predominant traits might be attributed to each one of them. Felice enters the world of hysteria as often as Clare takes a metaphysical flight of fancy. Clare comments specifically on her brother's feminized looks, describing him as "hermaphroditic" (22).

This psychic intimacy between the siblings attests to Williams's profound affection for his own sister, Rose, who was an inspiring figure for many of his female heroines (Parker, 524–26). The only one in his family to understand and share his preoccupations since childhood, Rose was—to his devastation—lobotomized at a young age and remained institutionalized for schizophrenia. The loss, not unlike Mallarmé's inconsolable mourning after his beloved sister's death, marked indelibly the playwright to the extent that brother-sister incest becomes in Williams's work a figuration of a profound psychic transaction through which two polar principles (gendered, or otherwise) interpenetrate to form a totality.

Alluding to such a reciprocal devotion between his sister and him, but also to his religious background which marked both his literary and libidinal imaginary (his maternal grandfather was a minister and young Williams was reared in rectories of the South), Felice's and Clare's family name is Devoto. Moreover, to express this paradoxically non-carnal, yet erotic, love for the sister, Williams turns to the *Song of Solomon* for his epigraph of *Out Cry*: "A garden enclosed is my sister . . ." The overwhelming biblical symbolism of this song, which transforms the virgin sister into the beloved, is coupled with Williams's *fin-de-siècle* symbolism of sexual reversibility, in which the completion of the fragmented self occurs in the passage from one sex to another, in the figure of the androgyne. Astutely, Parker relates *Out Cry*'s incestuous subtext to late romantic and symbolist works such as Poe's *The Fall of the House of Usher* and Villiers de L'Isle-Adam's *Axel*, while detecting in Williams's sexual preference for androgynous men a turn-of-the-century decadent sensibility (527), which valorized hermaphroditism from Baudelaire's giantesses to Mann's Tadzio.

Furthermore, the reversibility of the traits between brother and sister echoes on the characterological level the structural reversibility of this play, to which I pointed earlier in this essay, and which calls into question the play's verisimilitude by inverting its two dramatic frames. As Felice and Clare attempt to reconstruct their personal narrative, they, too, present each other with competing truths about their past, as well as with memories and identifications that sometimes overlap and othertimes diverge.

The family disaster began when their father, an astrologer and mystic, had to give up his spiritualist preoccupations under his wife's threat of institutionalization. The symbolic castration that the father experienced in his wife's denial of his spiritual virility led him to murder her and then kill himself. Left to decipher this violent legacy and to form some sort of narrative for their own survival, the siblings find themselves amidst the œdipal scene of "unlocking the heirlooms so that they spill their mystery, their unknown quantity, their memory, their silence, human impressions and faculties" (*Igitur,* 17). Felice appears on stage with the few belongings of his father, holding onto his astrological chart, and wearing his father's astrology shirt (11, 14). Clare unearths her birthstone ring given to her by her father (27). In their attempt to decode the meaning of the opal stone, the siblings polarize around the characterization of their parents: Clare agrees with her mother who considered opals "unlucky" prefiguring the murders committed by the father, whereas Felice accuses their mother as "frigid"—alluding to her emasculating capacities—and links her prejudice against the stone to her dislike of their father (27). This contrast between frigidity and spiritual pathos is displaced onto the siblings as well: the rationalist attitude of Clare, whose name alludes to lucidity, is opposed to the embattled idealism of Felice, whose name is associated with felicity and good fortune.

The other binary at work concerns the father's internal split between his high-minded mystical quest and his ultimate downfall. Clare points to this downfall when she compares the stage debris to a "shipwreck" (11), a signifier of past catastrophe, and in their case, of the paternal legacy. The father's spiritual loftiness ends in madness "spewing up wreckage" (11). Astrology and shipwreck, heaven and ocean, altitude and depth, the sublime and the bathetic—all gendered poles that split within the paternal imaginary—are metaphors preeminent in symbolist cosmology, and specifically Mallarmean in nature.[9]

Not surprisingly, it is the murderous event itself that becomes the locus of the most divergent interpretations and reconstructions between the siblings. In one of the scenarios they devise about how to relate this event to the outside world, Felice reverses the truth, transforming the mother into the murderess of the story: "what we saw was Mother with the revolver, first killing Father and then herself" (43). Clare objects to such an outright distortion, replying that, "A simple lie is one thing, but the absolute opposite of the truth is another" (44). Felice, then, justifies his distortion by pointing out the futility of Clare's desire to establish truth amidst the madness and to apply logic and chronology to uncontrollable and irrational forces: "What's the truth in pieces of metal exploding from the hand of a man driven mad by—!" (44).

Despite the two radically different accounts, this exchange remains exceptional in its frank admission of the event as murder. Frequently, both siblings insist on avoiding this term. Claiming to have been the exclusive witness to the double crime, Clare still calls it elsewhere an accident: "That night of the accident night, you ran to the foot of the stairs but not a step further, you blocked the steps, I had to force my way past you to the room" (26). In the second act, she stutters again euphemistically "the *un, inexplicable*—accident" (39, emphasis in the original). During one of their arguments, Felice reminds Clare of her confusion during the night of the "accident": "When terrible accidents happen, details get confused. Like you got confused the accident night? Ran downstairs and phoned a dead doctor [. . .]" (43). Clare's telephonic impotence, which is highlighted throughout the play in a number of abortive calls to several people, dates back to that fatal night when she was unable to get help. In a sense, death is exposed here as being always an accident, a metaphysical hiatus beyond cause and consequence, which suspends any act on our part and deprives us of a sound, proper, or efficacious decision. Utterly helpless at the critical moment, Clare called into the void.

Sleeping ever since in the bedroom of the crime with its ghosts, Clare is plagued by somnambulism: "Is it improper for me not to stay in one place? All night? Alone?" (27) she asks, agonizing over her own ghost-like errancy. Wandering around the house, both she and her brother refuse to exit it due to an overdetermined psychic burden: guilt, shame, fear, and resignation. For instance, in his first venture out of the house, Felice is quickly dissuaded by the startling presence of an enormous two-headed sunflower in the yard: "Botanists, you know botanists, they'll flock to New Bethesda to marvel at this marvel, photograph it for the—*National Geographic*, this marvel of nature. This two-headed sunflower taller than a two-story house which is still inhabited by a—recluse brother and sister who never go out any more. . . ." (29). The repetition of "marvel" alludes simultaneously to the fantastic and monstrous nature of this two-headed household, namely, to the persisting solace the siblings provide for each other, as well as to the incestuous isolation in which they are submerged.

Subsequent efforts to leave the house involve the rehearsal of absurd scenarios which prevent them from ever succeeding in their goal. Desperate in their isolation, both siblings remain paralyzed and feed off of each other's psychological impotence. Clare's attempt to leave near the end of the first act is yet another futile variation on the same theme. While she wishes to "go out calling" (32), she demands the company of Felice, who—of course—refuses on account of having to guard the house against "curious trespassers" (33). Afraid of leaving his habitual—even if terrifying—surroundings, Felice offers any excuse to stay, and the "curious trespassers" are as good as any, especially given the fact that Clare, in one of her unsuccessful phone calls for help, covers the family murder as an attack from a "housebreaker" (35). As the house gate marks the outermost limit of their existence, Felice seems to be ventriloquizing in his madness the paranoid animal creature of Kafka's "The Burrow":

At such times it is as if I were not so much looking at my house as at myself sleeping, and had the joy of being in a profound slumber and simultaneously of keeping vigilant guard over myself. I am privileged, as it were, not only to dream about the specters of the night in all the helplessness and blind trust of sleep, but also at the same time to confront them in actuality with the calm judgment of the fully awake. (334)

Just as Kafka's quadruped is thoroughly consumed by its obsession to defend its burrow, so Felice is perversely devoted to keeping vigilant guard over the house, and ultimately over himself: Felice's is the self-imposed disciplinary gaze that keeps watch over his desire to leave. Unlike Kafka's creature, however, that guards its burrow from the outside, Felice confines himself voluntarily inside. Eventually, whether ejected or incorporated by their house, both dwellers internalize it as the absolute law, the inescapable prison.

The house demands from the siblings; it locks them in and devours them while erecting itself as the quintessential "unalterable circumstance" of this play, an unconscious fixture—partly the imaginary desire for unity and belonging, and partly the internalized voice of the dead father, the symbolic law. Indeed, in the one time that Felice makes it barely outside the door, he hears the house behind summoning him back inside:

I feel so exposed, so cold. And behind me I feel the house. It seems to be breathing a faint, warm breath on my back. I feel it the way you feel a loved person standing close behind you. Yes, I'm already defeated. The house is so old, so faded, so warm that, yes, it seems to be breathing. It seems to be whispering to me: "You can't go away. Give up. Come in and stay." Such a gentle command! What do I do? Naturally, I obey. (55)

The expression "already defeated" signifies the œdipal recognition of a child who cannot overcome the paternal imperative. As children, Felice and Clare are defeated: unable to transcend their family of origin, they remain stranded within it, literalizing the symbolic model of the "family romance" in their quasi-incestuous love for each other. As artists, they are destitute like the old painter Clare describes, who was abandoned "in *rigor mortis* before a totally blank canvas" (11). Similarly, they are abandoned by their company, their audience, and forced to give a virtual performance with invisible props. "Put on your invisible jacket and your invisible tie" (50), says Clare to Felice, indicating the absurdity of their situation.

Consequently, the vision of the house symbolizes a double anxiety of influence—a psychic and an aesthetic one: who to be, or what to write, after the Father? This question is responsible for the existential passivity of the characters and the dramatic stasis of the play, both elements which make *Out Cry* an inheritor of Mallarmé's virtual theater; namely, a drama whose stakes are "not possible at the theater but requiring theater" (Mallarmé quoted in Gould, 141). One could assume that along with Felice, Williams, too, is pondering his own belated position in literary history, the way Mallarmé pondered the disappearance of the classic Muse, finding his consolation in the "Muse moderne de l'Impuissance." In the aftermath of the great tradition and of its exhaustion, the modern muse of impotence sings "a kind of negative poetry, a cult of absence and of the impossibility of being" (Delègue, 58, my translation). Williams's image of the house, as uncanny and prohibitive as the statue amidst the scenery, stands for this negative poetics, for what Clare and Felice recognized as the necessary impossibility (or impossible necessity) of their theater. Still stranded in the theater/home and unable to properly end their play, Clare speaks of the negativity that pervades their situation while facing that statue: "— Unalterable—circumstance—unaltered . . ." (64).

With all their efforts to leave the house doomed to failure, there remains one last move in this game: murder and suicide, following the parental model. Felice alludes to the possibility of Clare's suicide and links his refusal to leave the house with his concern that Clare might attempt to kill herself, if she is left unobserved. Clare refutes any suicidal wishes on her part, and to the contrary, accuses Felice of potential homicidal fantasies, explaining how threatened she feels by Felice's possession of their father's revolver (46).

Though unloaded this time, according to Felice, the murder weapon reappears as the critical prop toward the end of the play. After their last unsuccessful attempt to exit their home, Felice realizes that there is "nothing at all left to do" (58) other than (re)turning to the solution of the revolver. This constitutes the first of two endings of the play—the penultimate end, to use an oxymoronic figure of speech that will prove significant for the overall structure of the play.

Felice marks this turn of action in his speech by identifying it self-reflexively as a moment of novelty and improvisation within the play they perform: "And now I touch her hand lightly, which is a signal that I am about to speak a new line in *The Two-Character Play*" (58). In this "new line," he asks Clare whether she found the hidden cartridges. Her panicked and negative response is met by Felice's reproach: "Clare, you say 'yes,' not 'no'" (58). As Felice becomes the director of their play and their fate at this point, he refers to the still-present Clare in the third-person pronoun, as if she were absent, or a mere stage prop herself: "And then I pick up the property of the play which she's always hated and dreaded, so much that she refuses to remember that it exists in the play" (58). Subsequently, the dialogue condenses into a set of solipsistic stage directions uttered aloud by Felice, describing the arrangement of their potential execution: "Now I remove the blank cartridges and insert the real ones as calmly as if I were removing dead flowers from a vase and putting in fresh ones"; and later, "I put the revolver in the center of the little table across which we had discussed the attitude of nature toward its creatures that are regarded as un-natural creatures" (58, 59).

The revolver is aimed at them, as the "unnatural creatures" under discussion, but the climax does not arrive, and neither does a cathartic end. Instead, Felice substitutes the act of shooting the gun with the act of blowing soap bubbles in a metonymic regression from the adult decision of suicide to childhood games, from bullets to bubbles. Structurally, this scene repeats and inverts Clare's play with the soap bubbles in the beginning of this act (38). Beautiful and dreamy in its iridescence, a bubble is also the symbol of extreme fragility and transience, since it bursts so quickly, symbolizing a life cut prematurely: "Of course sometimes the soap bubble bursts before it rises, but this time please imagine you see it rising through gold light, above the gold sunflower heads" (59). With these words, Felice "mimes the action of blowing up soap bubbles" (59), in a gesture that empties out his capacity to pull the trigger, as well as denies him the real pleasure of an infantile game.

Consequently, the first ending consists in the impossibility to carry out the ultimate act in any other way than simulating it, or better yet, dissimulating it. The second ending follows only to reiterate the non-closure of the first one. While the former ending came as a result of their unsuccessful attempt to leave home, symbolizing a psychological dead end, the latter follows their equally unsuccessful attempt to exit the theater, marking an aesthetic dead end as well. Having to reenter the play to keep warm in the cold theater, Felice comforts Clare: "Don't worry about the ending, it'll come to us, Clare. I think you'll find it wherever you hid it" (69). In other words, the revolver will manifest itself at the right moment as the only solution, and demand their life. According to Felice, they will not even notice the moment of the end, since by then they will be intoxicated by the play, having given themselves completely to their art (70). They will go toward their end obeying art's supreme requirement: the death of the artist.[10]

However, the end consists again in another inconclusive scene, which foregrounds the siblings' existential nullification together with the impotence of the work of art to find proper closure. Seduced by the beauty of the sunflowers, instead of the soap bubbles, Felice and Clare stand by the window as the light around them evanesces. "The lights fade, and they accept it fading, as a death, somehow transcended" (72), read the stage directions in an uncanny echo of Igitur's supreme ambiguity: "He closes the book, stifles the candle with his chance-possessed breath and crossing his arms, lies down on the ashes of his ancestors" (*Igitur,* 20).

III

I have tried to establish that, in its preoccupation with the issues of psychological inaction and aesthetic failure, the poetics of *Out Cry* echoes symbolist concerns in general, and Mallarmé's philosophical meditations on the nature of death in particular. The parental shipwreck provides the symbolic stage upon which the incestuous children rehearse their madness as the disappearance of meaning: "The worst thing that's disappeared in our lives is being aware of what's going on in our lives," is Clare's diagnosis (62). Felice and Clare are frozen in a present, which when measured up to either their past or their future renders both these time zones signifiers of nullity: looking at the past, they recognize that which exists no more, while looking at the future, they anticipate that which will exist no longer. This nullity becomes most explicit in the play's refusal to offer a conventional ending, that is, an end which allows for a certain closure. Not only does the play abandon its own ending *qua* termination, but it presents us with two endings: a "penultimate ending," and a second ending which is practically a repetition of the former.

By way of concluding my own reading of a text that passionately affirms the inconclusive, I would like to suggest that it is this figure of the penultimate and its repeated deaths that links *Out Cry* most closely to Mallarmé's poetics of negativity and failure. True enough, *Out Cry* does not formally collapse back into the lyric form, affirming its dramatic failure, as did Mallarmé's theater. However, this play's resistance to conventional dramatic rules has been responsible for a history of failed productions and its general obscurity within the Williams repertory. The claustrophobic tone of the play, and its incessant repetition of motifs all the way to the double ending, is a kind of "overkill." This is, however, precisely what grants the play its truth: in refusing to depict death as a literal part of the action, *Out Cry* unfolds as the supreme game of putting death into words and yielding meaning out of nothingness. The suicide of the siblings never takes place, but remains always a subject of contemplation, perpetually postponed. Death, does not happen, but is named throughout the play in a number of metonymic chains. For instance, the space of the theater produces a chain of macabre spaces such as a mausoleum, a shipwreck, a prison, and a casket; similarly, the murderous father establishes his own moribund symbolic chain that includes magic, his "sacred flowers" which were replaced by the monstrous sunflowers in the yard, Clare's sinister birthstone ring, and the revolver. Most of all, however, this excessive symbolization of death, which overcompensates for the lack of action, is revealed at the play's double ending. As if one death were not enough, the characters are subjected twice to an almost identical death scenario. A symbolic overkilling in language counters the literal underkilling in reality.

Reading Mallarmé's claim that "the Penultimate is dead" ["La Penultième est morte"] in his prose poem "Le démon de l'analogie," Claire Lyu asks questions that pertain to the ending of *Out Cry*: "Would the dead penult somehow not be dead enough? But, if the penult has not died the first time, will it the second time? . . . or even the third time? Would this mean that the penult needs to be killed again and again infinitely, and that the penult always, and inevitably so, dies two or more times?" (565). Lyu's answer is that, "the penult does not contradict, but predicts the last" (567). "To be next-to-the last means inevitably and necessarily to touch the last and through this tangent, to already be the last," she writes (568), in a formulation that applies perfectly to the last two lines of *Out Cry*'s dialogue: "Magic is a habit," reads the penultimate sentence from Clare, which is immediately supplemented by Felice into the ultimate utterance, "Magic is the habit of our existence . . ." (72). Magic, often associated in the play with the fascination of childhood, with the sunflowers and the soap bubbles, is in their case also a signifier of death, since it was their father's magical preoccupations that led to the murder. In this sense, Clare's sentence can also mean that "death is a habit," and Felice's version that "death is the habit of our existence." Death is the fashion, the modality, in which their and our existence manifests itself.

This pattern of rendering explicit the dash, or ellipsis, of a previously unfinished statement, of uttering the unutterable and thus of repeating it, is constitutive of the structure of *Out Cry* as its dialogue constantly alternates between the penultimate and the ultimate. It is this kind of speech *in extremis* that leads Clare to ask of their dialogue, "Why are we talking to each other like this, like tonight was the end of the world and we're blaming each other for it?" (13). Clare's apocalyptic allusion refers to the fact that their language—despite, or rather precisely because of, its deterioration of meaning—bears a truth that comes from a space outside everyday life, from the space of death and revelation. The unfinished utterance of each sibling predicts and announces the response of the other sibling in the same way that the penultimate heralds the arrival of the end. Each sentence falls and folds back into the previous one in an endless chain of substitution of nouns for the "end." Felice alerts us to the Hegelian self-enclosure of the play, in which the end is already written in the beginning, as yet another level of the play's reversibility: "Just this evening, before you entered, I composed the opening monologue of a play that's—*closed* Unopened . . ." (67).

Through its incessant displacement and, thus, implicit repetition of the end, namely, through its over-symbolization of an unrealized death, *Out Cry* exposes the breach between language and reality. Indeed, the play posits death precisely in this inability to ground being and meaning in each other. The psychic and aesthetic impotence of the characters, to which I referred earlier on, corresponds to this severance of being from meaning, a severance which Lacan expressed with a bar that separates the signifier from the signified (164). Humans are who they are in their capacity to signify; yet insofar as they signify, they also negate being by subsuming it into meaning and language. Language, however, is far from being able to offer an affirmative solution to the ontological loss, since it cannot provide a definitive closure in the realm of semantics. The absurd scenarios of the siblings, and the ultimate failure of their "talking cure," demonstrate to the contrary that meaning is both endangered and endangering us: for what does it really mean to reach the end twice without ever reaching it?

"Finding the act useless because there is and yet there is no chance" (*Igitur,* 20), Felice and Clare give up the possibility of ever reaching the end, and propose, instead, an attitude of passivity in which they let the end happen. By abandoning the conclusion of *Out Cry* to a state of such radical ambiguity and indetermination, Williams the symbolist, refuses to end his play and, instead, gestures toward the end of theater.

NOTES

1. I am using this term consciously for its psychoanalytic overtones. The psychological and therapeutic aspects of the theater are as old as Aristotle's discussion of catharsis. Theater's healing nature is also shown by the fact that Epidaurus, the celebrated home of classical tragedy, was a version of an ancient spa where medicine and drama were both used as forms of treatment.

2. Entitled *The Two-Character Play*, the play-within-the play was also the title of the earlier, 1967 version of *Out Cry*. Williams revised *Out Cry* in 1975 and returned to its original title (Parker, 521).

3. The textual allusion to the chasm that separates the world of aesthetic integri-

ty from that of economic success unwittingly foreshadows Williams's own break with his agent, Audrey Wood, just before the 1971 Chicago opening of *Out Cry*. In his *Playboy* interview, Williams reveals that the break with Wood occurred after he had accused her of never wanting this play to succeed (6).

4. This is the ancient Greek term for actors, which survives in Modern English as an adjective for someone deceitful. The verb *hypokrinesthai* literally means to come under (*hypo*), to assume the judgment and decision (*krinein*) of another individual. Taking someone else's position, however, suggests not only a sympathetic approximation of the other's truth but also the imminent risk of misrecognizing and misrepresenting such truth.

5. For a systematic analysis of the symbolist influence in modern drama, see Deak.

6. See Lessing, *Laocoön*. In establishing the boundaries between the verbal and the plastic arts, Lessing's treatise argues that poetry is superior to painting or sculpture because the temporal nature of language does not fix our impression. Whereas the poetic representation of something ugly or violent is left to the imagination and transformed by the act of reading, the visual arts fix spatially and temporally the frightening as a permanent material presence. Contrary to the symbolists, however, Lessing argues that these differences are successfully reconciled in drama.

7. The fundamental differences between these two movements notwithstanding, critics have often linked them in their opposition to realism (Jackson, 20–25). Jackson also acknowledges that Williams's counterrealism positions him closer to the romantics and the symbolists, who are interested in the spiritual rather than the outward reality (27). Arguing for a mimetic reading of Williams, Fleche situates the playwright within realism, albeit a realism that is already complicated by the knowledge of its own aesthetic rules and conventions (18–19). According to Fleche, Williams's mimetic concerns lead him to consider both essence and appearance, inside and outside, so that his work is marked by the dialectic tension between expressionism and realism (89). Parker quotes Clive Barnes's remark that *Out Cry* "will one day be regarded as one of the most remarkable symbolist plays of the late twentieth century" (526). Asked about the writers that exerted influence on his work, or that he simply admires, Williams mentioned among others the symbolists Rimbaud and Rilke (*Playboy*, 8).

8. The original reads: "La *puissance* du hasard est telle qu'il porte en lui son contraire."

9. See Mallarmé's cosmogonic poem *Un coup de dés* in *Igitur, Divagations, Un coup de dés*.

10. This is one of Blanchot's central ideas in *The Space of Literature*. The death of the artist here is not related to Barthes's concept, in which the function of authorship is displaced, for instance, onto the reader. For Blanchot, as for Felice, the stakes are higher, since they involve an ontological battle between the author's being and the work's coming-to-being. The work, in order to *be* a work, must consume its author to the point of effacing him/her.

WORKS CITED

Blanchot, Maurice. *The Space of Literature*. Trans. Ann Smock. Lincoln: University of Nebraska Press, 1982.

Cohn, Robert Greer. *Mallarmé: Igitur*. Berkeley: University of California Press, 1981.

Deak, Frantisek. *Symbolist Theater: The Formation of an Avant-Garde*. Baltimore: Johns Hopkins University Press, 1993.

Delègue, Yves. *Mallarmé, le suspens*. Strasbourg: Presses Universitaires de Strasbourg, 1997.

Fleche, Anne. *Mimetic Disillusion: Eugene O'Neill, Tennessee Williams and U.S. .Dramatic Realism*. Tuscaloosa: University of Alabama Press, 1997.

Gould, Evelyn. *Virtual Theater from Diderot to Mallarmé*. Baltimore: Johns Hopkins University Press, 1989.

Heidegger, Martin. "The Origin of the Work of Art." *Basic Writings*. Ed. David Farrell Krell. New York: Harper, 1977.

Howe, Elisabeth A. "'Monologue ou drame avec Soi': *Igitur*." *Nineteenth-Century French Studies* 27.3 & 4 (1999): 356–65.

Jackson, Esther Merle. *The Broken World of Tennessee Williams*. Madison: University of Wisconsin Press, 1965.

Jennings, Robert. "Tennessee Williams: A Candid Conversation with the Brilliant, Anguished Playwright." *Playboy* (April 1973): 1–10.

Kafka, Franz. "The Burrow." Trans. Willa and Edwin Muir. *The Complete Stories*. New York: Schocken, 1971. 325–59.

Lacan, Jacques. "The Agency of the Letter in the Unconscious, or Reason since Freud." *Ecrits*. Trans. Alan Sheridan.New York: Norton, 1977. 146–178.

Lessing, Gotthold Ephraim. *Laocoön*. Trans. Edward Allen McCormick. Baltimore: Johns Hopkins University Press, 1984.

Lyu, Claire. "The Poetics of the Penult: Mallarmé, Death, and Syntax." *MLN* 113.3 (1998): 561–87.

Mallarmé, Stéphane. *Igitur*. Trans. Jack Hirshman. Los Angeles: Pegacycle Lady Press, 1974.

———. *Un coup de dés*. In: *Igitur, Divagations, Un coup de dés*. Paris: Gallimard, 1976.

Merleau-Ponty, Maurice. *The Visible and the Invisible*. Trans. Alphonso Lingis. Evanston: Northwestern UP, 1968.

Parker, R. B. "The Circle Closed: A Psychological Reading of the *Glass Menagerie* and *The Two Character Play*."*Modern Drama* 28.4 (1985): 517-534.

Williams, Tennessee. *Cat on a Hot Tin Roof*. Volume 3 of *Theatre*. New York: New Directions, 1971: 1–215.

———. *Out Cry*. New York: New Directions, 1969.

———. *The Two-Character Play*. New York: New Directions, 1969.

Memories and Muses
Vieux Carré and *Something Cloudy, Something Clear*

Bruce J. Mann[1]

"Any artist dies two deaths—that of his physical self and that of his creative power. Thus, the important part of me is really already dead."
——Tennessee Williams[2]

"Make voyages!—Attempt them!—there's nothing else. . . ."
——Lord Byron in *Camino Real*

During his final years, Tennessee Williams struggled with a desperate crisis of identity. No longer the successful younger playwright, after suffering a series of critical failures, and unable to accept what he had become, the older playwright existed in a kind of limbo, evident in his reference to himself as "the ghost of a writer" ("I Am . . . ")[3] Critics have paid little attention to these striking autobiographical works. *Vieux Carré* is considered to be derivative, a pale shadow of Williams's famous plays, while *Something Cloudy, Something Clear* is seen as diffuse and difficult to classify.[4] But I would argue that these are central, not marginal, works in the Williams canon, which deserve more study, not least for the remarkable window they open into the playwright's inner world. For that is where the plays are really set—not in a rundown rooming house or on the dunes—but in the depths of Williams's mind, at the roots of his imagination where his self was originally formed, an underworld of muses and memories where he searches for his lost sense of self.

This explains why both plays are so intensely self-reflective. Allusions to Williams's life and works resonate throughout the text. At every moment, we see someone or something that inspired the young playwright and found its way into his fictions. In *Vieux Carré*, for example, the sad, colorful residents of Mrs. Wire's rooming house obviously inspired many of his early short plays and later ones, as well. Here are the origins of *The Strangest Kind of Romance*, *Auto-da-Fé*, *Talk to Me Like the Rain and Let Me Listen . . .* , and, for that matter, *Battle of Angels* and *A Streetcar Named Desire*. In addition, there are allusions to important early muses, including his mother, grandmother, and nurse, and to such literary influences as William Saroyan, Edgar Allan Poe, and Anton Chekhov. Marked by similar allusiveness, *Something Cloudy, Something Clear* introduces Kip, the lover whose photograph Williams carried in his wallet for years, a special muse who surely inspired his theme of an ideal love lost but still sought (consider Skipper, whose name contains "Kip," in *Cat on a Hot Tin Roof*). And we also meet the ghosts of other real-life figures he loved, among them, his childhood friend, Hazel Kramer, whose relationship Williams draws from to write his short story, "The Field of Blue Children" (Leverich, 310). Again, the dramatic world is charged with his literary muses, including Rainer Maria Rilke and especially his beloved Hart Crane, the poet who most influenced him. Williams alludes to Crane by modeling *Something Cloudy, Something Clear* on his evocative "Voyages" poems.

Enhancing this effect is another striking feature, the interplay of two simultaneous points of view. On stage, we see the younger personae of Williams—the Writer and August—who serve as narrators and respond as they did at the time, inspired by everything around them. But the actual narrator, in both cases, is the older Williams, whose ghostly presence is felt constantly and whose thoughts we occasionally hear spoken by his younger self. Now in his final years, the aging playwright sees life much differently than he did back then. For him, revisiting the muses is difficult. These ghostly, dying figures no longer inspire him in the same way but instead remind him of disturbing things, such as how badly he behaved toward them in life, how he has lost his creative powers, and how close he is to death.

Williams must counterpoint these two selves, because they exemplify his inner struggle, the late-life crisis of identity mentioned earlier. Kathleen Woodward has dubbed it the "the mirror stage of old age" (109), after Lacan's mirror stage of infancy. One day in late adulthood, we discover in the mirror a jarring image of the older person we have become, which we cannot reconcile with the image of the younger self we think we are. This self-division fosters a sense of the Freudian uncanny, according to Woodward (104). But for an artist like Williams, the crisis is much more terrifying. Suddenly, he has become an older Other, separated and even estranged from his younger self. Unsure of his identity, he feels lost, lonely, and abandoned, an emotional orphan[5] cut off from his "mother," the nurturing powers which shaped his sense of self. This anguished condition is dramatized in *Vieux Carré*.

How can this late-life crisis be resolved? Writing in "The Orphan Archetype," Rose-Emily Rothenberg argues that orphans exploring their own identity should relive the trauma of separation, in order to bring out their pain and face the reality of their loss (192). Then, they need to build a stronger "autonomous" self by creatively reconnecting with the mother at her "archetypal source," the unconscious, to tap into nurturing forces there (192–3). This is analogous to what the aging Tennessee Williams does to resolve his emotional orphanhood. In *Vieux Carré* and

Something Cloudy, Something Clear, he relives the despair caused by his divided self, accepts the reality of his aging, and works to forge a new inclusive self by reconnecting with powers that, like a mother, shaped his identity. Both plays intimate that, near the end of our lives, all of us must return in our minds to our muses, the forces that gave birth to our identity, so that they may teach us how (or how not) to grow old, to assess our lives, and to prepare for death.

Based on an early short story, "The Angel in the Alcove" (1943) and a short play, *The Lady of Larkspur Lotion* (1939), *Vieux Carré* takes place in Mrs. Wire's crumbling rooming house at 722 Toulouse Street in the French Quarter, where Williams stayed during 1938 and 1939.[6] The play has little plot, focusing mostly on the shy young Writer, "myself those many years ago" (4), who interacts with the other residents: Jane Sparks, a would-be fashion designer; her lover, Tye McCool, a brutal strip-show barker; Nightingale, a quick-sketch artist dying of tuberculosis; Mrs. Wire, the mentally unstable landlady; Nursie, her Bible-quoting helper, and two manic, starving women, Mary Maude and Miss Carrie. What unfolds is the education of the artist, the shaping of his imagination as he soaks up bohemian life. "God, but I was ignorant when I came here!" the Writer tells Mrs. Wire. "This place has been a—I ought to pay you—tuition . . . " (66). In the play, the Writer converses with Jane, lusts after Tye, sleeps with Nightingale and then callously rejects him, helps Mrs. Wire, types in his alcove room, and finally runs away with a drifter named Sky, who resembles Val Xavier, the sexually attractive hero of *Battle of Angels*, the next play, incidentally, that would claim Williams's attention.

It was in this rooming house that Tennessee Williams found himself— "my true nature" (69)—and many of his muses. Almost everything we encounter in the dramatic world suggests an inspiration or a source for a play or story, including Beret, the cat, who turns up in *The Strangest Kind of Romance* (1942). Jane reminds us, in her speech patterns and desperate behavior, of Blanche DuBois in *A Streetcar Named Desire* (1947), and Tye exhibits Stanley Kowalski's brutality and sexual qualities. Mrs. Wire has the tenacity of Amanda Wingfield in *The Glass Menagerie* (1944) and the temper of Flora Goforth in *The Milk Train Doesn't Stop Here Anymore* (1963). Her bizarre behavior on the telephone may also remind us of Big Mama in *Cat on a Hot Tin Roof* (1955). Nightingale is a quick-sketch artist like Hannah Jelkes in *The Night of the Iguana* (1961), and he also resembles Doc, the burned-out physician, in *Small Craft Warnings* (1972) and Lord Byron in *Camino Real*. The desperate man and woman in *Talk to Me Like the Rain and Let Me Listen . . .* (1950) could have come from memories of Jane and Tye, and Mrs. Wire's outbursts about corruption in the Quarter appear to have inspired *Auto-da-Fé* (1941). Even more examples could be cited, including lines from later plays that might have originated here, for example, "Shh, walls have ears!" (26), a line spoken by Nightingale that is almost identical to one in *Cat on a Hot Tin Roof*.

For the aging playwright, however, returning to "this house" causes despair, because he is no longer his younger self. An emotional orphan, he cannot draw nurturing inspiration from his muses. When he looks at Jane, Nightingale, or Mrs. Wire, he sees only a frightening mirror image of himself. All three are also emotional orphans unable to accept what they have become—failed artists who feel old, abandoned, lonely, exhausted (none can climb the rooming house stairs without difficulty), and cut off from their younger self-images. In his desperation to reconnect with his muses, Williams enters into the characters of Jane, Nightingale, and Mrs. Wire but finds himself in a nightmare, experiencing again and again the shattering self-division of his identity crisis that has left him isolated and bereft of sanctuary.

Williams dramatizes his anguish in scenes that highlight the disconnection between the Writer and these characters. During the play, Jane, Nightingale, and Mrs. Wire become—in our eyes, too—emblems of the older playwright, and all are effectually betrayed or rejected by his younger persona, enacting the split and estrangement that causes Williams's despair. For example, when Jane learns that her blood disease is fatal, she is too shocked to share the news; but her anguish is conspicuous. The Writer ignores this, however, and chooses to look at the sexually attractive Tye sleeping on her bed. Pouring drinks, he asks her preference:

> JANE: Bourbon. Three fingers.
> WRITER: With?
> JANE: Nothing, nothing.
> [*The writer glances again at Tye as he pours the bourbon.*]
> Nothing . . .
> [*The writer crosses to her with the drink.*]
> Nothing . . . (53)

At the end of the play, he shows similar insensitivity, abandoning her even when he knows Tye will not return, an action that echoes Tom's leaving Laura in *The Glass Menagerie*, one of many echoes in *Vieux Carré* of this earlier memory play.

But it is in the relationship between the Writer and Nightingale that the split between younger and older selves is given its most evocative dramatic form. At the beginning of the second scene, before any words are spoken, we see in profile the silhouettes of Nightingale and the Writer, both suffering from aching loneliness, staring at the thin partition between their alcove rooms. In "The Angel in the Alcove," Williams writes about a young painter living in the house (129–32), but in *Vieux Carré*, he becomes an old painter, one who laments his decline from serious painting to quick-sketch artistry for tourists. Clearly, he has been reshaped to resemble the older Williams himself, his name deriving from the playwright's "private code word [in his journals] for sexual liaison or desire" (Leverich, 404). Nightingale comforts the Writer and sleeps with him, but the Writer ignores and then harshly rejects him, finding him unpalatable, not only because of his age but also because of his hacking cough and spitting of blood. The painter's agony over his own lost sense of self is something the Writer fails to understand, although when Nightingale, deathly ill, is carried out on a stretcher, he is shaken.

A final example of his divided self occurs during a late-night encounter with the normally corrosive Mrs. Wire. The Writer finds her drinking in the kitchen, and she tells him of her disappointment in him, and the other residents, for not testifying in her favor in court. (In a fit of madness, Mrs. Wire poured scalding water through the floor, injuring a photographer and his models.) Her speech describes the loneliness felt by the emotional orphan"

> MRS. WIRE: I only touch this bottle, which also belonged to the late Mr. Wire before he descended to hell between two crooked lawyers, I touch it only when forced to by such a shocking experience as I had tonight, the discovery that I was completely alone in the world, a solitary ole woman cared for by no one. You know, I heard some doctor say on the radio that people die of loneliness, specially at my age. They do. Die of it, it kills 'em. Oh, that's not the cause that's put on the death warrant, but that's the true cause. I tell you, there's so much loneliness in this house that you can hear it. Set still and you can hear it: a sort of awful—soft—groaning in all the walls.

> WRITER: All I hear is rain on the roof. (65)

The Writer's response exposes the enormous chasm between Mrs. Wire and her young, emotionally immature tenant. It is not bridged when the Writer claims her loneliness is unnecessary. "This house is full of people," he tells her. "People I let rooms to," she replies, "Less than strangers to me" (65). Originally a kind of surrogate mother to the young Tennessee Williams, Mrs. Wire becomes here more of a sibyl figure haunting the underworld in which the older Williams finds himself.

The final line of *Vieux Carré* inverts the Writer's earlier one. As he leaves the rooming house, the Writer speaks for the aging playwright, who bids farewell to these ghostly characters ("their voices are echoes, fading but remembered") and then announces: "This house is empty now" (116). What does he mean? For one thing, as mentioned earlier, the line suggests that "this house" is a mental landscape, the place in the playwright's mind where he stores his creative powers, and that they are gone; the older narrator all but acknowledges this earlier in the play, when he says: "the cash which is the stuff you use in your work can be overdrawn, depleted, like a reservoir going dry in a long season of drought" (44). But the final line also echoes the ending of *The Cherry Orchard* by Anton Chekhov, whom Williams revered. In that play, the elderly butler Firs is left behind in the house, presumably to die, suggesting that the fate of the older playwright is a similar one. While his younger self leaves to launch his career, his older self must remain behind, entombed, to await death.[7] This notion is perhaps reinforced by an allusion to Poe's "The Fall of the House of Usher." Since Mrs. Wire's haunted house recalls its famous predecessor, in which a character is buried alive, then in the final line Williams is declaring that the loss of his imaginative powers and the anguish of his divided self have left him feeling buried alive.

In *The Divided Self*, R. D. Laing writes that, for the schizophrenic, there is no sanctuary: "The place of safety of the self becomes a prison. Its would-be haven becomes a hell . . . It ceases even to have the safety of a solitary cell" (162). This describes the aging Williams and his characters in *Vieux Carré*, except the Writer (and perhaps Nursie). None has Laura's glass menagerie or Blanche's make-believe powers or Shannon's Mexican getaway. They all lament, like Nightingale late in the play, that they can find no sense of sanctuary; quoting the Bible to the Writer, who callously laughs at him, the painter cries: "Foxes have holes, but the Son of Man hath nowhere to hide his Head!" (92). *Vieux Carré* expresses the older playwright's inability to find sanctuary for his tortured self in the muses we have discussed and in others. There are allusions to his own mother ("Edwina, Edwina," cries a tourist in the courtyard); Ozzie, the childhood nurse who told him stories (Nursie represents her),[8] and the grandmother he loved, "Grand," whose angelic ghost appears to the Writer (26–27, 85). However, none of these is strong enough to overcome his identity crisis.

Nevertheless, *Vieux Carré* helps Williams. He relives his crisis; expresses his painful feelings; faces certain realities, such as his own aging, and realizes that he is no longer the person he thought he was. These are initial steps Rothenberg recommends for the orphan in trauma (192). But the playwright's identity crisis will continue until he literally re-creates himself from the point of view of his older self, reviewing his entire life and work and discovering its nature and meaning. That is what he accomplishes in his next memory play, *Something Cloudy, Something Clear*. He resolves his crisis by giving an identity to the older Other he has become and reconnecting with his memories and muses, not as nightmares this time, but as sources of self-discovery. This does not mean the task will be easy, however; because if the playwright is honest, he must see himself exactly as he was and now is, blemishes and all, which can be overwhelming.

Something Cloudy, Something Clear unfolds in the mind of the older Williams, who is recalling in 1980 events that transpired in Provincetown during the summer of 1940.[9] Funded by a small Rockefeller grant, Williams was there revising *Battle of Angels* when he met Kip Kiernan, his "first great male [love]" (*Memoirs,* 52). Described in the play as being "apparitionally beautiful," Kip was a Canadian draft dodger and dancer with whom Williams conducted a passionate but short-lived affair documented in letters to Donald Windham (7–12).[10] However, when the bisexual Kip chose to end the affair, Williams was devastated. For years afterward, he mourned the loss by carrying Kip's photograph in his wallet and by dedicating his first short story collection, *One Arm and Other Stories*, to him. The last time Williams saw him was in 1944 in the hospital room where Kip was dying of a brain tumor.

The play is expressionistic rather than realistic. It takes place amid the dunes where August, the playwright's young persona, lives in a deteriorating, largely roofless shack that is being reclaimed by nature's swirling sands, booming sea, and winds. In expressionistic terms, the set represents the ruins of the playwright's aging imagination, and in its liminal quality, it suggests the boundary between life and death, where the older Williams feels he resides. At the top of the dunes throughout the play, ghosts of real-life persons appear and speak, among them, the playwright's childhood love, Hazel Kramer; Frank Merlo, his devoted long-time lover who died of cancer, and the actress, Tallulah Bankhead, whom he first met that summer.

Adding to the strangeness of the dramatic world is what August calls the photographic "double exposure" effect (38). As in *Vieux Carré*, we hear Williams's older persona speaking through the young August; but here there is less delineation. They have almost become one, making the moment-to-moment switches in point of view seem natural, an indication in itself of the playwright's resolving his identity crisis. This is evident in a conversation between August and Clare, Kip's young companion:

> CLARE: How long will you go on working?
> AUGUST: Till I die of exhaustion.—But not now.
> [*Pause.*]
> No, a long time from now. Today I'd rather watch Kip dance.
> CLARE: I dance, too.
> AUGUST: I noticed that last night.
> CLARE: I thought you just noticed Kip. When you stare at him like you stared at him last night, you're not seeing into his—
> AUGUST: Mind? Spirit? Look, I work myself to the point of self-immolation before I go into P-town, and honestly, Clare, I don't go looking for rarefied minds or spirits. (14–15)

The setting and tone seem less strange, however, if we recognize the associations Williams is making. The same setting appears in an early short story, "The Poet," published in *One Arm,* in which a Hart Crane-like artist lives in a beach shack below the dunes and, in the month of August, produces a great visionary tale through ecstatic self-sacrifice and immolation (65–66). Thus, forty years ago, this setting emblematized the playwright's youthful imagination; now, the dunes and weather-beaten beach house represent his aging mental landscape. Also woven into the play are allusions to Rainer Maria Rilke's poems; in fact, in the final lines, August quotes from the tenth *Duino Elegy* (85). Williams loved Rilke, keeping a copy of his poems next to his writing desk (see Brown, 251; Jennings, 82). Many of Williams's favorite images were Rilke's, too—angels, roses, Orpheus, the unicorn—and judging by the allusions to Rilke in the title story of *One Arm*, he was reading him often during his early years.[11] *Something Cloudy, Something Clear* echoes Rilke in a number of ways. His *Sonnets to Orpheus* are dedicated to the memory of a young dancer who died,[12] just as Williams's play memorializes Kip. But it is more the tone and content of the *Duino Elegies*, their prophetic exploration of life, death, suffering, and the meaning of existence, that echo throughout Williams's play. More than one example could be given, but here are lines from the first elegy:

> They've finally no more need of us, the early-departed, one's gently weaned
> from terrestrial things as one mild you grows the breasts of a mother. But
> we, that have need of such mighty secrets, we, for whom sorrow's so often
> source of blessedest progress, could we exist without them? (31)

The timeless, expansive world of *Something Cloudy, Something Clear* and its concern with the relationship between the living and the dead seem to owes much to Rilke, just as the play's shape and theme owes much to Hart Crane, as I will discuss later.

The plot is spare. Kip and Clare stumble onto August's shack at the beach, and Kip practices his dance on an adjacent platform. They met the night before in town, but August does not learn, until the end, that Kip and Clare are dying, of brain cancer and complications from diabetes, respectively. In the shack, Clare, a non-historical character who exists in both past and present, urges August to care for the financially destitute Kip. She appeals to August's better side but realizes he is drawn to Kip for reasons other than caregiving. August negotiates at length with Kip, who is uncertain of his feelings, and finally sleeps with him, experiencing a fulfillment August calls "the parade" passing him by. However, Kip's feelings are not the same. In the meantime, August has negotiated a contract with his New York producers, the Fiddlers, and his play is accepted for production soon.

But this summary does not do justice to the play. In effect, we are seeing the older Williams watching his younger self, as if for the first time, and realizing what kind of person he was. The portrait is not flattering. August is selfish, insensitive, and sexually obsessed. When Kip fails to appear the first night, August agrees to sleep again with a drunken merchant seaman who vomits on the floor. Throughout the play, August treats Kip badly, taking advantage of his vulnerability and mocking his delays and excuses, never asking whether Kip loves him.

> KIP : . . . —Maybe I'll just take a little walk. It's late, I won't go far. [*He rises and starts off slowly.*]
> AUGUST: His voice, it sounded almost panicky. Was I that terrifying, forty years ago? [*He calls out.*] Stay in sight. If you don't, I'll pursue you. (65–66)

At one point, Clare suggests that August takes better care of his Victrola than people he likes, and the accusation rings true. Negotiating with the crude, powerful Fiddlers on the dunes, August fights valiantly for his play, refusing to do their rewrites and standing up for his rights as a dramatist. But not long after, when the gangster Bugsy Brodsky knocks down Clare, formerly one of his "firefly" girls, August stays in his shack, avoiding the conflict (54). He later deplores Bugsy's tactics but sees nothing wrong in using power himself to persuade Kip to sleep with him, and he ignores the physical toll his "amatory demands" (30) have made on the exhausted dancer. "The parade went by," August tells Clare the next evening, "it marched right by me, right by where I was waiting." Seeing Kip, a furious Clare replies: "He looks like it marched across him"(71).

These events prompt self-examination in the aging playwright. Was this an isolated case? Or has he continued to act in a similar fashion? The answer arrives with the return, in his mind, of the ghosts of Hazel Kramer, his St. Louis girlfriend; Frank Merlo, his lover who died of cancer in 1963, and Tallulah Bankhead. Appearing on the dunes, these ghosts converse with the aging playwright through August, who pays glowing tribute to them as persons he loved deeply. However, there is something unsettling about each appearance. To a one, they do *not* say they loved him. For example, August recalls that on his deathbed, Frank said, "'I'm used to you,'" when Williams offered to leave. "For a man as proud as Frank Merlo," August continues, "I guess that was a kind of declaration of love" (17). In addition, our own knowledge raises other concerns. We know that Williams was not always faithful to Merlo and that their relationship was ending when Frank was stricken (Spoto, 269–70). Also, in an interview, although not in the play, the playwright says he failed Hazel when she needed him (Jennings, 74), and he goes into a tirade with Tallulah, telling her she "pissed on my play," because of her camp rendering of Blanche DuBois.

What is being revealed to the playwright's older self is the dynamic that has given his life and art their meaning. The play's title alludes to this. *Something Cloudy, Something Clear* refers literally to the cataract in his left eye, which made it appear "cloudy." In symbolic terms, the eyes refer to his contradictory personality. His "clear" eye represents his gentler, spiritual side, the part of him interested in art, while the "cloudy" eye represents his darker side, the one "compulsively interested in sexuality" and also insensitive, cruel, and selfish. In his imagination, the clash of these opposing forces generated his greatest plays, which are battlefields pitting these two forces against each other: Blanche and Stanley; Blanche's own warring inner factions; the body/soul dichotomy of *Summer and Smoke*, and the spiritual Hannah and sensual Maxine of *The Night of the Iguana*. But in life, these contrasting impulses crippled him, making him a failure at human relationships. His "clear" side sought love, purity, and gentleness, while his "cloudy" side was selfish, insensitive, or wanted bodily satisfaction. If his "clear" side too often created unreal expectations, his "cloudy" side too often erupted, overcoming the "clear" one. The combination, he sees now, contributed to a self-destructiveness that made him hurt others, like Kip, Frank, and Hazel, and kept him from committing to love relationships or believing that others loved him (see Spoto, 270). "Being loved is a hard thing to believe," August tells Clare, who serves as a kind of conscience, "and to love is—." "Hard to believe, too?" she responds (24).

With these insights, the aging playwright finds his identity again, although what he discovers seems like cause for more despair, a litany of failed and lost loves in life to match all the lost loves in his plays: Laura's losing Jim and Tom, Blanche losing Allan and Mitch, Brick losing Skipper, Chance losing Heavenly, and so on. Williams escapes despair by turning to his greatest muse, Hart Crane,[13] and his "Voyages" poems, which help him interpret his actions. I find "Voyages" almost inscribed within *Something Cloudy, Something Clear*. The subject is astonishingly similar, Crane's love affair with Emil Opffer, and the setting seems identical—the seaside with its waves, sand, and bleached sticks (August carries some on stage in the final scene). In the second, third, and fourth "Voyages," Crane chronicles the passion he and his lover feel in language of "orphic intensity and musicality" (Mariani, 155), and at times, we can hear echoes of these poems in the play. Crane's extraordinary line, "Permit me voyage, love, into your hands . . . "

KIP: —Put the "Pavane" back on the victrola.

AUGUST: Yes— music.
[*He winds the phonograph and starts the "Pavane."*]
Still afraid? Of love?
KIP: Not of love, but —
AUGUST: What?
KIP: — The—other.—Please. I don't know what to do.
AUGUST: Will you accept my instruction?
[*Kip stares at him a moment, then slowly lowers his face. August waits, then takes Kip's hand.*]
—He could have easily broken away, but he didn't . . . (69–70)

This echo of Crane shows that, for Williams, making love to the handsome Kip was not just his "cloudy" side at work; he wanted the fulfillment Crane describes, a voyage with another into life's mysteries, and for a while, he believed his wish had come true.

In the fifth poem, Crane depicts the crushing failure of his relationship, because both have found other lovers, and in the icy final "Voyage," the mourning poet, in the wake of his loss, seeks a sign to help him understand the meaning of what happened.[14] According to Paul Mariani, he finds his answer in love's indestructibility:

> Lovers may and do betray each other, Crane too well knew. But that did not mean that the sacred idea of love need be compromised. Love remained unbetrayable because . . . because he needed it to be so. Love was a phoenix, dying and being continually reborn in the imagination, rising from its own spent ashes. (161)

This notion allows Williams to see his actions in a more forgiving light. He takes responsibility for the hurt he and his "cloudy" side caused, by depicting his own behavior in the play; but he can also interpret his failures in love as "voyages," excursions into the human heart that were valuable and contributed to the Platonic "idea of love." The word "love" (or a variation) appears more than thirty times in the play's eighty-five pages, an indication of this emotional orphan's desire to find it again near the end of his life. With Crane's guidance, he can do so, reconnecting meaningfully with those he loved, experiencing the only family he made, and bidding them a last, fond farewell.

At the end of *Something Cloudy, Something Clear*, August, Clare, and Kip share bread and wine on the beach (the play does not show the breakup of the affair). Suddenly, August kisses Clare repeatedly, calling her the Queen of his "Firefly Club" (81, 84). The reference seems obscure, but in a poem, "The Couple," Williams writes of once collecting fireflies with his sister, Rose (38), and we realize that, in the play, August is having a moment of communion with Rose and Kip, the two people he loved most; he is an Orpheus reunited with his lost Eurydices. In reality, having devoted his life to his work and provided so little space for others, Williams remains a lonely soul, yet this last night on the beach, looking back in time, he takes solace in what he has achieved and finds sanctuary in memories as he awaits the end of his life.

Perhaps now we can better understand the "mirror stage" of late adulthood; it provides both a rehearsal of and a preparation for death. If the fear of death is a fear of nothingness, then the onset of this crisis mimics death itself. In late-life plays like *Vieux Carré* and Eugene O'Neill's *The Iceman Cometh*, the characters are thrust into underworlds of despair, surrounded by ghostly figures, a means used by the playwrights to express their own feelings of being buried alive. By accepting their aging selves and transforming their ghostly muses into ancestors, as these writers do in *Long Day's Journey* and *Something Cloudy, Something Clear*, they reengage with life, though not without some despair remaining. Nothingness looms in the not-so-distant future. However, they know this and use their plays to begin to wean themselves from life, preparing for the final separation, the one their older selves must make, by visiting with ghosts of those who have already departed, muses who teach them again. *Vieux Carré* and *Something Cloudy, Something Clear* are striking contributions to this subgenre of late-life plays. While O'Neill's are undoubtedly the better and less esoteric works of art, Williams's haunting plays, written after his imaginative powers failed him, also deserve recognition as important and moving final statements.

NOTES

1. I would like to thank my wife, Kappa, for her encouragement. I also benefited from discussions with Natalie Cole, Robert Gross, Susan Hawkins, Robert Eberwein, and Rob Anderson. My thanks to all. Some of my research was made possible by an Oakland University Faculty Research Fellowship, for which I am grateful.

2. See Chandler interview (353), conducted after the premiere of *Something Cloudy, Something Clear.*

3. The play is produced in 1981, but in an interview, Williams indicates he was writing the play in 1979: "Now this play is written from the vantage point of 1979, about a boy I loved and who is now dead" (Rader, 169).

4. On *Vieux Carré*, see Rocha's summary/analysis, Simard as well as Adler. Adler explores the existence and some of the implications of the older narrator in the text (9). The most positive assessment comes from Gussow, who is sensitive to the self-reflective nature of the text. On *Something Cloudy, Something Clear*, see Isaac and Kolin, who summarizes critical responses by Frank Rich, Walter Kerr, Catharine Hughes, and John Clum (37–8). To describe the play himself, Kolin coins the term "postmodern memory play." Adamson, who directed the first production, writes a compelling and helpful introduction to the published script.

5. I am grateful to Lance Norman of Oakland University for this term.

6. *Vieux Carré* began as two separate short plays and was reworked by Williams at the urging of British director Keith Hack. See Rocha (185) and Clinton's interview with Hack. For details on Williams's New Orleans experiences, see Kenneth Holditch's articles. I wish to thank Patricia Brady, Director of Publications, and Joan L. Lennox, Docent, of the Historic New Orleans Collection for the opportunity to tour the building at 722 Toulouse Street.

7. The Writer also refers in the play to the short stories of William Saroyan (53).

Saroyan's popular 1933 story, "The Daring Young Man on the Flying Trapeze," features a young writer who dies alone of starvation in his room in the city, refusing to compromise his dreams while living in a world that remains indifferent or hostile to him (see Foster, 3–6); the situation finds echoes in *Vieux Carré*, with the young writer destitute and the older self feeling buried alive.

8. Simard makes this connection (72).

9. Leverich points out that *Something Cloudy, Something Clear* began its life as *The Parade*, a short play Williams apparently drafted after his affair with Kip ended (364). A copy of *The Parade* is in the collection of the New York Public Library for the Performing Arts at Lincoln Center, and as Leverich's research shows, it bears little resemblance to its later offspring, seeming to owe more to D. H. Lawrence, although the same setting of beach and dunes is used.

10. See also Leverich 361–68.

11. For example, on the first page, a character is described as looking "like a broken statue of Apollo, and he had also the coolness and impassivity of a stone figure," which suggests Rilke's famous poem, "Archaic Torso of Apollo." Later in the story, a minister recalls his childhood reaction to a panther at the zoo (22–23), an obvious echo of Rilke's "The Panther" (see Rilke, *Translations,* 159, 181).

12. Vera Ouckama Knoop. See the translator's notes in *Sonnets* (139–41).

13. For Crane's relationship with Williams, see Gross and Debusscher. Harold Bloom discusses Crane as Williams's "only" true literary precursor (2–5). In the foreword to a collection of Crane's letters, Paul Brooks writes that Crane was Williams's "idol": "Throughout the four decades of my friendship with Tennessee Williams, he remained obsessed by the Crane legend . . . " (vii).

14. My understanding of Crane's "Voyages" is indebted to Mariani's skillful and lucid interpretations (see 153–61).

WORKS CITED

Adamson, Eve. Introduction. *Something Cloudy, Something Clear*. By Tennessee Williams. New York: New Directions, 1995: viii

Adler, Thomas P. "The (Un)reliability of the Narrator in *The Glass Menagerie* and *Vieux Carré*." *Tennessee Williams Review* 3 (1981): 6–9.

Bloom, Harold. Introduction to *Tennessee Williams's* The Glass Menagerie. Ed. Bloom. New York: Chelsea, 1988: 1–5.

Bowles, Paul. Foreword to *O My Land, My Friends: The Selected Letters of Hart Crane*. Ed. Langdon Hammer and Brom Weber. New York: Four Walls Eight Windows, 1997: vii–viii.

Brown, Cecil. "Interview with Tennessee Williams," in *Conversations with Tennessee Williams*, ed. Albert J. Devlin (Jackson: University Press of Mississippi, 1986), 251–83.

Chandler, Charlotte. *The Ultimate Seduction*. Garden City: Doubleday, 1984.

Clinton, Craig. "The Reprise of Tennessee Williams' *Vieux Carré*: An Interview with Director Keith Hack." *Studies in American Drama, 1945–Present* 7.2 (1992): 265–75.

Crane, Hart. "Voyages," in *The Complete Poems and Selected Letters and Prose of Hart*

Crane, ed. Brom Weber (Garden City: Anchor, 1966), 35–41.

Debusscher, Gilbert. "'Minting their Separate Wills': Tennessee Williams and Hart Crane." *Modern Drama* 26 (1983): 455–76.

Foster, Edward Halsey. *William Saroyan: A Study of the Short Fiction*. New York: Twayne, 1991.

Gross, Robert F. "Consuming Hart: Sublimity and Gay Poetics in *SudSuddenly Last Summer*." *Theatre Journal* 47 (May 1995): 229–51.

Gussow, Mel. "Theatre: *Vieux Carré* by Williams is Revived." *New York Times* 5 April 1983, sec. 2: 13.

Holditch, W. Kenneth. "The Beginning of a Career: Tennessee Wiliams on Toulouse Street." *The Historic New Orleans Collection Quarterly* 13.1 (1995): 3–5.

———. "The Last Frontier of Bohemia: Tennessee Williams in New Orleans, 1938-1983." *Southern Quarterly* 23.2 (1985): 1-37.

Isaac, Dan. "*Something Cloudy, Something Clear*: Tennessee Revisited." *The Critical Response to Tennessee Williams*, ed. George W. Crandell (Westport: Greenwood, 1996) 278–82.

Jennings, C. Robert. "Tennessee Williams: A Candid Conversation with the Brilliant, Anguished Playwright." *Playboy* April 1973: 69.

Kolin, Philip C. "*Something Cloudy, Something Clear*: Tennessee Williams's Postmodern Memory Play." *Journal of Dramatic Theory and Criticism* (1998): 35–55.

Laing, R. D. *The Divided Self: An Existential Study in Sanity and Madness*. Baltimore: Penguin, 1965.

Leverich, Lyle. *Tom: The Unknown Tennessee Williams*. New York: Crown, 1995.

Mariani, Paul. *The Broken Tower: A Life of Hart Crane*. New York: Norton, 1999.

O'Neill, Eugene. *The Iceman Cometh*. New York: Vintage, 1946.

———. *Long Day's Journey into Night*. New Haven: Yale University Press, 1989.

Rader, Dotson. "The Art of Theater V: Tennessee Williams." *Paris Review* 23.81 (1981): 145–85.

Rilke, Rainer Maria. *Duino Elegies*. Trans. J. B. Leishman and Stephen Spender. London: Hogarth, 1939.

———. *Sonnets to Orpheus*. Trans. M. D. Herter Norton. New York: Norton, 1942.

———. *Translations from the Poetry of Rainer Maria Rilke*. Ed. and trans. M. D. Herter Norton. New York: Norton, 1938.

Rocha, Mark W. "*Small Craft Warnings*, *Vieux Carré*, and *A Lovely Sunday for Creve Coeur*," in *Tennessee Williams: A Guide to Research and Performance*, ed. Philip C. Kolin (Westport: Greenwood, 1998) 183–93.

Rothenberg, Rose-Emily. "The Orphan Archetype." *Psychological Perspectives* 14 (1983): 181–94.

Saroyan, William. "The Daring Young Man on the Flying Trapeze." *The Saroyan Special: Selected Short Stories*. Freeport: Books for Libraries, 1970: 36–39.

Simard, Rodney. "The Uses of Experience: Tennessee Williams in *Vieux Carré*." *Southern Literary Journal* 17.2 (1985): 67–78.

Spoto, Donald. *The Kindness of Strangers: The Life of Tennessee Williams*. Boston:

Little, Brown, 1985.

Williams, Tennessee. "The Angel in the Alcove." in *Collected Stories*. (New York: Ballantine, 1986), 125–32.

———. *Camino Real*. Volume 2 of *Theatre*. New York: New Directions, 1971: 417–591.

———. "The Couple." *Androgyne, Mon Amour*. New York: New Directions. 33–39.

——— . "I Am Widely Regarded as the Ghost of a Writer." *New York Times* 8 May 1977, sec. 2: 3

———. *Memoirs*. Garden City: Doubleday, 1975.

———. *One Arm and Other Stories*. New York: New Directions, 1948.

———. "The Poet." *One Arm and Other Stories*. 61–69.

———. *Something Cloudy, Something Clear*. New York: New Directions, 1995.

———. *Tennessee Williams' Letters to Donald Windham, 1940-1965*. Ed. Donald Windham. New York: Penguin, 1977.

———. *Vieux Carré*. Volume 8 of *Theatre*. New York: New Directions, 1992: 1–116.

Woodward, Kathleen. "The Mirror Stage of Old Age." in *Memory and Desire: Aging–Literature–Psychoanalysis*. Ed. Kathleen Woodward and Murray M. Schwartz. (Bloomington: Indiana University Press, 1986), 97–113.

Collapsing Resurrection Mythologies

Theatricalist Discourses of Fire and Ash in *Clothes for a Summer Hotel*

Linda Dorff

> *With the help of fire I will ascend to Ether again . . .*
> —August Strindberg, *A Dream Play* (1901)

> *The dead that have mastered fire live on, salamanders, in fire.*
> —D. H. Lawrence, "What Quetzcoatl Saw in Mexico" from
> *The Plumed Serpent* (1926)

> *I AM NOT A SALAMANDER!*
> —Tennessee Williams, *Clothes for a Summer Hotel* (1980)

The unpublished first draft of Tennessee Williams's *Clothes for a Summer Hotel* (dated April 1979) begins with an announcement to the audience that they are about to see a "ghost play" (1–1) that may represent "thin ice, very thin ice, for the metaphysical element isn't popular among the more literal-minded—who may be many among you" (1-1).[1] Such an ironic prelude may, indeed, have alerted audience members to pay less attention to literal details about the lives of Zelda and F. Scott Fitzgerald, who are its (ostensible) ghost-subjects, and to look more closely at its complex ghost-form. But by the time the play opened on Broadway March 26, 1980[2],—Williams's sixty-ninth birthday—this prologue had been cut and the "literal-minded" critical response was hardly a gift. Reviewers characterized the play as an attempt at biography that got its facts wrong, finding that it lacked "any real suggestion of the glamorous people the Fitzgeralds once had been" (Beaufort, 14). Giving voice to an earlier critical tradition that regards Williams's plays as thinly-veiled autobiographies, Thomas P. Adler claimed that Williams was "substituting the Fitzgeralds for the 'real life' portraits in *[The Glass] Menagerie*" (6).[3] Adler's speculation that the ghost characters stand for something other than the "real" Scott and

Zelda is perceptive, but their ghosts mask a more ambitious project than recapitulated autobiography. Like the meta-characters Lord Byron, Camille and Casanova from *Camino Real* (1953), the Fitzgeralds function as archetypal masks through whom Williams renegotiates his `own myths of artistic creation, death and resurrection. An ironic clue to this renegotiation is provided by the "demented woman" (222) Becky, who emerges from the asylum in which Zelda is confined to shout that she has "Transferred heads of stars!" (221). In the unpublished first draft she elaborates on this grotesquerie, claiming that she had been a Hollywood hairdresser who "invented the marcel . . . [in] my shop where I transferred famous heads, the head of Crawford, the Harlow, the Pickford for her come-back in a talkie" (1–7). While "transfer" refers to the marcel (wave) process, it also suggests severed heads transferred to different bodies, a connotation that gestures self-reflexively at the play's superimposition of the "heads," or identities of the Fitzgeralds onto bodies of discourse about resurrection that are drawn from D. H. Lawrence and August Strindberg. In the early 1940s Williams borrowed resurrection metaphors of fire and ash from Lawrence and Strindberg, recrafting them into his own phoenix-like dying artist myths. Forty years later, however, after two decades of late plays that insistently deny characters any lasting form of redemption, *Clothes for a Summer Hotel* ironically reverses Williams's earlier uses of fire and ash metaphors, collapsing his earlier modernist resurrection mythologies.

Fire and Purification: The Thesis Plays

Anti-resurrection discourse in *Clothes for a Summer Hotel* can be best understood by briefly examining the first clear evidences of resurrection structures in Williams's dramaturgy, which seem to emerge in two plays written in 1941: *I Rise in Flame, Cried the Phoenix* and *Auto-da-Fé*. These one-acts may be understood to constitute "thesis plays" because they present stripped-down, theoretical models of fire-and-ash resurrections that establish abstract paradigms for Williams's major "Broadway" plays.[4] Both represent fiery deaths as purifications, but whereas *I Rise in Flame, Cried the Phoenix* is an unabashed psalm to Lawrence in which Williams translates Lawrence's metaphors of sexual burning into his own vocabularies, *Auto-da-Fé* is clearly derived from Strindberg's chamber plays, in which fire consumes not only individuals but houses, purifying societies by unmasking false identities.

In its revisioning of the death of Lawrence, *I Rise in Flame* might be seen as an attempt to resurrect him at a time when modernism was dying, exposing the extent to which Williams's earlier plays look back to modernist ideologies. The impulse toward resurrection was fundamental to modernist works of literature and drama, which tend to resemble "purification rites" (Karl, 166), similar to apocalyptic scenarios in which the historic past, which is viewed as corrupt or obsolete, is swept away or rewritten (in modernist epics like *Ulysses* or *The Waste Land*), and replaced by a "new" (Jerusalem) order freed of normal constraints of time and space. Lawrence's work employed apocalyptic forms and scenarios in which fire or metaphoric burning was the medium of destruction and purification. His major redemptive archetypes were usually drawn from ancient myths involving fire, such as that of the phoenix, the "immortal bird" that is "burnt, burnt alive, burnt down/to hot, flocculent ash" (Lawrence, *Complete Poems,* 728) to rise again out of its ashes. Lawrence superimposed sexual burning onto other figures of resurrection, seen in his heretical novella *The Man Who Died,* in which the risen Christ is revisioned as being reborn in a fuller way after having sex with a female god.[5] Lawrence believed that resurrection is achieved through sexual touch, which he saw as the highest form of spirtuality,[6] a credo that Williams interpreted as "a belief in the purity of sensual life, the purity and the beauty of it" (Interview, 221). Fire is the primary metaphor Lawrence uses to signify sex, which is also linked to metaphors of the sun and blood when, for example, the sexual awakening of the *Man Who Died* is represented as a dawning sun that "sent its fire running along his limbs" (207).

Although *I Rise in Flame* utilizes Lawrence's metaphoric phoenix and sun, Williams's Lawrence is dying from the metaphoric burning of tuberculosis. In *Illness as Metaphor*, Susan Sontag notes that "fever in TB was a sign of an inward burning: the tubercular is someone 'consumed' by ardor, that ardor leading to the dissolution of the body" (20). Because tuberculosis was seen to aestheticize the sufferer in death, it became a Romantic metaphor for resurrection that Williams adopted in his apprentice works of the late 1930s.[7] In *I Rise in Flame*, Lawrence cries, "it's the fever! I'm burning, burning and still I never burn out" (69), subtly linking TB to Lawrence's dark sun metaphor, which represents a sexual life force that is "dark, throbbing, darker than blood" (Lawrence, *Ladybird*, 180). Williams's Lawrence dies like a great, blinding sun going down,[8] extending "his arms out like a Biblical prophet" who stretches "out the long, sweet arms of [his] art [to] embrace the whole world" (74), performing Williams's early thesis that art's visions consume the body in flame, purifying it.

The most significant (theatrical and literary) innovation Williams created in these one-acts was realized in his metonymic synthesis that fused Lawrence's image of an artist's burning body to Strindberg's metaphor of a house on fire. Building on the Lawrencean idea that "true fire is invisible" (*Ladybird,* 180), Williams recasts invisibility as theatrical transparency in Frieda's description of Lawrence's burning consumption:

> His body's a house that's made out of tissue paper and caught on fire. The walls are transparent, they're all lit up with flame! When people are dying the spirit ought to go out, it ought to die out slowly before the flesh, you shouldn't be able to see it so terribly brightly consuming the walls that give it a place to inhabit. (67)

Williams translates Lawrencean fire into his own metonym that expressionistically stages the terror of a dying soul seen through the transparent tissue paper "clothes" of the body. Although Frieda's speech does not suggest a resurrection, the play's title vehemently claims it for Lawrence.

The end of *Auto-da-Fé* literalizes the burning house-body metonym, staging a house in flames with the protagonist, Eloi Bordelon, inside. Like medieval and

Renaissance Spanish religious *autos*, *Auto-da-Fé* is an allegorical drama, but one that enacts a modernist purification rite, borrowing its subject and metaphors from one of Strindberg's lesser-known chamber plays, *The House that Burned*. *Auto-da-Fé* somewhat resembles Strindberg's *A Dream Play* and another chamber play, *The Pelican*, which end as houses burn. Although *The House that Burned* has already been reduced to ashes when the play begins, it has such striking parallels to *Auto-da-Fé* that it is clearly its primary source: Strindberg's house was set on a city block called "Morass" (146)[9], suggesting a "swamp of human pollution" (Johnson, "Introduction," 141), and Williams's house is set in the "fetid swamp" (134) of the Vieux Carré, in which "every imaginable kind of degeneracy springs up" (134). Strindberg's Stranger is a near-ghost who may have returned to his childhood home from the dead, embodying an abstract version of the "characterless" (53) type of character described in the preface to *Miss Julie*. In a direct allusion to Strindberg's text, Williams's Eloi calls himself "a stranger, a person unknown! I live in a house where nobody knows my name!" (140). As Elinor Fuchs has observed, character development in Strindberg's *To Damascus*, which also includes a Stranger, seems to be derived from an allegorical, "meaning-saturated landscape" (32). Similarly, in *The House that Burned*, the Stranger's character is developed as he rifles through the house's ashes, attempting to "read" (155) them as a text.[10] Observing that his father's bookcase has been reduced to a "scrap pile" (160) of ashes, he recalls his initiation into sexual knowledge through pornographic "printed work with illustrated jackets, which aroused my interests" (160) that was kept locked in the bookcase. *Auto-da-Fé* echoes this reference to pornography when Eloi is disturbed by a "lewd photograph . . . an indecent picture" (144) he discovers in the mail. In both plays, pornography is used as a representation of society's corruption of sexual desire, and Eloi burns the picture, his body and house, "for the sake of burning, for God, for the purification!" (141), as if to purge the larger social order.

Whereas Strindberg's chamber plays and other post-Inferno works are forerunners of expressionist drama and Williams's play arrives two decades after the vogue of expressionism, both use the burning house-body metonym in the service of social critique. Strindberg's houses are the antithesis of containers for the stable self, for they function as hiding places for the secrets of their inhabitants. Strindberg's late plays, and *The Ghost Sonata* in particular, are structured around scenes of unmasking in which the lies and secrets hidden in houses are exposed as the house burns down. When the mother's lies are revealed in *The Pelican*, the house is burnt down with the family inside, purifying their ashes. This typical Strindbergian resurrection structure differs from Lawrence's Western, semi-religious model in its debt to alchemy and Asian philosophy. The mytho-scientific approach of alchemy viewed fire as an agent of metamorphosis, reflected in the Daughter of Indra's claim that "with the help of fire I will ascend to Ether again" (*Dream Play*, 81). The suffering that Strindberg endured in his Inferno-madness was relieved when he discovered the philosophy of Emanuel Swedenborg, whom he called his "redeemer" (*Inferno*, 256). In his diary *Inferno*, Strindberg records his path to "spiritual purification" (256) and "salvation" (255). This personal resurrection experience is mirrored in parts of *A*

Dream Play, as when the Poet declares that "suffering is redemption, and death release" (85). Death is the "the only positive value in the Strindbergian fictional universe" (Rokem, 131), representing the great release from suffering in a hellish world.

Williams translated the burning body/house metonym developed in these thesis plays into an exemplar for the entrapment of his desperate visionaries in the early Broadway plays. This is seen in set directions for *The Glass Menagerie* (1945), which refer to apartment buildings that are *"always burning with the slow and implacable fires of human desperation"* (143). When Blanche finds herself in "desperate, desperate circumstances . . . Caught in a trap" (400), she rushes to the window crying out, "Fire! Fire! Fire!" (390) as if she were the burning house. *Orpheus Descending* (1957) offers the clearest articulation of the resurrection potential of the body-house figure as Val disappears into the flaming confectionary at the play's end leaving his snakeskin jacket/shroud behind. The use of mythic structure—particularly that derived from Christ and Orpheus—begins to fall away from Williams's plays beginning with *Suddenly Last Summer* in 1958, which he questions the viability of mythic strategies to present "a true story of our time and the world we live in" (*Suddenly*, 382). In the twenty-five years that followed, Williams's plays abandoned the structure of the family house to explore the liminal zones of bars, boarding houses, hotels and asylums. These transient spaces necessarily alter the configuration of the body-house figure, for the condition of homelessness marks these transient spaces Williams called "Dragon Country, the country of pain . . . an uninhabitable country which is inhabited" (*I Can't Imagine*, 138). In this theatrical territory of impossibility redemptive endings become impossible and do not appear again in the late plays.

Scattering the Ashes of Strindberg and Lawrence: Clothes for a Summer Hotel
While *I Rise in Flame, Cried the Phoenix* and *Auto-da-Fé* are plays of fire that lead up to heroic, burning purifications, *Clothes for a Summer Hotel* is an anti-heroic ghost play of ashes that rejects the earlier plays' redemptive paradigms. It was not a ghost play in its inception, however, in 1977 or 1978 when Williams first began writing a play under the working title *Tragedies of the Drawing Room*.[11] This draft was conceived as a play about the Lost Generation and included the characters of Gertrude Stein, Alice Toklas, Janet Flanner and Natalie Barney, as well as the Fitzgeralds and Gerald and Sara Murphy. Denying any attempt at docudrama, Williams noted at this early stage that "I draw these people intuitively. They are filtered through my particular set of sensibilities. It is by no means biographical in any part" (*Tragedies*, n.p.). This draft was apparently put aside until April 1979, when Williams rewrote it under the title *Clothes for a Summer Hotel (A Ghost-Play in 4 Scenes)*,[12] focusing on the Fitzgeralds and adopting the ghost format. Set outside Highland Hospital in Asheville, North Carolina[13] where Zelda Fitzgerald died in a fire in 1948,[14] the script draws many plot details from Nancy Milford's biography *Zelda*. Williams was not so much concerned with the facts themselves (or their accuracy) as he was with their poetic potential, as seen in the play's development of the ash-Asheville theme. It is possible that Milford's book may have initially suggested the ghost form to Williams, in its mention that Zelda felt Asheville to be "haunted" (Milford, 371), and when

Scott, lamenting the progression of Zelda's madness, says that "I cannot live in the ghost town which Zelda has become" (Milford, 319). Such references are of minor importance, however, for the basic ghost structure was obviously derived from Strindberg's chamber plays, *A Dream Play* and *The Dance of Death*. It is probable that inspiration also came from Strindberg's diary chronicling his own period of madness, *Inferno*, in which he makes reference to an asylum in which he was confined in as being near the "top of the hill" (184) like the Asheville asylum. At another point in the diary he describes people in a mental hospital as if they were the ghosts of Asheville: "I found myself in the company of spectres, faces like death's-heads, faces of the dying" (106).

The Fitzgeralds are the lens through which Williams recasts his resurrection tropes, seemingly because they are so antiheroic. Lawrence's resurrection metaphors are physically heroic, involving visceral deaths and sexual risings while Strindberg traces a spiritual path to redemption discovered through madness, isolation and bizarre journeys. But F. Scott Fitzgerald, read as a signifier, is the American poster boy for artistic failure, a pop culture icon standing for a malaise of success gone wrong through celebrity, alcoholism and crack-up. More people have heard his claim that "there are no second acts in American lives"[15] (and therefore, no come-back) than have read *The Great Gatsby*. And Zelda, by association and her debilitating madness, is culturally interpreted much the same way. Zelda and Scott are significantly different from other writers Williams has recreated as subjects of his dying-artist myths: for example, according to Williams's interpretation, Lawrence died of tuberculosis and through his burning, rose like a phoenix; Hart Crane's suicide leap into the Caribbean made him one with his subject, the sea; and Vachel Lindsay, wandering poet of the American plains drank Lysol, burning and purifying his body.[16] In contrast to these implied salvations through poetic deaths, when Williams transfers the heads of the Fitzgeralds (to use Becky's metaphor) onto other bodies of resurrection discourse appropriated from Strindberg and Lawrence, it may be heard/read ironically *precisely because* of their difference from Williams's earlier heroic poet-models.

Williams's late theatricalism foregrounds the artificiality/artifice of the denaturalized ghost form as an ultimate simulacrum, representing not the logic of the "real" or of reproduction (mimesis).[17] Instead, the ghosts and ghost-world of the play stage a reproduction of a reproduction—what Jean Baudrillard has defined as "that which is already reproduced. The hyperreal, . . . which is [already] entirely in simulation" (146). The play's theatricality foregrounds the simulated return to life of dead characters who usher in the realm of illogic, or the play's "world of make-believe" (214). Giles Deleuze theorizes that "the secret of the eternal return is that it does not express an order opposed to the chaos engulfing it. On the contrary, it is nothing other than chaos itself, or the power of affirming chaos" (264). In his "Author's Note" to *Clothes for a Summer Hotel*, Williams embraces this chaos and illogic:

> . . . all plays are ghost plays, since players are not actually whom they play. Our reason for taking extraordinary license with time and place is that

in an asylum and on its grounds liberties of this kind are quite prevalent: and also these liberties allow us to explore in more depth what we believe is truth of character. (202)

This note, which replaced the Prologue that was cut from the first draft, refers to licenses that are remarkably similar to those Strindberg claimed for the dream form in his "Explanatory Note" at the beginning of *A Dream Play*, in which he alerts his audience that the play attempts:

> to imitate the disconnected but apparently logical form of a dream. Everything can happen; everything is possible and likely. Time and space do not exist; on an insignificant basis of reality the imagination spins and weaves new patterns: a blending of memories, experiences, free inventions, absurdities, and improvisations. (19)

On the surface, it would seem as if Strindberg's note and play conscientiously violate many of the naturalistic tenets he argued for a decade earlier in his preface to *Miss Julie*, but the chamber plays actually realize the spirit of experimentalism that charactererized the preface to a much greater extent than the earlier play. To be sure, *Clothes for a Summer Hotel* owes its ghost form to the chamber plays, but while Williams's Author's Note seems to be an imitation, the play's metadiscourse opposes Strindbergian redemption from a late-twentieth-century postmodern perspective. This is accomplished through ironic emphasis on references to fire and ash that foreground the theatricality of the play's "mock-up" set that counterfeits (past) fire, its superimpositions of past and present time, its unmasking of writing as simulation and its denaturalized ghost characters.

Simulating the Asylum: Mock-up Facades

The set in *Clothes for a Summer Hotel* is dominated by the "'mock-up' facade" (204) of the asylum in Asheville, North Carolina where Zelda Fitzgerald was burned to "indistinguishable ash" (204) in a 1948 fire. The idea of ashes does not indicate, however, that it is the site of any sort of phoenix-like resurrection—instead, its *"unrealistically tall"* (204) gates and its "mock-up" style brand the set as a simulacrum that does not simulate reality, but calls attention to its artificiality. As Williams observes in his Author's Note, the notion of the ghost—the eternal return—conjoined with madness allows for the ultimate "license" to be taken, rupturing theatrical signifying systems that connect dramatic place (the idea of the "real" hospital) to stage space (how the asylum is represented on stage) (Issacharoff, 211–12). In calling attention to the "mock-up" nature of the asylum, the set exaggerates its theatricality, suggesting that only the shell, or ash, of theatrical simulation remains. When the asylum is referred to as a "madhouse" (214), it echoes Strindberg's vision of the world as both hell and a madhouse (inspired by Swedenborg). *A Dream Play* labels academia "an insane asylum" (39) and the

Stranger in *The House that Burned* says that he "thought the world was a madhouse!" (161). *The Ghost Sonata* continues Strindberg's indictment:

> Jesus Christ descended into hell—that was his journey on earth, this madhouse, this reformatory, this charnel house the earth; and the mad-men killed him, when he wanted to set them free, but the robber was released the robber always gets people's sympathy!—Alas for all of us. Savior of the world, save us; we perish! (227)

Williams had adopted the Strindbergian infernalist position that the earth is hell from the time of his early apprentice plays, such as *Not About Nightingales* (1938), and this (sometimes-barely-seen) philosophical underpinning runs throughout his canon. It is in late plays such as *Clothes* and *The Two-Character Play* (1967–1980), however, that the chamber plays' vision of the earth-as-madhouse comes fully forward. In a 1972 interview, Williams acknowledged that his drama was moving toward a different way of staging madness, saying "I think that I'm growing into a more direct form, one that fits people and societies going a bit mad" ("A Talk," 218). The madhouse-asylum in *Clothes*, however, is not represented with the modernist angst that permeates Strindberg's late plays, but presents it in a spirit of postmodern irony. For example, in a reference to Scott's movie scripts, Zelda asks him if Hollywood isn't called the "world of make-believe? Isn't it a sort of madhouse, too? You occupy one there, and I occupy one here" (214), establishing a theatrical-ist correlative between movies and the madhouse-theatre.

Visual allusions to fire and ash metaphors of Lawrence and Strindberg abound in the set, establishing a semiotic field that may be read as a silent (unsaid, ironic) level of the play's metadiscourse. A Lawrencean fire metaphor is staged as "a bush of flickering red leaves" (204), recalling several novels in which Lawrence deployed the symbol of the bush to stand for various types of primitive, animalistic and uncon-scious connections between humans and nature. This is illustrated in *St. Mawr* when Lewis' hair is repeatedly called a "bush" that flames with red color, signifying his robust undercurrent of sexuality. Lawrence alludes to the biblical burning bush in *Kangaroo* when Jack says, "If there was an individual inside the brightly burning bush . . . even if it was a sort of God in the bush, let him come out, man to man" (45). Here, Lawrence typically revisions his biblical source in a modernist frame, seriously daring God to jump out. Williams revisions Lawrence in a postmodern version of the bush:

> ZELDA: . . . can we turn the bench at an angle that doesn't force me to look at the flaming bush here?
> SCOTT: It's such a lovely bush.
> ZELDA: If you're attracted by fire. Are you attracted by fire?
> SCOTT: The leaves are—radiant, yes, they're radiant as little torches. I feel as if they'd warm my hands if I—
> ZELDA: I feel as if they'd burn me to unrecognizable ash. You see, the

demented often have the gift of Cassandra, the gift of—
> SCOTT: The gift of—?
> ZELDA: Premonition! I WILL DIE IN FLAMES! (219)

Williams's text ironically plays with the bush as a simulacrum, regarding it with a sort of winking, elbow-jabbing humor, as if to say, "See that symbol there? It's such a lovely symbol."

This was emphasized in Oliver Smith's set design for the play's 1980 premiere, in which the bush, like the asylum, was a mock-up, a cut-out of a bush, with a revolving light behind it to simulate flame. Rather than viewing the burning bush as a signifier of the identity of God ("I am that I am") that can, in turn, bestow a sense of identity to those who gaze upon it, Zelda feels fire will rob her of all identity, reducing her to "unrecognizable ash" that is not purified. Her claim to possess "premonition" is ironized by her ghosted state—she is already dead, and should, instead, be claiming to remember. But in Williams's collapsed time frames only the present tense is allowed.

Allusions to Strindberg's ash metaphors are found in the black smudges that mark the mock-up facade as if it had been "scorched" (206) by the 1948 fire, recalling *The House that Burned*, which, like *Clothes for a Summer Hotel*, takes place after the fire has occurred. Strindberg's house is in ashen ruins with only partial walls, as the fire took place in a distinct past time, but Williams's asylum is suspended in a weird limbo. In the play's dialogue, past episodes are linguistically recalled in the present tense, creating a ghost-negative effect that superimposes various times, disrupting linear logic. The set is also presented as a type of ghost-negative in which the "mock-up" asylum bears the marks of the past, but also appears as it might have in an earlier time: thus, Williams has specified that "the entire building must be in 'sudden perspective' so that the third (top) floor of it . . . is seen" (204). In this upper-story space, the past fire is theatrically recalled in the present time of the play when:

> *The upper stories light with flame and [Zelda] cries out, crouching, hand to her eyes. There is a ghostly echo of women burning at a locked gate. The intern/Edouard, the doctor, the two sisters, all rush toward her. Zelda waves them away.*
> ZELDA: Sorry, nothing happened, it was a trick of light . . .
> DR. ZELLER: May we continue without a disturbance of this kind.
> ZELDA: For what purpose? I don't understand the purpose.
> DR. ZELLER [*to intern*]: Explain!
> ZELDA: Yes, do!—Explain the inexplicable to me, please.
> [*All except the Intern/Edouard withdraw.*]
> INTERN: Shadows of lives, tricks of light, sometimes illuminate things.
> ZELDA: Not to us. To audiences of a performance of things past.
> (231)

In this scene, the simulated flickering of flame in the upper stories of the facade, along with the "ghostly echo of women burning at a locked gate" parodically echo the final image of *A Dream Play*, when Indra's Daughter enters the castle and "the backdrop is lighted by the burning castle and shows a wall of human faces, asking, sorrowing, despairing . . . " (86). Strindberg's final tableaux is offered as a serious formulation of a non-Western, modernist alternative to biblical resurrection myths, in which fire causes the castle's roof to bloom as a "giant chrysanthemum" (86). In Williams's play, the flickering of lights and sounds do not happen in any resurrectionist sequence, but seem to randomly flare up and are gone just as quickly. On the present-time ghosted stage, it is regarded as "nothing," only a simulated "disturbance," a theatricalist "trick of light." When Zelda says that such shadows illuminate nothing to "audiences of a performance of things past," Williams's text ironically gestures at United States audiences who are so steeped in realist dramas about the past that they cannot decode any other form.

Time: The Past—Still Always Present
The ghosts in *Clothes for a Summer Hotel* linger in a purgatorial state of present-time limbo, frozen in static moments that dissolve any possibility of future redemption. Unlike Williams's earlier "memory" plays that romantically displace characters into a past narrative frame, ghosts in this play speak of the past in the present tense, reminding the audience that "the past—[is] still always present" (280). Both Lawrence and Strindberg imagined a poetics that could conflate past and present times, as many modernists attempted to do.[18] In his 1918 essay "The Poetry of the Present," for example, Lawrence speculates about a "poetry of the immediate present . . . [in which] there is no perfection, no consummation, nothing finished. The strands are all flying, quivering and intermingling into the web" (*Complete Poems*, 182).[19] Strindberg suggested the idea as early as his preface to *Miss Julie* in which he describes his "characterless" characters as "conglomerates of past and present" (*Five Plays*, 54). In his chamber play *Stormy Weather*, when the Brother remarks that "one forgets the present . . . ," the Gentleman replies, "There isn't any present—what's right now is empty nothingness" (116). Both writers betray their respective desires to discover a time mode that will most accurately re-present reality. While Lawrence seems to feel he can directly reproduce time if he reaches out fast enough to grab its "quivering" physical essence, Strindberg prefigures the existentialist *nada*, suggesting that "now" is a vacuum.

In contrast to this, Williams's play with time deliberately produces a temporal confusion in which specific biographical dates—such as the 1948 asylum fire in which Zelda died, the 1940 date of Scott's death and the 1926 date of Zelda's affair with the aviator Edouard—are detached from a past time, dissolving the play's narrative structure into a juxtaposition of episodes that ruptures any sense of stable historical and/or biographical representation of its literary characters, presenting them as ghosted simulacra. Thomas P. Adler notes the confusion, proposing that the time of the play could be read in two ways, suggesting first that the play's action occurs briefly before the 1947 asylum fire (11). Although this view could be supported by interpreting Gerald Murphy's statement that "it will all be over in—one hour and forty-five minutes" (207) as a literal reference to when the fire will occur, Murphy's voice is said to be "*spectral*" (211), speaking as one already dead. When it is understood that all the ghosts speak of the past in the present tense, his observation becomes simply another ghostly displacement of past narrative into a present frame. Murphy's remark could be understood more accurately as a metadramatic reference to the actual playing time of the drama, allowing the "present" to be understood as the present time of performance in the theatre. Adler concedes that it is "equally possible" (Adler, 11) that the fire may have already occurred, citing Zelda's question, "Why should this be demanded of me now after all the other demands? —I thought that obligations stopped with death!" (212), which is a clear acknowledgment of her ghosted state. Williams notes that the degree to which characters "betray an awareness of their apparitional state" (204) may be a director's choice, privileging performance over text (in this instance).

Ghost Characters: Mist Over the Proscenium
The ghosts of Zelda and Scott have been disfigured by age and when they first meet, they do not recognize each other. Zelda sees Scott as "an impostor!— with] No resemblance to Scott" (211), overtly reading his ghost as an actor detached from any identifiable character. This is somewhat similar to Hummel's observation in *The Ghost Sonata* that his fiancée of sixty years ago "doesn't recognize me" (200), which develops the modernist theme that time and the repetition of modern, industrial life change appearances, masking people's souls. Most of Strindberg's apparitional characters in the chamber plays, such as *The Ghost Sonata's* Milkmaid and the Stranger in *The House that Burned* seem to embody this masked form of living death. In *The Ghost Sonata*, a family eats their "usual ghost supper" (207), so called because "They look like ghosts . . . And they've kept this up for twenty years, always the same people, who say the same thing" (208). Following his traumatic experience in World War I, Lawrence expressed that a similar condition had come over him, as if "my soul lay in the tomb—not dead, but with a flat stone over it, a corpse, become corpse-cold."[20] The modern death of the soul was noted by the Poet in *A Dream Play* in near-Shakespearean meter: "Now they're screaming because they have to die! Scream when they're born, and scream when they die!" (714). The Poet's modernist protest is echoed by Zelda, saying,"Between the first wail of an infant and the last gasp of the dying—it's all an arranged pattern of submission to what's been prescribed for us unless we escape into madness or acts of creation" (274).

These acts of mad creation are proliferated in the ghosts' theatricalist acknowledgments that they are performing various identities, for actors/characters have "multiple selves as well as what you call dual genders" (269). The ghosted characters are presented as performers against the theatricalist facade as "shadows of lives" (231) that cannot mimetically represent, but only suggest that "players are not actually whom they play" ("Author's Note," 202). When Zelda at first feels she cannot face Scott, the Intern tells her that she "must play it" (212) like an actress to which she replies, "As if it existed?" (212). Scott is exposed as a performer in references to his inappropriate costuming in unseasonable summer clothes. This idea may have come from Strindberg's *Ghost Sonata*, in which the apparitional Milkmaid is said to wear "summer clothes" (194). It also seems to echo a letter written by Lawrence upon his return from World War I in 1915, in which he says he has "a feel of grave clothes about me" (*Collected Letters,* 309). The inappropriateness of Scott's clothing seems to be akin to the mock-up set and other theatricalist devices, making his appearance even stranger and foregrounding his clothes as a costume.

Scott's "grave clothes" seem to go with Zelda's appearance as "a savage ghost in a bedraggled tutu" (274), her costume alone suggesting that she has not been "transformed" (258) or somehow resurrected, but is "more demented than ever, and now violent, too" (225). She changes clothing in a highly theatricalized ritual when the nuns "slowly lift their batwing sleeves [that] mask Zelda's costume change" (273) and then lower them to reveal Zelda in her tutu. This innovation is reminiscent of the Kabuki-inspired stage assistants in *The Milk Train Doesn't Stop Here Anymore* (1962) who change scenes in front of the audience. Williams, who was inspired by Noh and Kabuki theatre in the later years felt a kinship with Strindberg's interest in Japanese theatre and most likely derived this "masking" scene from a Kabuki technique that Strindberg utilized in *The Ghost Sonata*, in which an Asian-style "death screen" is placed in front of a dying character.

Writers And Writing: Dissolving Representation

Zelda's theatricalist attempts to dance and Scott's continual falling down are heavily encoded with allusions to Strindberg's work, making significant departures from resurrectionist discourse about writers and writing. In the April 1979 (unpublished draft), Gerald Murphy links Zelda's "dancing craze" to the "mediaeval aberration called Dancing Madness which coincided, I think, with some outbreak of the Plague, and people went dancing madly around until they fell in the filth and contagion of the streets" (1–6). In Strindberg's *Inferno*, he records a modern "dance of death" (245) in which he was told of an old woman who "dances, dances, indefatigitably, dressed like a bride . . . and weeps, too and fears that Death is coming to fetch her" (244). He apparently based parts of *The Dance of Death* on this story, in which the Captain performs a wild Hungarian dance before falling to the floor "senseless" (127). Williams borrows both physical movements—dancing and falling—as metaphors for artistic decline in *Clothes for a Summer Hotel*. Zelda ostensibly gave up her writing at Scott's request and replaced it with dancing, but she has "come late to the dance" and dances "more wildly" than the rest, feeling the music to be "a thousand knives at her breast" (223), threatening dismemberment. Scott, on the other hand, falls down throughout the play, theatrically physicalizing the myth of his decline. In *The Dance of Death*, following his collapse after the wild dance, the Captain, who like Scott, is a "famous writer . . . [but] of textbooks" (115), continues to "feel like I'm sitting and falling at the same time" (129). Williams parallels this when Scott is "about to fall" (258) with the theatrical sound effect of "the word 'fall' [that] is repeated as if an echo were fading into the wind" (258). Strindberg's *Dance*, however, tells the story of an anonymous marriage, whereas

Clothes relates the decline paradigm of the highly publicized "storybook marriage" (*Dance,* 278) of media icons, and so produces more contemporary meanings.

Williams also borrows Strindberg's key vampire metaphor to characterize the ways in which Fitzgerald, Ernest Hemingway and the Murphys have fed upon their subjects. In *The Dance of Death*, Alice's accusation that her husband is a "vampire . . . [who] bleeds excitement from other people, interfering with their lives, manipulating their destinies" (*Dance,* 143) is a domestic complaint, but Williams turns it into an indictment of Scott's writing process that exploited Zelda as its subject. She lashes out at him, crying "*What was important to you was to absorb and devour!*" (215). Scott claims that she is still "Mrs. F. Scott Fitzgerald" (279) even after death, but the fraudulence of representation itself that surrounds him in the theatricalist simulacra epitomized by a "fake countess" (222) and "counterfeit moon" (247) contradict his claim. Their attempts to represent each other prove to be as faulty at capturing life as photography, as Zelda observes: "Photographs are a *petit souvenir* but not a good likeness at all. They can't penetrate the flesh, they have no heart, no fury, no explosion of molten—I was about to say fire" (251). They play with "fictitious names . . . but [are] not Daisy and not Gatsby" (242), and cannot tell whether stories are "true or apocryphal" (264). The episodes in which Zelda and Scott attempt to capture the past are marked by the "lunatic" (215) space of the madhouse/theatre as "fantasy world[s]" (208) and "hallucinations" (223), which cannot tell any recognizable "secret called truth" (253), for their words are "wasted, . . . blown away" (276), dissolving the episodes with the relentless sound of wind sweeping across the stage, a wind also punctuates *The Dance of Death*. Just as Hemingway modeled his characters on his first wife, Hadley, so he accuses Scott of writing "Zelda and Zelda and more Zelda. As if you'd like to appropriate her identity" (268). Scott insists that his wife be addressed as his creation: "Mrs. Fitzgerald, not—Zelda . . . " (225), explained by Zelda as "the part he created for me. Mrs. F. Scott Fitzgerald. Without that part, would I ever have been known[?]" (248). He discourages what he sees as Zelda's attempt "to compete with my success as a writer" (209), claiming that Zelda's material was nothing but "a beautiful but cloudy, indistinct mirror of mine" (209). The doctor, however, defends Zelda's writing, saying that she "sometimes struck a sort of fire in her work that—I'm sorry to say this to you, but I never quite found anything like it in yours, even yours, that was equal to it . . . " (259). Zelda rejects her role as "Mrs. F. Scott" at the play's end, shouting "I'm not your book! Anymore! *I can't be your book anymore! Write yourself a new book!*" (280).

In contrast to the relatively self-aware "performances" of the Fitzgeralds, Hemingway maintains an essentialist position, saying, "Fuck it!—You know as well as I know that every goddam character an honest writer creates is part of himself" (269), setting himself up for Scott to point out that Hemingway sometimes wrote of men as having "dual genders" (269). Scott reminds him of a night in France when Hemingway treated him with uncharacteristic tenderness, and Hemingway recalls that "You had the skin of a girl, mouth of a girl, the soft eyes of a girl" (270), admitting that this was "disturbing" (270) to him. Zelda also feminizes Scott, asking if women chase him "because you're so pretty they think you must be a secret one of them?" (235). Attempting to backpedal, Hemingway contradicts his earlier claim that characters are part of a writer's "self," claiming that his story "Sea Change," about homosexuality, was written from a detached point of view, because "it's my profession to observe and report all kinds of human relations" (271). Facing the audience, Hemingway says "There I stop it, this game" (272) of theatrical confession, breaking out of the episode as if to protect his "cold, hard pride" (272) from further assault by Scott's notions about "multiple selves" (269).[21]

No Purifications

It is tempting to project resurrectionist meanings onto Zelda when Williams's stage directions describe her as having "the majesty of those purified by madness and by fire" (213), but, as specific considerations of resurrection unfold in the play, it becomes clear that there is no permanent salvation for her or the others. Zelda ironically rejects being mythologized as any symbol, declaring:

> ZELDA: I AM NOT A SALAMANDER! —Just tell him that.
> INTERN: Salamander, she said?
> SCOTT: The salamander does not exist, never did; it is a mythological creature that can live in fire and suffer no hurt of [*Scott utters a gasp, almost a sob.*]—injury from—the element of fire.
> ZELDA: I am not a salamander. Do you hear? You've mistaken my spirit for my body! Because my spirit exists in fire does not mean that my body will not be consumed if caught in fire behind the barred gates and windows on this windy hill. (226)

Whereas Scott would write her as a mythological creature with a spirit that lives in fire without burning, Zelda more closely resembles another Williams's lizard—the iguana—trapped at the end of a rope, marked for certain death and consumption. The Intern moronically repeats "Salamander, sal-a-mander" (226) acknowledging that (along with most audience members) no one knows what it means. In medieval literature and alchemy, the salamander's myth was a parable of resurrection similar to that of the phoenix. In various mythic versions,[22] the salamander was thought to be able to live in fire due to its cold-bloodedness. It fed on flames and exhaled them, becoming a symbol of "transcendence of the material to the spiritual" (David Williams, 201–202). Lawrence used the salamander as a metaphor of resurrection in the poem "What Quetzcoatl Saw in Mexico" from *The Plumed Serpent*: "The dead that have mastered fire live on, salamanders, in fire" (*Collected Poems,* 796).[23] Although Strindberg refers to a phoenix in *Stormy Weather*, his only overt reference to one is from his diary, *Inferno*, in which he reports seeing (or hallucinating) "gruesome and fantastic shapes" (222) that included salamanders and dragons. These figures would have been relevant to him as an alchemist, for the salamander was the primary symbol for the transforming element of fire in alchemy.[24] When Zelda cries "I AM NOT A SALAMANDER!" it represents Williams's direct rejection of the resurrectionist ideologies of Lawrence's phoenix and Strindberg's ashes that are "hauled out into the country to make the soil fertile" (*House,* 176) with new growth arising from them like a phoenix.

Clothes for a Summer Hotel traces Zelda's search for salvation, which she attempts and fails to find in art and men. She looks to her aviator-lover Edouard for a savior. "Aviator" phonetically resembles "Xavier," the last name of Val, who functioned as the savior Christ/Orpheus figure in *Orpheus Descending.* A would-be savior, Edouard asks, "Could I have saved you?" (249), while Zelda dreams that he might "crash in fire" (251) doing acrobatics. But he had been too concerned with earthly practicalities to soar in imagination and from the after-death present time of the play he reveals that he was no hero but simply "gradually . . . *grew old*" (251). The Intern who doubles as Edouard encourages her to look on Scott as a Christ who "died for attempting to exist as both" (273) a gentleman and an artist, reminding her that he "rose again from the dead" (274). Zelda ironically rejoins, "And ascended to the lawn of Highland Hospital" (274), lampooning resurrection, Scott and the play that brought him there. She says that resurrection is "the Everlasting ticket that doesn't exist. The lies of Christ were such beautiful lies, especially on the night before crucifixion on The Place of the Skull" (274).[25]

Zelda's final plea to Scott for help asks that the asylum staff gather her ashes and scatter them. The first draft contains an expanded and more revealing version of this monologue, in which Zelda asks:

> . . . if the bodies of nine ladies on the top floor which is barred are reduced to indistinguishable though isolate mounds of ash, a little galaxy of the transferred heads and bodies of stars, scatter all to the wind, the constant wind sweeping this tallest hill called Sunset. There is the purification!—dispersed to the wind and scattered on the sea . . . " (April 1979, 4–20)

Nancy Milford reports that following her "real" death, Zelda's body was identified by a (dancing?) slipper lying under it, providing Williams with the image of mounds of ashes. But like the "demented" Becky, Williams's text plays with his own "little galaxy of transferred heads and bodies" of resurrection discourse, occasionally swapping the Fitzgeralds' heads for those of Lawrence and Strindberg. While Zelda seeks a scattering purification that could have been written by a modernist, *Clothes for a Summer Hotel* questions the viability of such representations in the late twentieth century. No purification is forthcoming, and the set, with its simulated flickerings of fire and unrecognizable ash remains static, in a ghosted, shell-like theatrical paralysis.

NOTES

1. The first draft from which this quotation is derived (and all subsequent "April 1979" quotations) is held as part of the José Quintero Papers in Special

Collections at the M. D. Anderson Library of the University of Houston.

2. *Clothes for a Summer Hotel* previewed first in Washington D.C. at the Kennedy Center on January 29, 1980. From there, it moved to another out-of-town preview at Chicago's Blackstone Theatre on February 26, 1980. It opened on Broadway at the Cort Theatre on March 26, 1980 and ran only until April 6, 1980. The production was directed by José Quintero, with set design by Oliver Smith and costumes by Theoni Aldredge. Geraldine Page played Zelda, Kenneth Haigh was Scott, with Robert Black was Hemingway.

3. Although on the surface, *Clothes for a Summer Hotel* would not seem to portray Williams or his family, the play was still subjected to autobiographic approaches, reflected in Thomas P. Adler's claim. Adler does go beyond the autobiographical stratagem, however, to point out similarities between the dramatic structures of Yeatsian purgatorial drama and *Clothes for a Summer Hotel*. Using a slightly different approach, Ruby Cohn argues against the "tedious cliché" (12) that all of Williams's plays are autobiographical, instead viewing it as a biographical "tribute" (16) to the Fitzgeralds' marriage.

4. I would consider Williams's verse drama *The Purification*, which was first written in 1940 and rewritten in 1944, to be another one-act "thesis play." Partially inspired by Lawrence and Federico Garcia Lorca, the play presents another image of burning purification, in which a character chants: "I burned /I burned/I burned . . . " (64). He is a (Lawrencean) "burnt-out shell of longing that drove [him] to violence" (40). Another character, The Son (a Christ image), is the visionary of the play, who is the only character capable of translating his sexual burning (for his sister) into an act of purification when he stabs himself, bringing on a rain storm which washes and purifies the desert. While *Auto-da-Fé* and *I Rise in Flame* place more emphasis on burning through fire and fever, *The Purification* stresses the purifying rain over fire imagery.

5. Jill Franks notes that Lawrence "travesties the Bibles 'I am risen' by interpreting it to mean 'my penis is erect'" (143), remaking him as a "pagan hero" (144) of fertility/virility.

6. See Jill Franks, 5–6.

7. The visionary nature of subjectivity in Williams's early plays is expressed through metaphors of disease, in which vision—which is equivalent with revelation in these plays—produces a partial or complete erasure/disfiguration of the stable subject of realist ideology. In other words, to see visions is to become broken and/or to die. Such expressionist moments of subjective vision can be located in Williams's earliest full-length "apprentice" plays, written in the late 1930s, such as *Candles to the Sun* (1935, unpublished) and *Not About Nightingales* (1938–1939), in which the characters see burning, infernalist visions that critique society, and in *Spring Storm* (1937) and *Stairs to the Roof* (1940), in which metaphoric visions equate love and sexuality to burning.

8. It is likely that the play's end is partially derived from Frieda Lawrence's autobiography that links "those last days of his [with] rays of the setting sun" (288).

9. Unless otherwise indicated, all quotations from Strindberg's plays are taken

from *A Dream Play and Four Chamber Plays*, trans. Walter Johnson.

10. Freddie Rokem observes that it seems as if the houses and other inanimate objects in the chamber plays "have become articulate" (133). Brian Rothwell also comments on houses in the chamber plays, noting that "the house, then, is a theatrical expression of the hold of the past, of the complexity of human relationships and of the spiritual state of the actors" (156).

11. This early draft and assorted loose pages are held by The Harvard Theatre Collection (see Works Cited).

12. This is the version referred to as "First typed draft" (April 1979) in Works Cited.

13. Asheville, North Carolina was the birthplace of Thomas Wolfe, another influence on Williams. In an unpublished letter to Paul Bigelow dated April 12, 1950, he notes that he has been reading Wolfe, and in another letter to Bigelow in January 1952, jokes that "I am compared to Thomas Wolfe as he would have written had he controlled his style!" (Tennessee Williams Papers, Rare Book and Manuscript Library, Columbia University).

14. In his stage directions, Williams misidentifies the date of Zelda's death in the asylum fire as taking place in the "autumn of 1947" (204), whereas it actually occurred on March 10, 1948. Williams seems to make occasional errors in reproducing dates and the titles of the Ernest Hemingway stories to which the play refers (see Note 20). Williams, however, made it clear that his exegetical plays about writers (such as Lawrence and Crane), were not biographies but his own (re)interpretations of parts of their lives.

15. Fitzgerald's quote is drawn from an unfinished novel, *The Last Tycoon*, he was writing in 1940 at the time of his death.

16. Williams's one-act play about Hart Crane's death is entitled *Steps Must Be Gentle*, probably written in 1947 and withheld from publication until 1980. It is collected in *The Theatre of Tennessee Williams, Volume 7*. Williams also wrote a one-act play about Vachel Lindsay's death, entitled *Suitable Entrances to Springfield or Heaven*. At the time of this article, it remains unpublished.

17. While I choose to approach ghosting through the play's theatricalist foregrounding of simulacra, it is also important to consider the influence that Noh and Kabuki theatre had on Williams's use of the ghost. Allean Hale has done pioneering work in this area, (see her articles in Works Cited) focusing on the development of *In the Bar of a Tokyo Hotel* (1969). She points out that, in contrast to Western theatre, Noh drama frequently employs ghosts to symbolize "the character and his double, or opposite spirit" ("Secret Script," 366), who achieve transcendence by re-performing their lives through a ritualized play.

18. Gertrude Stein, for example, experimented with a "continuous present," which she theorized in "Composition as Explanation" and practice in several works, such as "Melanctha."

19. Williams's personal library at his Key West home contained several works by Lawrence including *Apocalypse, Complete Poems* and *The Man Who Died*.

20. This quote is taken from a letter to Lady Cynthia Asquith on 31 January

1915, from *The Collected Letters of D. H. Lawrence,* 309.

21. In this passage, Williams has misidentified the story Hemingway describes as "The Sea Change," which is actually to be found in *Death in the Afternoon,* an error that Hemingway scholars rushed to point out. For articles on Williams's errors about Hemingway stories, see essays by Hays and Monteiro in Works Cited.

22. According to David Williams, "The salamander was considered monstrous in the Middle Ages specifically because of the element of fire in its constitution. According to Pliny, the salamander's ability to inhabit fire arose from its extraordinary coldness; it was, in other words, the opposite of fire, and a contrary so powerful as to be able to extinguish flames by its touch. In addition to Pliny's view, another version described the monster as having its natural dwelling in fire, upon which it also fed. Not surprisingly, living on such a diet the salamander exhaled flames. The animal's ability to pass through or even inhabit fire was, again, taken as a sign of the transcendence of the material to the spiritual. It is likely because of this symbolism that the cabalists proposed the salamander as the sire of Zoroaster." See 210–212.

23. Lawrence identified with the work of Carl Jung, who, like Lawrence, appropriated archetypes from ancient sources. Jungian analyst Michael Adams notes that to a Jungian, "the psychoanalytic process is comparable to the alchemical process: the individuals (patient and analyst) are like substances (*prima materia*) in a vessel. When they are heated in this fiery process they are, like the salamander, burned but not consumed—that is, they are psychically transformed" (Adams interview).

24. Jung notes that "the salamander symbolizes the fire of the alchemists . . . The salamander is also the 'incombustible sulphur'—another name for the arcane substance from which the lapis [the philosopher's stone] or fillius is produced" (142).

25. *The Everlasting Ticket* is the title of a play about Joe Orton that Williams worked on in the early 1980s. To date, only fragmentary pages have been found.

WORKS CITED

Adler, Thomas P. "When Ghosts Supplant Memories: Tennessee Williams' *Clothes for a Summer Hotel.*" *The Southern Literary Journal* 19:2 (Spring 1987): 5-19.

Baudrillard, Jean. *Simulations.* Trans. Paul Foss, Paul Patton and Phillip Beitchman. New York: Semiotext(e), 1983.

Beaufort, John. Review of *Clothes for a Summer Hotel. Christian Science Monitor* 27 March 1980: 14.

Cohn, Ruby. "Tributes to Wives." *Tennessee Williams Review* (Spring 1983): 12–17.

Deleuze, Giles. *The Logic of Sense.* Trans. Mark Lester. New York: Columbia University Press, 1990.

Fuchs, Elinor. *The Death of Character: Perspectives on Theatre after Modernism.* Bloomington: Indiana University Press, 1996.

Hale, Allean. "Noh and Kabuki in the Drama of Tennessee Williams." *Text and Presentation: A Journal of the Comparative Drama Conference* (1994): 37-41.

———. "The Secret Script of Tennessee Williams." *The Southern Review* 2:27 (April 1991): 363–75.

Hays, Peter L. "Tennessee Williams 'Outs' Scott and Ernest," in *The Author as*

Character: Representing Historical Writers in Western Literature, ed. Paul Franssen and Ton Hoenselaars (Madison: Fairleigh Dickinson University Press, 1999), 253–63.

Issacharoff, Michael. "Space and Reference in Drama," *Poetics Today* 2:3 (Spring 1981): 211–24.

Johnson, Walter. "Introduction to *A House That Burned*." August Strindberg. *A Dream Play and Four Chamber Plays*. Seattle: University of Washington Press, 1973. 137–41.

Jung, Carl. "Paracelsus as a Spiritual Phenomenon," *Collected Works*. v. 13. Ed. Sir Herbert Read *et al*. Princeton: Princeton University Press, 1967: 109–89.

Karl, Frederick R. *Modern and Modernism: The Sovreignity of the Artist, 1885–1925*. New York: Atheneum, 1985.

Lawrence, D. H. *The Collected Letters of D. H. Lawrence*. Ed. Harry T. Moore. New York: Viking, 1962.

————. *The Collected Poems of D. H. Lawrence*. Eds. Vivian de Sola Pinto and Warren Roberts. New York: Viking Press, 1964.

————. *Kangaroo*. New York: Penguin, 1980.

————. *The Ladybird*, in *The Ladybird, The Fox and The Captain's Doll*, ed. Dieter Mehl (Cambridge: Cambridge University Press, 1992), 157–221.

————. *The Man Who Died. St. Mawr and The Man Who Died*. New York: Vintage, 1960.

————. *The Plumed Serpent: Quetzalcoatl*. Intro. William York Tindall. New York: Alfred A. Knopf, 1951.

Milford, Nancy. *Zelda: A Biography*. New York: Harper and Row, 1970.

Monteiro, George. "Tennessee Williams Misremembers Hemingway." *Hemingway Review* X.1 (Fall 1990): 71.

Rokem, Freddie. "The Representation of Death in Strindberg's Chamber Plays." in *Strindberg and Genre*, ed. Michael Robinson. (Norwich: Norvik Press, 1991), 119–36.

Rothwell, Brian. "The Chamber Plays." in *Essays on Strindberg*, ed. Carl Reinhold Smedmark (Stockholm: Beckmans Bokförlag, 1966), 29–38.

Sontag, Susan. Illness and Metaphor. New York: Farrar, Straus, and Giroux, 1978.

Strindberg, August. "Author's Preface." *Miss Julie*. Strindberg: *Five Plays*. Trans. Harry G. Carlson. New York: Signet, 1984. 50–61.

————. *The Dance of Death, Parts I and II*. in *Strindberg: Five Plays*, Trans. Harry G. Carlson (New York: Signet, 1984), 103–208.

————. *A Dream Play and Four Chamber Plays*. Trans. Walter Johnson. Seattle: University of Washington Press, 1973. 17–90.

————. *Inferno. Inferno* and *From an Occult Diary*. Trans. Mary Sandbach. New York: Penguin, 1979. 95–274.

Williams, David. *Deformed Discourse: The Function of the Monster in Mediaeval Thought and Literature*. Montreal: McGill-Queens University Press, 1996.

Williams, Tennessee. *Auto-da-Fé*. Volume 6 of *Theatre*. New York: New Directions, 1981: 129–151.

————. *Clothes for a Summer Hotel*. Volume 8 of *Theatre*. New York: New

Directions, 1992: 201–80.

———. *Clothes for a Summer Hotel: A Ghost Play in Four Scenes.* Tms. "First typed draft, April 1979." José Quintero Papers. University of Houston, Houston, Texas.

———. *Clothes for a Summer Hotel: A Ghost Play in Four Scenes.* Tms. "April–September 1979." José Quintero Papers. University of Houston, Houston, Texas.

———. *Clothes for a Summer Hotel.* Tms. Director's (Quintero's) script for Broadway production, with production cues, director's notes and revised pages dated 3/14, 3/20/, 3/21 and 4/3. José Quintero Papers. University of Houston, Houston, Texas.

———. *The Glass Menagerie.* Volume 1 of *Theatre* New York: New Directions, 1971: 123–237.

———. *I Can't Imagine Tomorrow.* Volume 7 of *Theatre.* New York: New Directions, 1981: 133–150.

———. *I Rise in Flame, Cried the Phoenix.* Volume 7 of *Theatre.* New York: New Directions, 1981: 55–75.

———. Interview with Jim Gaines. "A Talk about Life and Style with Tennessee Williams." *Saturday Review* (29 April 1972): 25–29.

———. *The Purification.* Volume 6 of *Theatre.* New York: New Directions, 1981. 28-77.

———. *A Streetcar Named Desire.* Volume 7 of *Theatre.* New York: New Directions, 1971: 238–419.

———. *Suddenly Last Summer.* Volume 3 of *Theatre.* New York: New Directions, 1971: 343–423.

———. *Tragedies of a Drawing Room.* Early unpublished draft fragment of *Clothes for a Summer Hotel.* ca. 1977–78. Tennessee Williams Papers. The Harvard Theatre Collection.

Previously unpublished material by Tennessee Williams printed by permission of The University of the South, Sewanee, Tennessee. Copyright © 2000 by the University of the South. Grateful acknowledgment is also given to the Tennessee Williams Papers at the Harvard Theatre Collection, the Houghton Library, Fredric Woodbridge Wilson, Curator, and to the José Quintero Papers at the Special Collection Division of M. D. Anderson Library at the University of Houston.

"Nothing Unspoken"

The Notebook of Trigorin and *The Seagull*

Rhonda Blair

> "What writers influenced me as a young man? Chekhov!
> As a dramatist? Chekhov!
> As a story writer? Chekhov!
> D. H. Lawrence, too, . . ."
>
> (Williams, quoted in Devlin, 331)

In the summer of 1934 when he was first becoming a playwright, Tennessee Williams discovered the works of Anton Chekhov in the Southwestern University and Main Street libraries in Memphis. This marked the beginning of Williams's life-long attraction to Chekhov and his work, and his claiming of the Russian author as a great influence (*Memoirs*, 40–41).

Critics have made much of the similarities and resonances between Chekhov's and Williams's plays—the qualities of lyricism, poignancy, the bittersweet vision of life, the resemblances among certain characters in the plays, and a basic humanity shared by the writers—and there are times when the two authors are indeed notably similar in tone and temper. An opportunity for comparing these two playwrights in detail is provided by the 1997 publication of Williams's *The Notebook of Trigorin*, subtitled "a free adaptation of Anton Chekhov's *The Seagull*."

Representative of the many critics who compare the two playwrights is Felicia Hardison Londré, who writes that "[Williams] often depicts Southern society as characterized by an attitude of romantic melancholy or by a kind of aristocratic decay, very like the Russian milieux of his favorite author Chekhov" (34). Similarly, Francis Donahue compares the two writers in terms of their sensitivity, their focus on "weak" characters and the "sensitive misfits of this world," their creation of moods of nostalgia and preoccupation with memory; she finds Williams superior for his ability to create dramatic tension through strong clashes of will (214–215)[1].

However, basic differences in Williams's and Chekhov's dramaturgies and world views have been noted as far back as Louis Kronenberger's review of the Broadway premiere of *The Glass Menagerie*:

> For in its mingled pathos and comedy, its mingled naturalistic detail and gauzy atmosphere, its preoccupation with 'memory,' its tissue of forlorn hopes and backward looks and languishing self-pities, *The Glass Menagerie* is more than just a little Chekhovian. But Chekhov worked from within, as Mr. Williams does not; and successfully on more than one level, as Mr. Williams does not quite; and in such a way that his comedy and pathos coalesced, where Mr. Williams's—except where Miss Taylor makes them blend-emerge separately. (16)

This points toward what one finds in comparing *The Notebook of Trigorin* and *The Seagull*.

By the early 1970s Williams was talking about doing a production of *The Seagull*; he wanted to recuperate the play based on his deep love for it and his view that it needed to be theatricalized and updated in order for a modern American audience to appreciate Chekhov's story fully. Williams was given an opportunity to act on this desire in 1980 when the Vancouver Playhouse commissioned him to write his own version of *The Seagull* for their 1981 season opener (Hale, xii). Following a troubled process in which, according to Allean Hale, neither Williams nor the theatre was satisfied, the Playhouse produced *Notebook*. Williams continued to work on the play until his death two years later. It was produced at the Colony Studio Theatre in Los Angeles in 1982, but did not receive another production until 1996 at the Cincinnati Playhouse, when a final version was staged.

Williams's adaptation is clearly his, and not Chekhov's, play, with characteristics that place *Notebook* firmly within Williams's universe. *Notebook* substantially alters elements of narrative, character, emotional tone, and structure. The adaptation does away with what Williams calls Chekhov's "reserve" and seeming non-theatricality, replacing it with an explicitness and psychosexual darkness not found in the Russian play. In comparing the two texts, it is possible to see how Williams uses Chekhov's story as a ground for working through recurring issues and motifs central to his own writings and personal struggles—in short, how Williams uses his idea of Chekhov's play as a "screen" on which to project his own personal and specific vision.

The following comparisons and impressions—generally based on easily available information—occurred to me as I considered the two playwrights and their scripts, providing a framework for the discussion which follows:

Williams:	Chekhov:
American, mid-20th century	Russian, turn of the 20th century
wrote *Notebook* at age 69, in 1980	wrote *Seagull* at age 36, in 1896
asserts values	explores ambiguitie
judgmental (Puritan/American)	non-judgmental
Christian atheist	
writer as spiritual/moral patient	writer as spiritual/moral doctor/diagnostician
the sick child	the healthy child
the hypochondriac adult	the tubercular (dying) adult
gay, single, sexually active	straight, single, sexually active
totalizing statements	statements of ambiguity/indirection
simple action	complex action
triangulation in one-on-one dialogue	directness, explicit of implicit, in one-on-one
("Do you want him? her?)	"I know you
("I want you")	desire him/her"
enmeshed characters	autonomous characters with
desires/longings	
lust/ sex	familial and romantic love/desire/
longing	
morality	happiness/ fulfillment

In *Notebook* and *Seagull* respectively, Williams and Chekhov play out two disparate themes: Chekhov, a comedy of the complexity of human desires in work and love; Williams, a tragedy of how human cruelties drive people to madness and suicide. A difference between the authors is where they stand in relationship to their narratives, which are related to aspects of their identifications—Chekhov as objective doctor, Williams as suffering patient/victim. Chekhov is not "inside" of his narrative, insofar as his text does not indicate a strong personal identification with any of the characters, or his need to have them speak "for" him, in that none of the major characters "stands for" Chekhov (though, certainly, he has traits in common with a number of them, in terms of his occupations as writer, doctor, and person of the theatre). Conversely, Williams seems strongly identified with the two writer characters: he replays a version of the Tom/Amanda relationship through Treplev and Arkadina, turning this into a struggle to the death between flawed, weak son and monstrously egocentric and self-deluding mother[2]; Trigorin becomes a world-weary, bisexual writer much younger than Arkadina, dependent on her for his success in a way in which he is not in Chekhov's version. In *Notebook*, the older writer in fact becomes an important source of comfort and encouragement for the younger (this can even be viewed as the older "Tennessee" comforting young "Tom"), as they struggle with their relationships to the mother figure who is the source of their well-being and even survival. Related to this is a general diminishment of tenderness in many of the characters' relationships; with *Notebook* I often have a question of why the characters stay together, if they dislike each other so much, while in Chekhov most of the characters have a warm attachment to at least one other character to hold him or her there.

Chekhov's play is essentially polyphonic, multifocal, even underdetermined in terms of dramatic action and character attitude, with four characters at the play's center and supporting characters closely interwoven into the core action; *Seagull's* group scenes have multiple points of focus and different concerns for the various characters. Williams's play tends to simplify this, with Arkadina becoming the spine and central character of the play; in *Notebook*, group scenes tend to have a single point of focus for the action. With great consistency, Williams tells us how to feel about his characters. Possibly most significantly, *Seagull's* ending is open-ended: we are not shown the characters' reactions to Treplev's shooting himself, but are left without closure, and all of the characters but one are going on with their lives at the play's end. Conversely, in *Notebook* we see servants carrying Treplev's body from the lakeside toward the house (in an image resonant of the ending of *Hamlet*), as all the characters react to his death and Arkadina, downstage center, performs her pain (98). Williams is attracted to victims; Chekhov is interested in survivors.

Almost all of the characters in Williams are focused from the play's beginning on their failures and the impossibility of finding fulfillment; they are relatively fixed at the play's start. They have desires, but little hope. This at times changes a character's action from attempting to win another character's love or loyalty to blaming another character for his or her pain and failure; from a positive to a negative kind of energy. The nature of this energy is connected at times to an explicit sexualization of a character's desires.

What follows is an act-by-act comparison of the two texts, focusing on Williams's adaptations and transformations of the Russian play.

Act I

A comparison of the first few lines between Masha and Medvedenko, returning from a walk, sets out basic differences. Chekhov's opening:

> MEDVEDENKO: Why do you always wear black?
> MASHA: I'm in mourning for my life. I'm unhappy.
> MEDVEDENKO: Why? [*Thoughtfully.*] I don't understand . . . You're healthy and your father, though he's not rich, he makes enough. Life's much harder for me than for you. I only make twenty-three rubles a month and they still take money out for my pension, but I don't go around in mourning.
> [*They sit.*]
> MASHA: The problem isn't money. Even beggars can be happy.
> MEDVEDENKO: Theoretically, yes, but in reality it goes like this: there's me, my mother, my two sisters, a little brother, and a twenty-three ruble salary for all of us. You have to eat and drink. You need tea and sugar. Tobacco. And that's how it goes.[3]

Williams's opening:

MEDVEDENKO: Masha, tell me, why do you always wear black? [*she is obviously inattentive to him.*]
You've got no reason to be depressed. You're in good health. Your father's well-off. [*He takes her hand.*]
MASHA: Don't, please don't. I'm touched by your feeling for me but I just can't return it, that's all.
MEDVEDENKO: If I were not so wretchedly poor, twenty-three rubles a month!
MASHA: It isn't a question of money. I could love a beggar if . . .
MEDVEDENKO: The beggar was Constantine. Isn't that so?
MASHA: His mother treats him as one—loves him?—Oh, yes, but love can be cruel as hate. She will despise his play this evening and make no secret of it and she'll be coldly polite, polite as ice to Nina, you'll see. It will be clear that she's what she believes she is, the star that's the greatest in Russia. She probably thinks she's the greatest star in the world. (1)

In Williams, major points of conflict are presented explicitly in the first lines, with little room for ambiguity. Mourning and unhappiness (in a literary reference drawn from Maupassant's *Bel-Ami*) are exchanged for a different emotion—depression. There is immediately a physical overture of desire from Medvedenko, a meek, kind character in Chekhov, which is firmly rebuffed. Williams's Medvedenko explicitly confronts Masha about her desire for Treplev; this is not the way for a lover to woo successfully, but is rather a way to accuse and blame. Arkadina is front and center from the first page, demonized as megalomaniacal and self-deluded; even non-intimates of the actress speak of her destructiveness and weaknesses. This is a prickly, rather than a pastoral, place. This prickliness continues as Medvedenko describes his "witch of mother" (shades of Amanda), his "homely as heifers" sisters, and uncontrollable brother; Masha has already rejected "poor stupid" Medvedenko's "very curious proposal" to become a member of his "appalling family" (2). If Masha dislikes Medvedenko so much, why is she out walking with him? Characters seem bound by loneliness, lust, insecurity, and habit, without affection.

Williams extends Chekhov's brief (virtually three line) scene in which Masha and Medvedenko cross over with Treplev and Sorin substantially into one in which Treplev coaches the workman building the stage, Sorin complains about aging, Masha makes overtures to Treplev, and she and Medvedenko gossip about Arkadina and Trigorin. Treplev enters alone, dramaturgically "detached" from his uncle Sorin, who, in Chekhov, is a source of support and love for the young man. Masha hyperbolically praises Treplev's play, saying that it will be performed all over Russia, causing Treplev to accuse her of drinking (3); these things are *in potentio* in Chekhov till later. Upon entering, Sorin immediately speaks of the emotional pains of aging and of his fear of being left alone by Constantine; ironic self-awareness is laced with desperation: Chekhov's "Whether you want to or not, you go on living . . . " is exchanged for "Want to sleep it [life] away, yes, keep falling asleep. Wake up?— Why? For what?" (4). Williams's focus on sex and age continues in Masha and Medvedenko's discussion of whether Arkadina and Trigorin are lovers or just traveling companions—something which would have been understood in Chekhov's culture—and the fact that in *Notebook* Trigorin is made closer in age to Treplev than to Arkadina. In Chekhov, they are late thirtiess, twenty-five, and forty-three, respectively. In Williams, Arkadina's age is ambiguous because, though Treplev says she is forty-three, other characters regularly refer to her as being over fifty. This becomes another way of "collapsing" the two writers into each other and reinforcing the idea of Mother-as-hag. Before exiting, Masha deflects yet one more marriage proposal from Medvedenko and asks for a cognac; the pressure and dysfunction are reinforced.

The extended scene between nephew and uncle is notably reduced by Williams, and its focus shifted. Treplev's extended struggle with his thoughts and feelings about art, his mother, the theatre, and class is reduced from a series of long, detailed speeches to a single speech. This is the first instance in which Williams alters what might be called a character's "arias:" extended monologues or semi-monologic passages of passion—either shortening them or converting them into more dialogic structures. Here, Treplev has a short speech about how his mother does not love him and a few lines about the need for new forms in art; this increases the play's emphasis on the psychological, even Oedipal, problems related to Arkadina, while largely eliminating the social context and aesthetic issues with which Treplev is struggling. The sense of family connection is further diminished as Sorin describes his sister's shame and embarrassment about him, his age and his demeanor; this is counter to the explicit affection between brother and sister in Chekhov, and diminishes Sorin's past professional and public life. In a significant rewriting, Trigorin enters alone to encourage, and even mentor, the young writer—and to ask him to join him for a swim; Trigorin becomes the younger writer's "cheerleader," even as this, Trigorin's polymorphous sexuality, specifically his homosexuality, is introduced (8). From the start, he is a stand-in for Williams.

Williams's Nina lacks mobility, and she does not love Treplev. She enters, having narrowly escaped a sexually threatening carriage ride with a stranger (9); she's vulnerable, dependent, seemingly without agency, unlike Chekhov's Nina, who rides in on her own horse and who enters laughing as well as crying. Nina's stepmother is sexualized and later demonized (she's the Bohemian one, and Arkadina later calls her a harlot [25]). Treplev kisses a reluctant Nina ("*Pause. With a loud intake of breath he kisses her. She smiles sadly.*" 10), while in Chekhov they kiss each other when she tells him, "My heart is full of you." This Nina has a different emotional journey; if she is not in love with Treplev—even as she is interested in meeting Trigorin—, there is less change, less for her to lose, less for her to leave behind. It also changes Treplev, in that his love is hopeless from the start. This Nina substantially criticizes Treplev's play and explicitly states her lack of desire for him ("I do love you, Kostya, but not in this way") (13), while Treplev is overtly jealous of Nina's interest in Trigorin. This imbalanced, tenuous relationship contrasts to the playful, even erotic one in the older play.

The bleakness of sexual relationships is reinforced in the brief scene between Dorn and Polina. In Chekhov, she is importunate and he puts her off, but with a reminder that there has been much good in his relationships with women, and that he has always been honest. Williams's Dorn says nothing about the goodness in these relationships, and connects honesty to his statement that "men—such as I—need the attention of women, not one woman, but women" (14); he is actively engaged in seeking multiple partners, while Chekhov's Dorn has implicitly given this up— or at least pursues it with discretion. Dorn likes and is liked by no one, yet he makes passes at all of the female characters, speaks leeringly of women in general, and keeps turning up at the estate like a bad penny; thus, Chekhov's dispassionate doctor, with his history of past love affairs and his direct but honest friendships with a number of characters, becomes a destructive, compulsively active hedonist in Williams4. Given that Dorn has more stage time than almost any other character in both versions of the plays, he has a significant impact on the general tone of the play.

Upon the group's entrance to see Treplev's play, Arkadina immediately participates in interchanges which establish her intractability. There is an extended set-up for the start of the play, in which her neuroses, jealousies, and people's fears of her are continuously in focus: Sorin pulls Treplev aside to tell him to let Arkadina participate in his play in order to assuage her, Arkadina chides her son for the makeshift nature of his platform, while Trigorin whispers urgently to her, "Be kind tonight, it's their night, you've had so many stages, allow them to have this platform " (17). The text of Treplev's play is truncated, used primarily to demonstrate Nina's incompetence as an actor and the lack of respect given to Treplev and his work by his community. Because of the abbreviation of his play's text, we get less of a sense of him as an artist and the issues about artistic endeavor. Nina cannot remember her lines and needs much coaching, and she has a grotesque sneezing fit. When Treplev stops the play and "staggers as if drunk upstage to the bench" (21), it is Trigorin who goes to comfort him. Trigorin returns to criticize Arkadina in front of the group, something which never occurs in Chekhov (21).

The aftermath of the play's collapse is compressed and selected lines of action are driven forward directly. Arkadina's explosive aria about why she is so angry with her son's art is cut, as is the group's subsequent recovery from the debacle. Nina reenters almost immediately—into an atmosphere of anger and blame, not the reestablished pastoral quietness of a group listening to music coming from across the lake. Arkadina is barbed in congratulating Nina, evincing little tenderness or charm— "You did the best you could without any training, my dear, you must not feel humiliated" (22)—, and then she tries to rush Nina home and away from Trigorin. Instead, Nina approaches Trigorin to show him her house across the lake; he then sees her off to the carriage—right in front of Arkadina (24). Explicit pursuit is withheld by Chekhov until the end of Act II, when Trigorin and Nina approach each other with more caution and nuance . She is less interwoven into the life of the estate: she is attached not through affection for Treplev and Sorin, but predominantly through the outsider Trigorin.

There is no uncomplicated solace for Treplev. When he returns, Dorn insults his masculinity and his art, then exits. Again, it is Trigorin who reenters to encourage the younger man (a function served by Dorn in Chekhov), even as he has just returned from making overtures to Nina; this makes him similar to Arkadina in relationship to Treplev, carrying in himself simultaneously a power to save and to destroy the young man. The central energies of the play are consolidated in a few characters, rather than flowing more fluidly among the group. There is also a marked example of Williams's characters' self-dramatization. When Masha enters, calling Treplev to his mother, Williams has the young man say, "Tell her I've gone away, and please, all of you, leave me alone, don't keep coming after me with these *bits of consolation, scraps thrown to a whipped dog*" (italics mine, 27). Chekhov has her stop with "Don't come after me!"

Trigorin takes on more of the comforting and *raissoneur* functions ascribed to Dorn in the original. The writer consoles Masha, eliminating the father/daughter subtext given to Dorn and Masha in *Seagull*. The final moments of the act also provide a key indicator of fundamental differences in the playwrights' world views. Through Trigorin, Williams asserts the presence of a God and a strong moral—both of which would have been anathema to Chekhov:

> How tortured you both [Masha and Treplev] are by it [youth]. And by love. Unrequited . . . Well. Youth, love, they're worth the price, worth it no matter what a . . . How bewitching the lake is! It's telling you something. What the lake tells us is what God tells us—we just don't know his language. (28)

Conversely, Chekhov's Dorn keeps it simple and human scale:

> They're all so nervous! They're all so nervous! And so much love . . . Oh, bewitching lake! Tenderly. But what can I do, my child? What? What?

Act II

Here *Notebook* is set in a garden, following lunch and wine, rather than on a croquet lawn before lunch. Dorn makes repeated jibes at Arkadina about her age, rather than humoring her, and explicitly flirts with Masha, telling her he has a prescription that would cure her melancholia: "Drop by my office before it opens tomorrow or after it closes" (30). The negativity continues as Dorn prescribes "resignation" for Sorin's ailments, and Sorin himself indicates how he has given up, essentially victimized by life; conversely, Chekhov's Sorin refuses hopelessness and says he wants to live as much as he can, regardless of his age, health, and limited resources.

Williams truncates the scene between Arkadina and Shamraev, in which he refuses to give her a carriage, so that in roughly five lines it culminates in Arkadina's impulsive announcement that she is leaving. In Chekhov, the scene is at least in part about how a delicate balance of power is maintained between a self-important but infatuated estate manager and the great actress—we have a sense of relationship and history. Also, the brevity of Williams's beat provides little context for the characters' impulsiveness and strong action; they do not try to work the conflict through before he resigns and she says, "We're leaving." Interestingly, this eliminates one of the times when we see Arkadina-as-great actress in full sail, moving from charm and cajolery to fury and deep, if flamboyant, offense. It is as though Williams wants to keep Arkadina's interactions focused on her son, her lover, and Nina, and does not want to distract the audience with a "minor" conflict.

Polina and Dorn are then left alone, and she asks a question that an audience might ask itself about a number of relationships in the play: "How is it possible that a woman can find a man despicable as I find you, know you to be, and yet still long to be with him?" (36), and proceeds to catch him in a lie about his age. Williams's Dorn, who embodies a kind of clear-eyed honesty in Chekhov, is as caught up in the quest for continued youth as Arkadina is, and preys sexually on all the women around him. When Nina returns from the house, Polina goes off, tearing up the flowers the young woman has given to Dorn, but Dorn, rather than going in to give the actress and her old brother valerian drops, straightens his cravat and puts the moves on Nina. Rather than the soliloquy in which Nina articulates her delight in discovering that famous artists are no different from others and which gives us a sense of her inner life, Williams substitutes Dorn making a pass at her: "You need a tonic, my dear. I'm heavily booked today but if you could drop by my office, say, at half past six " (38).

In Chekhov the brief scene between Treplev and Nina, in which he presents her with the dead seagull and which is a point of no return for the two characters, is structured so that it culminates with Treplev's outpouring about the failure of his "stupid play," employing a rich array of images to describe his pain, connecting it not just to Nina, but to all the others and to his own failures and weaknesses; this outpouring—a mini-aria, rather than a dialogue—creates a sense of the complexity of Treplev's pain and passion. Thus Treplev knows he is at least in part responsible for his failure. Williams's young man blames only Nina for his pain, not admitting in anyway that his play might have been flawed (40). The blame lies with others.

The motor of Chekhov's extended scene between Trigorin and Nina is Trigorin's helpless obsession for writing, sparked by Nina's enthusiastic fantasy about the artist's life and, only later, their gradually and indirectly acknowledged attraction to each other. In Williams the two characters go immediately to the steamy, sexually driven parts of their lives. In an instance of triangulation, the older writer begins by describing to Nina how Arkadina is the source of much of his unhappiness. Arkadina is not mentioned in Chekhov's scene; indeed, in the entirety of *Seagull* Trigorin never once refers to—much less complains about—Arkadina's career or her work. Conversely, in *Notebook* Trigorin describes at length the tedium of traveling with Arkadina, being forced to listen to her rehearse *Medea* in a small train compartment (41), and Arkadina's unrelenting hold on him. He focuses on his relationship and his desire to talk with Nina at length about their "interior worlds," rather than on what it is like to be a writer and his struggles (42). He triangulates again, asking about Treplev and Nina's feelings for him in order to find out how attached she is; this discussion leads Nina to say, in a comment that diminishes Treplev, "May I say you're the only writer of my acquaintance who understands the female character" (44)[5]. In Chekhov's scene, Treplev is mentioned only once, when Nina answers Trigorin's question about where the dead seagull came from. Trigorin's longest speech in this scene in *Notebook* is primarily about his struggles with deficient virility. Obsession with writing figures into this, but the core of the speech is sexual. A fellow artist praises Trigorin for the accuracy of his portraits of women, but the praise quickly turns to contempt:

> He went on to say that I had a certain softness about me, in my eyes and—Well. He was implying that I was deficient in—virility for—the practice of such a totally masculine profession as that of writing. I realized that. I stopped blushing. I looked at him, straight in the eyes and I doubt that my eyes were soft then. I said to him, "You are excessively delicate in your attack on me for a change. Now why is that? What do you really mean? I doubt that I don't know or anyone at this table doesn't know, so why hesitate to say it straight out like the shameless hack you are?"

> He said nothing. I went on staring straight at him. Finally he did speak—A single obscene word, drank down his wine and spat it onto my face . . . (44).

While Chekhov's Trigorin escapes to the theatre or fishing when he is done with a piece, Williams's writer runs to "Sicily or to Venice or a Greek island and—[turns] for a while into a simply—mindless—beast . . . " (45). Trigorin's bisexuality, effeminacy, and promiscuity are overt, allowing us to both align him directly with Williams's biography and judge him for what seems to be an irresponsible promiscuity, as an immoral person. In Chekhov, there is no indication that Trigorin is anything other than monogamous with Arkadina, except for his liaison with Nina (or at the very least he is discreet).

Again, Williams cuts Trigorin's "aria" in half and shortchanges his obsessive ruminating about writing, his humorous hyperbole about his youthful anxieties, and the nationalistic Russian strain in his writer's desire. The focus is on sexual desire, as when Nina tells him that he is spoiled by success:

> TRIGORIN: I would prefer, much prefer, to be loved by—
> NINA: —By?
> TRIGORIN: One . . .[*touching her face*]
> NINA: You mean as a—
> TRIGORIN: Known and completely understood by just one.
> NINA: You're not able to see that you are? (45)

This is reinforced by the explicit and psychologized interchanges between them which follow, in which Nina tells Trigorin that the lake and Kostya must let her go, and that she has to escape them in order to accomplish her life, while Trigorin warns her:

> . . . I hope that when you leave for the excitement, the lights of what is called the world—cities, theatres, cafes—I hope most earnestly it won't turn bitter and you won't be haunted as I am—by the regrets and-the guilt of abandoning someone or something—that held you in a dream. Forgive me these sentiments, Nina—it's only the music, the mist . . . (47–48)

The negativity and self-referentiality are Williams. In Chekhov, the characters' impulses toward each other are expressed indirectly, for example, her efforts to draw him out about his writing, his "I don't really want to go," his idea for the short story about the young girl who is like the seagull; the only warning or textual foreshadowing in Chekhov is the "idea for a short story." A mutual expression of desire does not occur until the end of Act III. Williams is far more sexual, direct, and foreboding.

Act III

Williams's opening scene in this act between Masha and Trigorin is more hyperbolic than Chekhov's. Masha is explicitly drunk from the first (she even hallucinates that more people than Trigorin are listening to her) and instead of an understated response to her announcement that she will marry Medvedenko ("I don't see why that's necessary"), Trigorin asks, "Are you reconciled to an action as drastic as that?" This Masha, acutely aware of and attached to her pain, asserts that Treplev, who has shot himself, is "not as seriously hurt as [she has] been for a long time" (49). Drinking more copiously than Chekhov's character, she expresses disgust at the idea of sharing Medvedenko's bed. Hypersexuality and self-pity replace slightly alcoholic forthrightness, toughness, and slyness. The dramaturgy of her departure is altered in relationship to Nina's entrance: in Williams, Nina enters after Masha has asked for the inscribed books from Trigorin, making this scene a discrete, separate unit; in Chekhov, Nina is the specific motivation for Masha to leave the room, reinforcing Masha's jealousy, her awareness of the energy between Nina and Trigorin, as well as her "dislocatedness" within the play as a whole. Some of the "connective tissue" is eliminated.

In the ensuing scene, Trigorin and Nina speak directly of their attraction to each other, Trigorin even asking Nina why she is attracted to him and not to Treplev, "such a romantically handsome young man who was driven to shoot himself for you." They mutually agree to meet later, because Nina has an "indiscreet confession" to make (52). Chekhov's reference to the seagull, and Trigorin's association of it with Nina, are eliminated, making space for Trigorin's metaphoric association of Nina with his notebook.

The core of Act III is Arkadina's "trial by fire"; she faces, one by one, the three main men in her life—her brother, her son, her lover—in increasingly pressured and high stakes situations. The actress' brother is in failing health, her son has shot himself and is deeply sad and angry, and her lover's faithfulness is being compromised by a much younger woman. In Chekhov these scenes build both internally and also one upon the next, so that by the end of her scene with Trigorin, there is a sense of Arkadina having come through a series of ordeals as a glorious survivor, not visibly altered or scarred, still the grand diva. This changes in Williams; the affectional dimensions of the scenes are altered, so that they carry less weight. Arkadina is less "present" to her men. The scene between the actress and her ailing brother emphasizes Arkadina's concerns about Nina pursuing Trigorin; her selfishness is highlighted substantially, as she carefully puts on an expensive Parisian hat, even as she is saying she does not have money for clothes for her son and that he's "handsome enough to be attractive in rags" (55). In the rewriting of the scene, its dialogic rhythms are altered and the pressure between the siblings' conflicting objectives to please each other and her need to avoid poverty and his need to get some help for his desperate nephew are diffused.

The Arkadina-Treplev scene is altered in interesting ways, with some sections expanded and others cut. A two-line interchange in Chekhov becomes an extended exchange about Shamraev's abuse of Sorin and the old man's desperation to escape to the city, and about Arkadina's encouraging her son to give up writing and do small parts on the stage (a completely new thread); hyperbole occurs again as Arkadina calls herself "Russia's most prominent actress" (57)—in Chekhov, she is merely very successful. Instead of Treplev's peacemaking gesture of asking his mother to change his bandage, Williams' mother and son immediately engage in an extended disagreement. The most extreme alteration comes in their fight, which is reduced to five lines and focuses entirely on Trigorin, including his "swimming with Yakov." Williams eliminates the elements of conflict between them having to do with family relationship and art, as well as the "going for the jugular" nature of Chekhov's fight. In Chekhov, Trigorin is the catalyst, but the fight transforms and escalates into an explosive confrontation about mother's and son's failures, in each others' eyes, *as artists*—the identity that matters most deeply to each of them. When Treplev collapses at his mother's horrendous name-calling (her "Decadent!," "Kiev merchant! Parasite!," "Beggar!," culminate in "Nobody!"), she becomes, however momentarily, a tender, repentant mother, appalled by her own behavior. There is a soft, though flawed, heart to their relationship, between the mother and her little boy, a tenderness and love which make the awful wounds they inflict on each other all the more painful. In *Notebook*, the fight is less traumatic and Treplev is less obviously devastated by his mother's attack.

Williams's Trigorin is dependent on Arkadina in ways that he is not in Chekhov. She is responsible for his professional success, having introduced him to the right people who could publish and promote his writing; she controls his professional survival. Chekhov's Trigorin is independent, well-established by the time he and Arkadina become involved. In *Notebook* Arkadina moves from literally shouting reminders of his dependence to playing the Southern belle—she "sprains" her ankle and needs his assistance (61). There is little sensuality in this scene; the eroticism of the tactics found in Chekhov is not here, namely her kissing and embracing of him, as she talks about both her desire for him and how he is the greatest writer in Russia. Rather, sex surfaces as a means for blackmail, when Arkadina confronts Trigorin with his "perversion," based on a photograph she has found in his papers of a beautiful Italian boy in a bathing suit, inscribed "Con Amore" (62). She threatens to out Trigorin if he leaves her, and he capitulates. He stays with her out of fear and dependence, rather than desire. The *Seagull* Arkadina's "aria" of seduction and desire in this scene, a masterful performance of her female desirability and her manipulation of male ego, is substantially altered. *Notebook* substitutes a barbed dialogue culminating in a threat of blackmail; Trigorin relents—"a coward—morally flabby" (63). The relationship is founded on mutual fear—his of her power over his professional fate, hers of being alone without a sexual partner, regardless of whether he is attracted to her. In Chekhov, Arkadina needs Trigorin so that she can continue to prove her attractiveness and desirability (to herself as well as others); he stays with her because it is the most comfortable, pleasurable, easy thing to do. In Chekhov, Trigorin stays because he has "no will of [his] own," unconnected in any way to moral stigma—he is simply a soft touch when it comes to attractive, willful women. In Williams, blackmail and shame replace desire, flattery, and pleasure. The interdependence in Williams is fraught with negativity and judgment, while in Chekhov it is based on desire, comfort, and familiarity—ultimately, they know each other well and *accept* each other.

For all three men in Williams, Arkadina is a version of the Great Mother, the source of life and death, prosperity and annihilation; there is no place where they can stand on their own apart from her. Williams is playing out one more version his fascination with the all-powerful mother figure, the destructive, controlling old(er) woman who is the root of life and misery. In Chekhov, at least two of the men—Sorin and Trigorin—have a place where they are able to stand apart from her.

The end of Act III is substantially restructured in *Notebook*, again emphasizing the corrupt nature of sexuality and placing Arkadina at the center. The entourage prepares for departure, as in Chekhov, but they do not then exit to empty the stage, allowing Trigorin to reenter to find Nina alone for their brief interchange. Instead, the company sits for a moment of silence and prayer per the Russian custom. Trigorin sees Nina outside on the lake shore and goes to her, claiming he has left his new notebook outside (65). Thus we have a dual scene, Arkadina and the rest inside, praying, while Trigorin and Nina have a lakeside exchange, permeated with guilt and corruption, as Treplev lurks in the bushes, unseen by them. When Nina tells Trigorin she is going to Moscow, he *"thrusts a number of bills lingeringly down the bodice of her white dress. Constantine's eyes open at this moment: he makes a slight cry, unheard"* (67). Trigorin asks, "You understand how the world turns on—successfully practiced—duplicity? On cunning lies? [*She gasps and nods, unable to speak. He continues, with face contorted.*] Then stay here!" When Nina cries out and crouches on the bench, he *"crouches beside her and kisses her repeatedly with abandon "* (68). The focus then shifts to Arkadina, who sends the others on and waits alone in the house for Trigorin's return, a *"dignity and tragedy in her stoical isolation."* As they exit she says, "Take me to the carriage . . . [*She takes his arm and they cross off slowly together.*] We've much to discuss privately on the train . . . " Williams emphasizes Trigorin's obscene decadence, rather than Nina's dreams and youth and the attraction they hold for the jaded writer. Rather than Nina's excitement, Arkadina's self-conscious torment is the focus of the act's end. Thus, paradoxically, even as the performance of Arkadina's power as a woman and an actress is undercut by the truncation of her scenes with the three men and Williams's narrowing of her repertoire of performative tactics, he nonetheless keeps her center stage.

Act IV

Williams draws out the first scenes in this act considerably, slowing the action's movement and making it less dense and compressed. He provides more facts and psychological "information," reducing the emotional fluidity and mystery in the play and trading "saying" for "being" in his characters. Conflicts and sexual feelings implicit in *Seagull* are explicitly developed at length in the first scene between Masha and Medvedenko. The schoolteacher talks about how he desires Masha's snowy white body, hidden under her black clothes, and accuses her of having had sex with Treplev because "I don't believe you'd spend three nights here unless he'd finally accepted you" (73). Her revulsion is noted a number of times, and he eventually clutches at her, even tearing her dress. In Chekhov, the focus is on responsibilities to family—the child at home—not on sexual desire. Any ambiguity about what they heard crying out by the stage the night before is eliminated as they tell us that Nina is back in town.

A small but telling modification of a concrete action in the first two French scenes is an example of how implicit connections among characters and the way that their desires are embodied nonverbally are unravelled in *Notebook*. Characters are isolated, and embodiment, or behavior, is exchanged for statement. Here Masha makes up a sofa bed for Sorin as she speaks to her husband; this removes a simple concrete motive for Treplev and Polina to enter together as they do in Chekhov (they are united by their affection for the old man and their desire to take care of him). This also removes a physical excuse for Masha to get away from Medvedenko, offering to help make Sorin's bed and thereby getting into Treplev's good graces. Description reigns as Medvedenko asks to speak to Treplev privately, ostensibly about Masha, and as Treplev explicitly rebuffs Polina's importunings and Masha's efforts at connection (74–75); in *Seagull*, he simply exits in silence. There is a loss of subtlety in how humiliations are negotiated.

Sex, madness, and hyperbole are present in the ensuing scene between daughter and mother. Polina believes Masha has a chance of winning Treplev, because, "now that he knows he's lost Nina forever to her madness, he might suddenly appreciate your devotion" (75). While the question of Nina's sanity or madness is, I believe, always a question to be explored by actor and director in *The Seagull*, Williams asserts that the young woman is insane. Moments of lyricism, such as Masha's brief waltz to Treplev's offstage piano playing, are cut. More cheap sex is added as Masha and Polina deal with their mutual desperation—Masha's fear of ending up "a drunken prostitute on the streets," and Polina's having gone to Dorn's clinic and saying, "Take me, take me" (76).

Medvedenko reenters, wheeling in Sorin, followed by Dorn, as cynical as ever, and soon thereafter by Treplev. The animus among the men is unabated. In *Notebook*, Sorin is not humorously self-ironizing; he and Dorn are not old friends. Sorin's compassion and empathy for others are eliminated as he focuses solely on himself. There is an edgy negativity to everyone's mood, whereas there are various configurations of compassion in Chekhov, for example, Dorn and Treplev for the physically ailing Sorin, and Sorin for the spiritually ailing Treplev. Williams's Treplev goes so far as to challenge Dorn to a duel for saying insulting things about Nina. (Interestingly, at no point in *Notebook* does he ever challenge Trigorin.) Chekhov's ironic, tough-love interchange between Dorn and Sorin about desire and about the inevitability and sadness of aging and mortality (e.g., Sorin's "The Man Who Wanted To" story) is exchanged in Williams for one in which Treplev and Sorin are confronted with Dorn's crassness and hedonism on the subject of death. Chekhov's Dorn loves Genoa, his favorite city abroad, because it is possible to lose oneself among the crowds in the street, to dissolve into "a single world spirit"-an almost Buddhist view of the pleasures of the dissolution of ego. In Williams's character, pleasure is connected to sexual appetite:

> DORN: Any large Italian city pleases me. They're full of well-fleshed women that smile at me on the street and—
> CONSTANTINE: He means whores.
> DORN: Not necessarily, just women unencumbered by an excess of propriety . . . (78–79)

The question remains. If, as Masha says, "we all know what [Dorn] is, all of us despise him" (79), why does he continue to come back to the estate, and why is he allowed to come back?

The Seagull's extended account of Treplev's and Nina's trials over the preceding two years, including his description of how he followed Nina fruitlessly, of her performances and letters, and how she signed herself "the seagull" is eliminated in *Notebook*. This removes Treplev's articulation of what his last two years have been like, and thus a foundational element of his development and unfolding as a character in this act—preparation for his ultimate meeting with Nina and for the shooting.

Arkadina returns to the estate (which she calls "my home!," something she never does in Chekhov) because the theatre critics have turned against her and her tour is failing (81), not because she has been summoned to come quickly because her aging brother may be dying. In Williams, she is running away from failure, rather than running toward her sibling—another version of the fading, self-deluding belles, the Amandas and Blanches. This change eliminates a kind of normative continuity and skews the action toward melodramatic despair. In Chekhov, Arkadina and Trigorin are doing well, while the younger people are struggling—

there is vitality somewhere and life will go on. Williams's changes continue to keep Arkadina at the center of the dramatic impulse of the play. She is suffering, in crisis from her public and professional humiliations. She is crushed, not in her element, not revelling in her triumphs. Williams again chooses failure, rather than continuing success; part of Chekhov's point is that she is a glorious, flawed survivor, in contrast to her mortally weak son. Williams makes structural changes in the large group scene. Treplev is more explicitly confrontational and rude to Trigorin, exchanging the communal dimension of this segment for a more *mano-a-mano* structure. Medvedenko stays onstage significantly longer, softening Masha's rejection of him and lessening the sense of his marginality and humiliation within the group. Treplev is kept onstage at his desk throughout: this diminishes the sense of the young man's restlessness and unease by eliminating his pained exit upon discovering that Trigorin has not read his story, his offstage piano playing, and his reentering and pacing as he looks out onto the turbulent lake. This also eliminates the group's discussion of Treplev and his writing, including the following telling words from *Seagull*:

> TRIGORIN: He's unlucky. He's never been able to find his real voice. There's something strange, vague about it—at times it's even irrational. There's not one living character in his writing.
> DORN: But I believe in Konstantin Gavrilovich. He has something! He has something! He thinks in images, his stories are colorful, clear, and they move me deeply. It's just a shame that he doesn't have a definite purpose. He creates impressions, nothing more, but you can't get far on impressions alone. Irina Nikolaevna, are you glad your son's a writer?
> ARKADINA: Imagine, I haven't read him yet. There's never time.

Williams's Trigorin remains more interested in swimming with Yakov than in fishing (85). Arkadina no longer controls the lotto game for, as she tries to tell false stories of her triumphs, she " *observes with embarrassment that no one is listening to her. She dabs her tearful eyes at the mirror*" (84); her victimhood, aging, and lack of agency are reinforced. Shamraev's star-worshipping attachment to Arkadina and his reference to having had the seagull mounted are eliminated; he is in the scene primarily to tell his son-in-law he can't have a horse. (The bird is mentioned only when it is revealed near the end of the act.) Williams's characters are together because they have nowhere else to go and are stuck with each other.

In the final scene between Treplev and Nina, Williams minimizes the importance of art and the artist's struggle, eliminating Treplev's soliloquy about what art is and what matters to him in his own art. This passage of self-examination is gone, altering the psychological preparation for Treplev's reception of Nina significantly. Unlike Chekhov's, Williams's Nina has been visible for some time, peering in at the window, so she has seen everyone, including Trigorin, by the time she enters. This loses a key moment of discovery in *Seagull*, in which Nina learns of his presence by hearing him laughing in the other room; this changes a primary element in the given circumstances and discoveries in the scene, and thus its rhythms and energies.

Williams's Nina is not so obviously hungry and tired when she enters, making few references to physical thirst, hunger, and weariness; her distress is predominantly psychological. She explains the seagull metaphor for Treplev (and for us), never once using the phrase "I am a seagull," and describes the artist's lot in a psychologizing, rather than an emotional/poetic, way:

> A sea gull. To whom does a sea gull belong? Can they feel love? It must be a thing of the moment, then flight again and even when flying together seem to be each—alone [. . .] Oh, I know the Spartan require-ments of an artist, how one thing after another has to be discarded, those things that are just for effect, to please vulgar tastes, such as—sentimentality—extravagances of manner. But suppose the aspiring artist divested himself of all these false adornments and underneath them found there was nothing left that his audience could see? The audience, seeing nothing, would say, "There is nothing to see." (88–89)

The moment-by-moment negotiation of whether they will keep talking to each other, or whether she will run out into the night, is exchanged for a discursive dia-logue about their lives, their pains and dreams. Williams's Treplev seems more con-trolled; the passionate, iterative begging of Nina to stay is gone, because Nina's repeated, but aborted, efforts to leave are eliminated as well. This changes the sense of the characters' emotional extremity and volatility, especially Treplev's, and there-fore decreases the pressure being put on Nina, in terms of her struggle to find a way to leave that is not totally devastating to him. Williams's focus on plot-driven sus-pense and story, rather than on the negotiation of a complex relationship, is reflect-ed in his Treplev being kept in the dark about the specifics of Nina's liaison with Trigorin until this point—most significantly that she has had a child. This is a major change in Treplev's psychological "terrain," for it presents late in the play a new, melodramatic discovery with which he must deal. (It seems unusual, given his attachment to Nina and the way that circles of family and friends communicate, that he would not already know this.) Nina's inner life is also substantially altered, in that her child, rather than dying in infancy as it does in Chekhov, has been given up for adoption to a couple "in a new world. It has a lovely name—America . . . " (91).[6]

Nina's arias about her struggles and eventual embracing of her lot—the journey of her soul—are broken up into dialogue with Treplev, changing his action from one of essentially taking her in, drinking in every moment with her, and seeing how his sense of faith cannot compare to hers, to one of challenging her through dialogue. The changes and turns in Nina's inner action are diminished. In Chekhov, if one goes with a direct reading of her words, she moves from describing the harshness of her life, to an assertion of her faith and her work, to asking Treplev to come see her when she's a great actress, to a *cri de coeur* of her passionate, desperate love for Trigorin, to an embracing of the happy pure past, to an extended recitation of lines from Treplev's play. In Williams, Nina compares an artistic vocation to a bastard

child—that mustn't be given away; any pleasure or peace is conditional, never directly asserted, as in the following in which the negative qualifiers virtually erase the
asserted positive and the omnipresent mother once again surfaces and is critiqued:

> NINA: . . . Look, Kostya, my friend. In our work what's important isn't
> fame, isn't glory, not those things I dreamed of which satisfy your
> mother. What's important? Only to endure. . . To be able to bear the
> vocation, writing or acting, never give it away like a bastard child.
> (92–93)

Similarly, a significant conditional is inserted when Nina asks Treplev, "When
I'm a great actress, if ever promise you'll come to see me" (93); in Chekhov there is
no self-doubt, no self-diminishing: "When I become a great actress, come and see
me."

In Williams, Treplev's final moments alone are as follows:

> I don't know why I should find it necessary to practice a profession
> when I have just a passing talent. [He notices the letter [Nina] gave
> him [to mail].] Just the city and country and the last names of the peo-
> ple. [Silence. He tears up all his manuscripts and throws them under the
> desk. He exits into the garden.] (93)

In Chekhov:

> [After a pause.] It'll be bad if someone sees her in the garden and tells
> Mother. It might make Mother angry. [In the next two minutes he silent-
> ly tears up his manuscripts and throws them under the table, then he
> unlocks the right door and exits.]

It is interesting that, at this culminating moment, Williams would *not* make
Arkadina a focal point for her son's despair, and seemingly makes the primary
motive for Treplev's suicide his failure as a writer, rather than his failure on multiple
fronts.

Following this, when the group reenters from dinner, Williams gives Arkadina
and Trigorin a long dialogue regarding the vicissitudes of aging and the loss of beauty and youth. This extends the amount of time before the gunshot, decompressing
and deflecting the tension related to Nina's departure and the young man's final
moments on stage. The scene throws increasing emphasis on the humiliations of
aging and Arkadina's and Trigorin's persistent exposing of each others' vulnerabili-
ties, as the focus is drawn away from the two younger characters. When the gunshot
is heard, the amount of language and activity around the event and the aftermath is
altered and expanded. Trigorin grabs Arkadina and wildly dances with her to keep
her from following Dorn out (96). Dorn returns to pull Trigorin aside to break the
news of Treplev's suicide; rather than the play ending at this moment, Masha con-

fronts Dorn, breaking into a "crazed laugh" and physically striking him (97). Treplev's body becomes visible by the lake as Masha and Polina *"move helplessly about as if under deep water."* Dorn moves to Arkadina, who has sensed what has happened, and asks her to take a bow for her part in this special "occasion," her son's suicide. The play ends as her son's corpse is brought upstage:

> *Clapping a hand over her mouth, Irina now staggers up from the lotto table. She backs slowly downstage to the footlights. The audience in the theatre confronts her, as she turns about. The instinct of nearly a lifetime prevails and she bows. Her face is a tragic farewell to her profession, her life, to her deeply loved son: her victim.* (98)

The focus at the end is on the actress-mother, the source of all power for good and evil, not on the held moment of the group. It is a diva's theatrical "tragic farewell," not Chekhov's *sotto voce* caesura—a moment before the next thing happens, as life goes. Williams provides complete closure—the world has ended in some irreversible way: in Nina's madness, Treplev's suicide, and the ignominious end of Arkadina's career and the loss of her son. In Chekhov, we do not know really what those remaining will do, though the play's narrative moves open-endedly beyond the final curtain: Nina is distressed and has a rough life, but she is pursuing her calling and is not (if you take the text directly) mad; Arkadina's career is in fine shape, and her relationship with Trigorin, from what the text gives us, is reliable. And, because the play is open-ended and because there is at least tenuous community, there is hope for some comfort somewhere.

Ultimately, *The Notebook of Trigorin* is a quintessential Williams play, inspired by the bolder outlines of Chekhov's narrative and Williams's felt kinship with the Russian writer. Unlike *The Seagull*, it is dominated by universal humiliation and failure in both life and work, as well as the impossibility of tenderness or fulfillment in any quarter. While there is at least some small compassion in Chekhov's agnostic Russian play, Williams's Christian American one is unrelievedly dark and hopeless, in spite of its grotesque comic elements. In order to appreciate what Williams has done, *Notebook* must be taken on its own terms, separated from any comparison with its source of inspiration. *Notebook* is not *The Seagull*. It is a bleakly funny, wonderfully gothic and even grotesque melodrama. It is a no-holds-barred, take-no-prisoners script with great energy and boldness, and-in direct contradiction to Chekhov-absolutely nothing unspoken.

NOTES

1. For a sampling of useful comparisons of Williams and Chekhov, see Bloom, Kernan, Adler, Quintus, and the essays by Bigsby, Debusscher, Londré and Roudané in Roudané.

2. This has a kind of interesting reflexivity, since *The Seagull* has been viewed as a source of inspiration for *The Glass Menagerie*, as discussed in detail in Gunn.

3. Anton Chekhov, *The Seagull*, Act I, unpublished translation by Rhonda Blair. All quotations from *Seagull* are from this version.

4. This view of Dorn eliminates the subtext of his parentage of Masha; this was explicit in Chekhov's initial version of play, but was excised at the direction of the censor. See Rayfield, 382.

5. There is an interesting resonance here with Williams's own notable ability to "write women."

6. This latter is also an example of a number of references and statements in Williams (including Medvedenko's ignorance of *Hamlet*) that indicate a lack of familiarity with Russian culture at the end of the nineteenth century.

WORKS CITED

Adler, Thomas P. *A Streetcar Named Desire: The Moth and the Lantern*. Boston: Twayne, 1990.

Bloom, Harold, ed. *Tennessee Williams's* The Glass Menagerie, New York: Chelsea House, 1988.

Chekhov, Anton, *The Seagull*, Rhonda Blair, trans. unpublished manuscript.

Devlin, Albert J., ed. *Conversations with Tennessee Williams*, Jackson: University Press of Mississippi, 1986.

Donahue, Francis. *The Dramatic World of Tennessee Williams*. New York: Frederick Ungar, 1964.

Gunn, Drewey Wayne. "'More than Just a Little Chekhovian: *The Sea Gull* as a Source for the Characters in *The Glass Menagerie*." *Modern Drama* 33:3 (1990): 313–321.

Hale, Allean. Introduction to *The Notebook of Trigorin: A Free Adaptation of Anton Chekhov's The Sea Gull*. New York: New Directions, 1997: ix–xx.

Kernan, Alvin B. "Truth and Dramatic Mode in the Modern Theater: Chekhov, Pirandello, and Williams." *Modern Drama* 1:2 (1958): 101–114 .

Londré, Felicia Hardison. *Tennessee Williams*. New York: Frederick Ungar, 1979.

Kronenberger, Louis. "A Triumph for Miss Taylor," 2 April 1945, 16, cited in George W. Crandell, ed. *The Critical Response to Tennessee Williams*. Westport: Greenwood, 1996.

McCann, John S. *The Critical Reputation of Tennessee Williams: A Reference Guide*. Boston: G. K. Hall, 1983.

Presley, Delma E. *The Glass Menagerie: An American Memory*. Boston: Twayne, 1990.

Quintus, John Allen. "The Loss of Dear Things: Chekhov and Williams in Perspective," *English Language Notes*, March 1981.

Rayfield, Donald. *Anton Chekhov: A Life*. New York: Henry Holt, 2000.

Roudané, Matthew C., ed. *The Cambridge Companion to Tennessee Williams*, New York: Cambridge University Press, 1997.

Williams, Tennessee. *Memoirs*. Garden City: Doubleday, 1975.

——*The Notebook of Trigorin: A Free Adaptation of Anton Chekhov's The Sea Gull*. New York: New Directions, 1997.

——*Tennessee Williams' Letters to Donald Windham 1940–1965*, ed. Donald Windham, New York: Holt, Rinehart and Winston, 1977.

Selected Bibliography

Primary Sources

Plays

Williams, Tennessee. *Auto-Da-Fé. Twenty-Seven Wagons Full of Cotton and Other One-Act Plays.* Norfolk, New Directions, 1945: 107–120; Volume 6 of *Theatre.* New York: New Directions, 1981: 131–51.

————. *Battle of Angels. Pharos* 1–2 (1945): 1–109; [with *Orpheus Descending*] New York: New Directions, 1958; Volume 1 of *Theatre.* New York: New Directions, 1971: 1–122; rev. ed. New York: Dramatists Play Service, 1975.

————. *Camino Real.* Norfolk: New Directions, 1953; Volume 2 of *Theatre.* New York: New Directions, 1971: 417–591.

————. *The Case of the Crushed Petunias. American Blues.* New York: Dramatists Play Service, 1948: 22–32.

————. *Cat on a Hot Tin Roof.* New York: New Directions, 1955. Rev. ed. New York: New Directions, 1975; Volume 3 of *Theatre.* New York: New Directions, 1971: 1–215.

————. *The Chalky White Substance. Antaeus* 66: 467–473.

————. *Clothes for a Summer Hotel: A Ghost Play.* New York: Dramatists Play Service, 1981; New York: New Directions, 1983; Volume 8 of *Theatre.* New York: New Directions, 1992: 201–280.

————. *Confessional. Dragon Country.* New York: New Directions, 1969: 151–196; Volume 7 of *Theatre.* New York: New Directions, 1981: 153–96.

————. *The Dark Room. American Blues*. New York: Dramatists Play Service,
1948: 15–21.

————. *The Demolition Downtown. Esquire* 75.6 (1971) 124–27, 152; Volume 6
of *Theatre*. New York: New Directions, 1981: 331–58.

————. *The Eccentricities of a Nightingale* [with *Summer and Smoke*]. New York:
New Directions, 1964; Volume 2 of *Theatre*. New York: New Directions,
1971: 1–111.

————. *The Frosted Glass Coffin. Dragon Country*. New York: New Directions,
1969: 197–214; Volume 7 of *Theatre*. New York: New Directions, 1981:
199–214.

————. *The Glass Menagerie*. New York: Random House, 1945; Rev. ed., London:
John Lehmann, 1948; Rev. ed. New York: Dramatists Play Service, 1948;
Volume 1 of *Theatre*. New York: New Directions, 1971: 123–237.

————. *The Gnädiges Fräulein. Esquire* 64.2 (1965): 102, 130–34; New York:
Dramatists Play Service, 1967; *Dragon Country*. New York: New
Directions, 1969: 215–62; Volume 7 of *Theatre*. New York: New
Directions, 1981: 217–62.

————. *Hello from Bertha. Twenty-Seven Wagons Full of Cotton and Other One-Act
Plays*. Norfolk, New Directions, 1945: 183–193; Volume 6 of *Theatre*.
New York: New Directions, 1981: 231–44.

————. *I Can't Imagine Tomorrow. Esquire* 65.3 (1966): 76–79; *Dragon Country*.
New York: New Directions, 1969: 131–150; Volume 7 of *Theatre*. New
York: New Directions, 1981: 133–50.

————. *I Rise In Flame, Cried the Phoenix*. New York: New Directions, 1951; Rev.
ed,. New York: Dramatists Play Service, 1951: *Dragon Country*. New York:
New Directions, 1969: 55–75; Volume 7 of *Theatre*. New York: New
Directions, 1981: 59–75.

————. *In the Bar of a Tokyo Hotel*. New York: Dramatists Play Service, 1969;
Dragon Country. New York: New Directions, 1969: 1–53; Volume 7 of
Theatre. New York: New Directions, 1981: 3–53.

————. *Kingdom of Earth (The Seven Descents of Myrtle)*. [one-act version] *Esquire*
67:2 (1967) 98–100, 132, 134; [full-length versions] New York: New
Directions, 1968. Rev. ed. New York: New Directions, 1969; Rev. ed.,
Volume 5 of *Theatre*. New York: New Directions, 1976: 121–214.

————. *The Lady of Larkspur Lotion*. *Twenty-Seven Wagons Full of Cotton and Other One-Act Plays*. Norfolk, New Directions, 1945: 65–72; Volume 6 of *Theatre*. New York: New Directions, 1981: 81–105.

————. *The Last of My Solid Gold Watches*. *Twenty-Seven Wagons Full of Cotton and Other One-Act Plays*. Norfolk, New Directions, 1945: 75–85; Volume 6 of *Theatre*. New York: New Directions, 1981: 93–105.

————. *Lifeboat Drill*. Volume 7 of *Theatre*. New York: New Directions, 1981: 281–96.

————. *The Long Good-Bye*. *Twenty-Seven Wagons Full of Cotton and Other One-Act Plays*. Norfolk, New Directions, 1945: 161–75; Volume 6 of *Theatre*. New York: New Directions, 1981: 203–27.

————. *The Long Stay Cut Short, or The Unsatisfactory Supper*. *American Blues*. New York: Dramatists Play Service, 1948: 33–42.

————. *Lord Byron's Love Letters*. *Twenty-Seven Wagons Full of Cotton and Other One-Act Plays*. Norfolk, New Directions, 1945: 123–132; Volume 6 of *Theatre*. New York: New Directions, 1981: 155–67.

————. *A Lovely Sunday for Creve Coeur*. New York: New Directions, 1980; Volume 8 of *Theatre*. New York: New Directions, 1992: 117–200.

————. *The Milk Train Doesn't Stop Here Anymore*. New York: New Directions, 1964; rev. ed. London: Secker and Warburg, 1964; Volume 5 of *Theatre*. New York: New Directions, 1976: 1–120.

————. *Mooney's Kid Don't Cry*. *American Blues*. New York: Dramatists Play Service, 1948: 5–14.

————. *The Mutilated*. *Esquire* 64.2 1965: 95–101; New York: Dramatists Play Service, 1967; *Dragon Country*. New York: New Directions, 1969: 77–130; Volume 7 of *Theatre*. New York: New Directions, 1981: 81–130.

————. *The Night of the Iguana*. New York: New Directions, 1962; Rev. ed. New York: Dramatists Play Service, 1963; Volume 4 of *Theatre*. New York: New Directions, 1972: 247–376.

————. *Not about Nightingales*. Ed. Allean Hale. New York: New Directions, 1998.

————. *The Notebook of Trigorin: A Free Adaptation of Anton Chekhov's The Sea Gull*. Ed. Allean Hale. New York: New Directions, 1997.

———. *Now the Cats with Jeweled Claws.* Volume 7 of *Theatre.* New York: New Directions, 1981: 299–330.

———. *Orpheus Descending.* [With *Battle of Angels*] New York: New Directions, 1958; Volume 3 of *Theatre.* New York: New Directions, 1971; 219–342.

———. *Out Cry.* New York: New Directions, 1973.

———. *A Perfect Analysis Given by a Parrot. Esquire* 50:4 (1958): 131–34; New York: Dramatists Play Service, 1958; *Dragon Country.* New York: New Directions, 1969: 263–78; Volume 7 of *Theatre.* New York: New Directions, 1981: 265–78.

———. *Period of Adjustment: High Point over a Cavern. A Serious Comedy.* New York: New Directions, 1961; Volume 4 of *Theatre.* New York: New Directions, 1972: 125–246.

———. *Portrait of a Madonna. Twenty-Seven Wagons Full of Cotton and Other One-Act Plays.* Norfolk, New Directions, 194: 89–104; Volume 6 of *Theatre.* New York: New Directions, 1981: 109–27.

———. *The Purification. Twenty–Seven Wagons Full of Cotton and Other One-Act Plays.* Norfolk, New Directions, 1945: 31–62; Volume 6 of *Theatre.* New York: New Directions, 1981: 41–77.

———. *The Red Devil Battery Sign.* New York: New Directions, 1988; Volume 8 of *Theatre.* New York: New Directions, 1992: 281–378.

———. *The Remarkable Rooming-House of Mme. Le Monde.* New York: Albodocani Press, 1984;

———. *The Rose Tattoo.* New York: New Directions, 1951; Volume 2 of *Theatre.* New York: New Directions, 1971: 257–415.

———. *Small Craft Warnings.* New York: New Directions, 1972; Volume 5 of *Theatre.* New York: New Directions, 1976: 215–300.

———. *Something Cloudy, Something Clear.* New York: New Directions, 1995.

———. *Something Unspoken. Twenty-Seven Wagons Full of Cotton and Other One-Act Plays.* Norfolk, New Directions, 1945: 219–238; Volume 6 of *Theatre.* New York: New Directions, 1981: 275–96.

———. *Spring Storm.* Ed. Dan Isaac. New York: New Directions, 1999.

————. *Stairs to the Roof: A Prayer for the Wild of Heart that Are Kept in Cages*. Ed. Allean Hale. New York: New Directions, 2000.

————. *Steps Must be Gentle*. New York, Targ Editions, 1980; Volume 6 of *Theatre*. New York: New Directions, 1981: 317–27.

————. *The Strangest Kind of Romance. Twenty-Seven Wagons Full of Cotton and Other One-Act Plays*. Norfolk, New Directions, 1945: 138–58; Volume 6 of *Theatre* . New York: New Directions, 1981: 171–200.

————. *A Streetcar Named Desire*. New York: New Directions, 1947; Rev. ed. New York: New Directions, 1950; Rev. ed. New York: Dramatists Play Service, 1953; Volume 1 of *Theatre*. New York: New Directions, 1971: 239–419.

————. *Suddenly Last Summer*. New York: New Directions, 1958; Rev. ed., New York: New Directions, 1959 Volume 3 of *Theatre*. New York: New Directions, 1971: 343–423.

———— . *Summer and Smoke*. New York: New Directions, 1948; Rev. ed., London: John Lehmann, 1952; Volume 2 of *Theatre*. New York: New Directions, 1971: 112–256.

————. *Sweet Bird of Youth. Esquire* 51.4 (1959): 114–30, 132–34, 136, 138, 140, 142–55; Rev. ed. New York: New Directions, 1959; Volume 4 of *Theatre*. New York: New Directions, 1972: 3–124.

————. *Talk to Me Like the Rain and Let Me Listen. . . . Twenty-Seven Wagons Full of Cotton and Other One-Act Plays*. Norfolk, New Directions, 1945: 209–18; Volume 6 of *Theatre*. New York: New Directions, 1981: 265–72.

————. *Ten Blocks on the Camino Real. American Blues*. New York: Dramatists Play Service, 1948: 43–77.

————. *This is the Peaceable Kingdom, or Good Luck God*. Volume 7 of *Theatre*. New York: New Directions, 1981: 333–65.

————. *This Property is Condemned. Twenty-Seven Wagons Full of Cotton and Other One-Act Plays*. Norfolk, New Directions, 1945: 197–207; Volume 6 of *Theatre*. New York: New Directions, 1981: 247–61.

————. *Tiger Tail*. [with *Baby Doll*]. New York: New Directions, 1991

————. *The Travelling Companion. Christopher Street* 58 (1981): 32–40.

———. *Twenty-Seven Wagons Full of Cotton. Twenty-Seven Wagons Full of Cotton and Other One-Act Plays.* Norfolk, New Directions, 1945: 3–28; Volume 6 of *Theatre.* New York: New Directions, 1981: 3–38.

———. *The Two-Character Play.* New York: New Directions, 1969; Rev. ed. New York: New Directions, 1979; Volume 5 of *Theatre.* New York: New Directions, 1976: 301–70.

———. *The Unsatisfactory Supper.* [with *Baby Doll*] New York: New Directions; 1956; Volume 6 of *Theatre.* 297–313.

———. *Vieux Carré.* New York: New Directions, 1979; Volume 8 of *Theatre* . New York: New Directions, 1992: 1–116.

———. *Will Mr. Merriwether Return from Memphis? Missouri Review* 22.2 (1997): 89–131.

Collaborations
Williams, Tennessee, and Donald Windham. *You Touched Me!* New York: French, 1947.

Screenplays
Williams, Tennessee. *Baby Doll.* New York: New Directions, 1956; [with *Tiger Tail*], New York: New Directions, 1991.

———. *Stopped Rocking and Other Screenplays.* New York: New Directions, 1984.

Novels and Short Story Collections
Williams, Tennessee. *Tennessee Williams Collected Stories.* New York: New Directions, 1985.

———. *Eight Mortal Ladies Possessed: A Book of Stories.* New York: New Directions, 1974.

———. *Hard Candy: A Book of Stories.* New York: New Directions, 1954.

———. *The Kingdom of Earth, with Hard Candy, a Book of Stories.* New York: New Directions, 1954.

———. *The Knightly Quest: A Novella and Four Short Stories.* New York: New Directions, 1967. Rev. ed. [under title *The Knightly Quest: A Novella and*

Twelve Short Stories] London: Secker and Warburg, 1968.

―――. *Moise and the World of Reason*. New York: Simon and Schuster, 1976.

―――. *One Arm, and Other Stories*. New York: New Directions, 1948.

―――. *The Roman Spring of Mrs. Stone*. New York: New Directions, 1950.

―――. *Three Players of a Summer Game and Other Stories*. London: Secker and Warburg, 1960.

Verses
Williams, Tennessee. *Androgyne, Mon Amour: Poems*. New York: New Directions, 1977.

―――. *In the Winter of Cities: Poems*. Norfolk: New Directions, 1964.

Nonfiction, Letters, and Interviews (Selected)
Williams, Tennessee. *Conversations with Tennessee Williams*. Ed. Albert J. Devlin. Jackson: University Press of Mississippi, 1986.

―――. *Five O-Clock Angel: Letters of Tennessee Williams to Maria St. Just, 1948–1982*. With commentary by Maria St. Just. New York: Alfred A. Knopf, 1990.

―――. *Memoirs*. Garden City: Doubleday, 1975.

―――. *Tennessee Williams' Letters to Donald Windham 1940–1965*, ed. Donald Windham. New York: Holt, Rinehart and Winston, 1977.

―――. *Where I Live: Selected Essays*, ed. Christine R. Day and Bob Woods. New York: New Directions, 1978.

Secondary Sources (Selected)
Brooking, Jack. "Directing *Summer and Smoke*: An Existentialist Approach." *Modern Drama* 2:4 (1960): 377–85.

Rejecting the mind/body dichotomy as central to *Summer and Smoke*, Brooking sees Alma and John as existentialist figures who have achieved freedom by the final curtain. Useful as a director's essay on the play, and praiseworthy for its refusal to moralize.

Crandall, George W., ed. *The Critical Response to Tennessee Williams*. Westport: Greenwood Press, 1996.

An excellent collection of reviewers' responses to Williams in production.

_____. *Tennessee Williams: A Descriptive Bibliography*. Pittsburgh: University of Pittsburgh Press, 1995.

An invaluable reference book, detailing all of Williams's publications.

Derounian, Kathryn Zabelle. "'The Kingdom of Earth' and *Kingdom of Earth*: (*The Seven Descents of Myrtle*): Tennessee Williams's Parody." *University of Mississippi Studies in English* 4 (1983): 150–58.

Though generally dismissive of Williams's later work, Derounian argues that *Kingdom of Earth* coheres through its thoroughgoing use of parody.

Dorff, Linda. "Babylon Now: Tennessee Williams's Apocalypses." *Theater* 29:1 (1999): 114–21.

Looking at the motif of apocalyptic disaster throughout Williams's writing, Dorff links it to the influence of expressionism. Special attention is given to *The Red Devil Battery Sign*. Followed by a brief dramatic fragment from the 1980s.

Fleche, Anne. *Mimetic Disillusion: Eugene O'Neill, Tennessee Williams, and U.S. Dramatic Realism*. Tuscaloosa: University of Alabama Press, 1997.

For Fleche, O'Neill and Williams are the two major American playwrights who contemplated the limitations and contradictions of realism in their dramas. Focusing on Williams in chapters on *Menagerie* and *Streetcar*, Fleche brings an impressive knowledge of post-structuralist theory to bear on these two canonical works.

Fritscher, John J. "Some Attitudes and a Posture: Religious Metaphors and Ritual in Tennessee Williams' Query of the American God." *Modern Drama* 13:2 (1970): 201–15.

In an intriguing combination of psychoanalytic and religious interpreta-tions, Fritscher sees both the Old Testament God of Wrath and New Testament God of Love in Williams's drama. Williams, fearful of passivity since his childhood illness, both resists and sees the need to submit to these figures of divinity.

Gronbek-Tedesco, John L. "Absence and the Actor's Body: Marlon Brando's Performance in *A Streetcar Named Desire* on Stage and in Film." *Studies in American Drama, 1945–Present* 8:2 (1993): 115–26.

> In a skilful blend of observation, theory and cultural criticism, Gronbeck-Tedesco provides an important reading of the most legendary performance of a Williams character.

Gross, Robert F. "Consuming Hart: Sublimity and Gay Poetics in *Suddenly Last Summer*." *Theatre Journal* 47 (1995): 229–51.

> Using Williams's play to provide a queer revision of Edmund Burke's theory of the sublime, Gross argues that the Gothic horrors of *Suddenly Last Summer* exist in a tension with the playwright's deep and erotic relationship to the works of gay predecessor Hart Crane.

_____. "The Pleasures of Brick: Eros and the Gay Spectator in *Cat on a Hot Tin Roof*." *Journal of American Drama and Theatre*. 9:1 (1997): 11–25.

> Starting from the specular pleasure of watching Brick in his silk pajamas, Gross argues that *Cat* offers two major strategies of interpellation—a hysterical identification with Maggie, and a melancholic identification with Brick.

Jackson, Esther Merle. *The Broken World of Tennessee Williams*. Madison: University of Wisconsin Press, 1965.

> Tracing Williams's career through *The Night of the Iguana*, Jackson presents Williams's plays as a paradigm of dramatic writing at mid-century, stressing its links to romanticism, existentialism, and expressionism.

Kimball, King. "The Rebirth of *Orpheus Descending*." *The Tennessee Williams Journal* 1:2 (1989–90): 18–33.

> Marking the occasion of Peter Hall's successful London revival of *Orpheus Descending* in 1988, King charts the changes that Williams made to the play over the years, and analyzes the play as an exploration of the artist.

Kleb, William. "*Streetcar*, Williams and Foucault." In *Confronting Tennessee Williams's A Streetcar Named Desire*." Ed. Philip C. Kolin. Westport: Greenwood Press, 1993: 27–43.

> Kleb suggests intriguing similarities between Williams and the French theorist Michel Foucault. Both writers, Kleb argues, chart out a landscape of

death, sexuality and madness, in which characters struggle to control through the power of knowledge and manipulation of discourse. Intriguingly links Alfred Kinsey's sexological studies and *Streetcar* in their common insistence on verbalizing the 'truth' of sexuality.

Kolin, Philip C. *Tennessee Williams: A Guide to Research and Performance.* Westport: Greenwood Press, 1998.

A very useful reference guide, with biographical background, bibliography, a summary of major critical approaches, and an overview of major productions and screen adaptations.

_____. *Williams: A Streetcar Named Desire.* Cambridge: Cambridge University Press, 2000.

From the original production to incarnations in experimental theatre, ballet and opera, this infomrative and very readable volume is the fullest production history of a Williams play to date.

Leverich, Lyle. *Tom: The Unknown Tennessee Williams.* New York: Crown Publishers, 1995.

The first of a projected two-volume biography of Williams, left uncompleted upon Leverich's death in 1999. Well written, highly regarded by scholars, and far superior in its meticulousness to any other biography of Williams.

Murphy, Brenda. *Tennessee Williams and Elia Kazan: A Collaboration in the Theatre.* Cambridge: Cambridge University Press, 1992.

A very useful and well-documented positivist history, tracing Kazan's collaboration with Williams on the Broadway premieres of *Streetcar*, *Camino Real*, *Cat*, and *Sweet Bird of Youth*. Murphy convincingly argues that these four productions created a highly influential style that juxtaposed realistic objectivity with expressionist subjectivity.

Pagan, Nicholas. *Rethinking Literary Biography: A Postmodern Approach to Tennessee Williams.* Rutherford: Fairleigh Dickinson University Press, 1993.

Drawing on insights from a range of post-structuralist critics, most notably Roland Barthes and Jacques Derrida, Pagan ingeniously explores the expanse of Williams's textuality. Rejecting traditional literary biography as naive about the status of the author, Pagan immerses himself in a much freer and synchonic exploration of Williams's work.

Palmer, R. Barton. "Hollywood in Crisis: Tennessee Williams and the Evolution of the Adult Film." In *The Cambridge Companion to Tennessee Williams*. Ed. Matthew C. Roudané (Cambridge: Cambridge University Press, 1997), 204–31.

A careful analysis of the situation of American film industry in the years after the Second World War, noting the conditions that made it possible for 'art fims' on the European model to emerge out of Hollywood at that time. Dubbing *Streetcar* "the first adult film," Palmer shows how the film versions of Williams's plays had a distinct influence on American films of the 1950s and '60s.

Phillips, Gene D. *The Films of Tennessee Williams*. Philadelphia: Arts Alliance, 1980.

A useful guide to screen versions of Williams's works, with plot summaries, analysis and discussion of reception.

Savran, David. *Communists, Cowboys and Queers: The Politics of Masculinity in the Work of Arthur Miller and Tennessee Williams*. Minneapolis: University of Minnesota Press, 1992.

In contrast to Arthur Miller, whose realistic writings embody a liberal humanist project, Savran presents Williams as a writer whose surrealistic tendencies repeatedly resist closure and fragment unity. A thoughtful and highly influential analysis.

Schiavi, Michael R. "Effeminacy in the *Kingdom*: Tennessee Williams and Stunted Spectatorship." *Tennessee Williams Annual Review* 1:2 (1999): 99–113.

Schiavi argues that the figure of Lot in *Kingdom of Earth* has been unjustly attacked by critics, and that Lot's effeminacy has been taken as representative of the failure as a play as a whole. Rather, the figure of Lot shows Williams trying to dramatize the figure of the effeminate male in a way that can resist interpretative violence.

Schlatter, James. "*The Red Devil Battery Sign*: An Approach to a Mytho-Political Theatre." *Tennessee Williams Annual Review* 1:1 (1998): 93–101.

Schlatter demonstrates how Williams uses archetypes of character and behavior that distinguished his earlier work in *The Red Devil Battery Sign*, but reworked in a play that is at once mythic and deeply political, grounded in the political concerns of the mid-1970s.

Schlueter, June. "'We've Had This Date with Each Other from the Beginning': Reading Toward Closure in *A Streetcar Named Desire*." In *Confronting Tennessee Williams's* A Streetcar Named Desire. Ed. Philip Kolin (Westport: Greenwood, 1993), 71–81.

Drawing primarily on the reception theory of Wolfgang Iser, Schlueter focuses on the climactic confrontation between Blanche and Stanley as a confrontation of two competing narratives. There is a pleasure generated in this bringing together of the two narratives into an aesthetic whole, but the repugnance generated by the rape simultaneously creates a discoherence that creates problems in reading the final scene.

Smith, Harry. "Tennessee Williams and Jo Mielziner: The Memory Plays." *Theatre Survey* 23:2 (1982): 223–35.

A thoughtful overview of scene designer Jo Mielziner's contributions to the Broadway productions of *Menagerie*, *Streetcar* and *Summer and Smoke*. Smith stresses the delicacy and lyricism of Mielziner's settings for these plays, noting how his work on *Streetcar* softens the brutality of the script. Sees *Summer and Smoke* as the high point of the collaboration.

Spector, Susan. "Alternative Versions of Blanche duBois: Uta Hagen and Jessica Tandy in *A Streetcar Named Desire*." *Modern Drama* 32:4 (1989): 545–560.

A careful documentation of the differences in two notable early performances of Blanche. While Tandy's intepretation showed a Blanche who was extremely vulnerable and emotionally unstable from the start, Hagen's Blanche was driven insane by the brutal environment presided over by Stanley Kowalski.

Vowles, Richard. "Tennessee Williams and Strindberg." *Modern Drama* 1:3 (1958): 166–171.

A noted Strindberg scholar observes the orientation toward Strindberg in Williams's work as early as *You Touched Me!* Though sceptical of direct influence, he sees a powerful affinity between the two playwrights in philosophy, dramatic action and theatrical effects.

Weales, Gerald. "*Period of Adjustment*: High Comedy over a Cavern." *Journal of American Drama and Theatre* 1:1 (1989): 25–38.

Acknowledging the "uneasy place" of this domestic comedy in the Williams canon, Weales traces its history, and then analyzes the strange coexistence of 1950s Broadway comic charm and bleakness throughout it.

Contributors

RHONDA BLAIR is a director, solo performer, and actor. Her writing appears in *Method Acting Reconsidered, Upstaging Big Daddy, Women and Performance, Theatre Topics,* and *Theatre Journal.* Her solo performances include *I Used to Be One Hot Number* and *American Jesus.* She has translated *The Seagull* and *The Cherry Orchard,* and has directed *The Seagull* twice. One of her first roles in high school was Cornelia in Williams's *Something Unspoken.* She is professor of theatre at Southern Methodist University.

FRANK BRADLEY is chair of the Department of Performing and Visual Arts and artistic director of the Wallace Theatre at the American University in Cairo. He has taught and directed in universities throughout the United States and Egypt, and has written on American drama and theatre semiotics.

THOMAS GREGORY CARPENTER teaches in the English Department at Lipscomb University in Nashville. He recently completed his dissertation on masculine identity in the plays of Tennessee Williams and August Wilson, and he has presented scholarly papers at the Tennessee Williams Festival in Clarksdale, Mississippi, the William Inge Festival in Independence, Kansas, and the Edward Albee Festival in Valdez, Alaska.

LINDA DORFF unexpectedly passed away while this book was in press. She was assistant professor of theatre history, theory and criticism in the School of Theatre at the University of Houston. She was completing a book entitled *Disfigured Stages: The Late Plays of Tennessee Williams.* In addition to editing a book of interviews, *Working with Tennessee,* she was producing and directing a documentary for public television, entitled *Dragon Country: The Late Plays.* She was about to edit of the forthcoming volumes of New Directions' *The Theatre of Tennessee Williams*. Her contribution to the study of Williams, especially his late plays, was great, and she is missed by her many colleagues, students and friends.

LAUREN FRIESEN is the director of playwriting and associate professor of theatre history at the University of Michigan-Flint. His recent publications include the one-act *Wildflowers*, and essay in the German quarterly *Maske*, "The Problem of Transcendence in Modern Playwriting," and "Vondel, Sudermann and Kliewer: Stretching the Invisible Canon of Mennonite Playwriting" in *Mennonite Quarterly Review*. He edits the annual *Best Student One-Acts* for Dramatic Publishing Company.

JOHN L. GRONBECK-TEDESCO is associate dean for the College of Liberal Arts and Sciences at the University of Kansas and Editor of the *Journal of Dramatic Theory and Criticism*.

ROBERT F. GROSS teaches theatre at Hobart and William Smith Colleges, where he has directed productions of *Out Cry*, *Suddenly Last Summer* and *Small Craft Warnings*. He is the author of *S. N. Behrman: A Research and Production Sourcebook*, and the editor of *Christopher Hampton: A Casebook*.

STEPHANIE B. HAMMER is a professor of comparative literature at the University of California-Riverside. She has written articles on George Lillo, Arthur Schnitzler, Christopher Hampton, Peter Handke and Wendy Wasserstein. Her book on the plays of Friedrich Schiller, *Schiller's Wound: From Crisis to Commodity* will appear in December 2000 with Wayne State University Press.

BRUCE J. MANN is associate professor of English at Oakland University in Michigan, where he teaches drama and modern literature. He has published articles on Tennessee Williams, Eugene O'Neill and Sam Shepard and served as dramaturg for Meadow Brook Theatre. he is the editor of the forthcoming volume, *Edward Albee: A Casebook*.

KALLIOPI NIKOLOPOULOU is the Andrew Mellon Assistant Professor of Comparative Literature at Vanderbilt University. She is currently working on a man-uscript entitled "Reading the Disaster: The Ethics of Negativity in the Poetry of Paul Valéry and Paul Celan."

MICHAEL R. SCHIAVI is assistant professor of English and coordinator of ESL at New York Institute of Technology's Manhattan Campus. His work has appeared recently in *The Tennessee Williams Annual Review* and *The Journal of American Drama and Theatre*. He also has essays forthcoming in *The Quarterly Review of Film and Video*, Continuum's *Companion to Twentieth-Century Theatre*, and the antholo-gy *A Doorway, A Dawn, A Dusk: Queer Lives in the Theatre*.

ANN WILSON teaches in the School of Literatures and Performance Studies in English at the University of Guelph, Ontario, Canada. Her scholarly interests focus on issues of gender, class and race in the context of nationalisms.

Index